Contents

Music and Copyright

Second edition

Edited by Simon Frith and Lee Marshall

Edinburgh University Press

© in this edition Edinburgh University Press, 2004
© in the individual contributions is retained by the authors

Edinburgh University Press Ltd
22 George Square, Edinburgh

Typeset in Ehrhardt
by Hewer Text Ltd, Edinburgh, and
printed and bound in Great Britain by
The Cromwell Press, Trowbridge, Wilts

A CIP record for this book is available from the British Library

ISBN 0 7486 1812 0 (hardback)
ISBN 0 7486 1813 9 (paperback)

The right of the contributors
to be identified as authors of this work
has been asserted in accordance with
the Copyright, Designs and Patents Act 1988.

Contributors

Simon Frith is Professor of Film and Media at the University of Stirling, and editor of *Popular Music. Critical Concepts* (Routledge, 2004).

Steve Greenfield is Senior Academic and Course Director of the LLB, School of Law, University of Westminster, and co-author of *Film and the Law* (Cavendish, 2002).

Friedemann Kawohl is a Research Fellow at the Centre for Intellectual Property Policy and Management, Bournemouth University, Visiting Lecturer at Musikhochschule Trossingen, and author of *Urheberrecht der Musik in Preussen 1820–1840* (Schneider, 2002), a historical analysis of German music copyright.

Martin Kretschmer is Professor of Information Jurisprudence and joint Director of the Centre for Intellectual Property Policy and Management, Bournemouth University, and Visiting Professorial Fellow at the Queen Mary Intellectual Property Research Institute, University of London.

Dave Laing is an independent researcher based in London. He was formerly Reader in Music at the University of Westminster. Recent publications include 'Music and the Market: The Economics of Music in the Modern World' in *The Cultural Study of Music*, edited by Martin Clayton, Trevor Herbert and Richard Middleton (Routledge, 2003).

Lee Marshall is a Lecturer in the Sociology of Culture at the University of Bristol, and author of *Bootlegging: Romanticism and Copyright in the Music Industry* (Sage, 2004).

Guy Osborn is Course Leader in the LLM Entertainment Law at the University of Westminster. Recent publications include *Regulating Football. Commodification, Consumption and the Law* (Pluto Press, 2001).

Anthony Seeger is Professor of Ethnomusicology at the University of California at Los Angeles and Director Emeritus, Smithsonian Folkways Recordings. He is author of *Why Suyá Sing, A Musical Anthropology of an Amazonian People* (updated edition with CD, University of Illinois Press, 2004) and editor (with Shubha Chaudhuri) of *Global Perspectives on Audiovisual Archives in the 21st Century* (Seagull Books, Calcutta, 2004).

Paul Thèberge is Canada Research Chair of Technological Mediations of Culture at the Institute for Comparative Studies in Literature, Art and Culture at Carleton University, Ottawa, and author of *Any Sound You Can Imagine: Making Music/Consuming Technology* (Wesleyan University Press, 1998).

Ruth Towse is Reader in Cultural Industries at Erasmus University, Rotterdam. Recent publications include 'Copyright and Cultural Policy for the Creative Industries' in *Economics, Law and Intellectual Property*, edited by Ove Granstrand (Kluwer Academic Publishers, 2004).

Jason Toynbee is a Lecturer at the Institute of Popular Music, University of Liverpool, and author of *Making Popular Music: Musicians, Creativity and Institutions* (Arnold, 2000).

Roger Wallis is Visiting Professor (Multimedia) in the Media Technology Research group at the Royal Institute of Technology Stockholm. Recent publications include (with A. Edström-Frejman) 'Can diversity be a profit-maximising strategy? The apparent incompatibility of deregulation policies, media concentration and audience access to range of choice' in *Proceedings of the 2003 COST A20 conference on New Media Paradigms*, Pamplona, 2004.

CHAPTER 1

Making Sense of Copyright

Simon Frith and Lee Marshall

The first edition of this book was published more than a decade ago, in 1993. As the original introduction argued, the book reflected growing professional and academic interest in copyright law. Two reasons were suggested for this interest: first, new technologies for the storage and retrieval of knowledge, sounds and images were posing complex problems for legal definitions of work, authorship and use; second, the related globalisation of culture was impelling multinational leisure corporations to seek the 'harmonisation' of copyright regulations across national boundaries. Either way, the legal concept of 'intellectual property' and its financial value had become an issue. For music industry analysts, in particular, a business that had been studied in the 1960s and 1970s as manufacture, producing commodities for sale to consumers, had come to be understood in the 1980s as a service, 'exploiting' musical properties as baskets of rights.

This was not then (and probably is not now) the way in which most people understood a music industry still routinely described as 'the record business', a business dominated by the major 'record labels'. To this day, music business success is measured in record sales, music business problems by record sales decline. Musicians are more likely to celebrate writing a song or releasing a record than 'creating a basket of rights' and, for consumers, copyright law is undoubtedly an arcane and jargon-ridden area of interest. What are 'mechanical' or 'neighbouring' rights? Where is the 'public domain'? What is the difference between 'rights in perfor-mance' and 'performance rights'? Between the Berne Convention and the Rome Convention? Who, besides a few record company lawyers, cares?

If it does nothing else, we hope this book explains why you should. For anyone with any interest in music, copyright is vitally important, more important than any other concept in making sense of the variety of social practices that make up 'the music industry'. Copyright provides the framework for every business decision in the industry. Who gets

recorded? What do they record? How and where they are marketed? Who
is allowed to use their song? Who makes money from this performance?
Who is allowed to use their image? Who makes money from that? Will this
song be heard on the radio? Used on a TV commercial? Feature in the
background of a cinematic film? Can you get a ringtone of your favourite
track? Can you arrange it? Sample it? Download it? Copy it for a friend?
All these questions concern copyright. Copyright, one might say, is the
currency in which all sectors of the industry trade.

Ignoring copyright thus means ignoring one of the key structural
features of the music industry and this collection is intended to help
students of popular music understand the vital role that copyright plays in
what they are studying. This introduction will offer an idiot's guide to
copyright terms while later chapters provide both an exploration of key
theoretical assumptions and a discussion of how copyright affects everyday musical practices. No prior understanding of copyright is assumed –
indeed, prior ignorance can be quite useful when approaching this topic
because the aporias and contradictions of copyright can seem more
apparent. As Jessica Litman once put it:

> Although writers have suggested that members of the public find the idea of
> property rights in intangibles [like a piece of music] difficult to accept, there seems
> to be little evidence that members of the public find the idea of a copyright
> counterintuitive. Rather, the lay public seems to have a startlingly concrete idea of
> what copyright is and how it works, which has little to do with actual copyright law.
> (Litman 1991: 3–4)

At the time Litman was making a mildly ironic point about lawyers'
capacity for arrogance and self-delusion. A dozen years later, as the
Record Industry Association of America begins legal proceedings against
random individuals for downloading tracks using peer-to-peer software
(and the British Phonograph Industry threatens to follow the RIAA lead),
the remark reads like a prescient and sober warning. There is now an even
bigger gap between the lay and professional understanding of copyright as
copyright holders dramatically increase its scope. Their remarkable
success in lobbying governments for legal change, to put this another
way, is due in no small part to the lack of public understanding of what the
new laws imply. There is another kind of irony here. Most lay people (not
least journalists) believe that digital technology is such a systematic
financial threat to record companies and the artists signed to them that
the various technological and legal attempts to prevent digital 'theft' have
been in vain. In the first edition of this book, for example, most
contributors wrote about sampling (the first copyright issue really to

interest popular music scholars) as a new kind of composition process which would, in the end, necessitate new definitions of authorship, originality and the public domain. The views of someone like the Turtles' Mark Volman (on being sampled by De La Soul) seemed plainly anachronistic:

'Sampling is just a longer term for theft . . . Anybody who can honestly say sampling is some sort of creativity has never done anything creative.' (quoted in McLeod 2001: 89)

In the event, as Kembrew McLeod notes, by the beginning of the new century sampling was being regulated systematically by the 'old' copyright system, with 'sample clearance houses' emerging, used by both artists and labels to sort out sample licences and fees. By the end of the 1990s nearly all major publishing and recording companies had followed the lead of EMI and employed staff 'whose sole job was to listen to new releases that may have contained samples of its property' (McLeod 2001: 89). Clearing samples had become increasingly expensive and administratively time-consuming, which, in turn, had had a variety of effects on how sample-based music like hiphop is produced. For example:

When Public Enemy wanted to sample a bit of Buffalo Springfield's 'For What It's Worth', the group discovered that it would be cheaper for them to have the song's original vocalist Stephen Stills sing the part of the song they were going to sample.' (McLeod 2001: 94)

The history of sampling suggests another reason why musical copyright is an important issue to understand: the music business was the first sector of the entertainment industry to experience the 'threat' of digital technology, and has therefore been at the forefront of the campaign for new legislation to deal with it. There is a familiar story of unexpected technological consequences here: the industry's adoption of the digital format of CDs in the early 1980s, and its brilliantly successful campaign to persuade consumers to shift from vinyl to CD, can be said to have saved record companies from a serious economic crisis. But in storing music as bits of information, record companies were also undermining the material distinction between production and reproduction (or original and copy) on which copyright law rests. In retrospect it seems technologically inevitable that machines to play CDs would eventually be replaced by machines to play and write CDs, by devices that could retrieve digital-musical information for new uses.[1] It was for this reason that the Internet (a new means of *distributing* digital information) was immediately perceived as much more of a threat to record companies than to, say, book publishers or broadcasters, who have been slower in developing their use of digital technology.

These issues will be discussed further in the course of this book, but before laying out our guide to copyright terms, we would like to make one final point about the importance of rhetoric for copyright practice. A common theme of all the chapters here is that the legislative response to digital technology has not only vastly increased the scope of copyright but has also done so in a way which benefits corporate interests at the expense of those of both artists and consumers. What's being described here is a legislative trend that began with the World Intellectual Property Organisation (WIPO) Convention in Geneva in 1996. Signatories to the international treaties drawn up by the WIPO Convention in Geneva agreed to update their national copyright laws so as to give authors, performers, publishers and record companies the right to authorise and require payment for the distribution of their work on the Internet and other computer networks. The result in the USA was the Digital Millennium Copyright Act (DMCA) of 1998, which expanded US legislative protection for intellectual property to digital materials, and, in Europe, the EU Copyright Directive of 2001, which became law in the UK at the end of October 2003 as the Copyright and Related Regulations Act.[2]

There are three points to be made here about these laws. First, the chances are that most readers of this book will not have heard of them – even readers who are avid music makers and consumers. Copyright is not normally taken to be a topic of political or public interest. It is rarely written about in newspapers or featured in policy debate. This means, second, that the rationale of copyright laws and why they matter tends to be determined by the interest of the corporate lobbyists who have driven the legislative changes of the last decade.[3] Our third point follows: while the corporate argument is framed as 'bringing copyright law into line with the new environment' (which is, indeed, a common sense thing to do), from an academic perspective what has actually happened is that the original principles of copyright have been surreptitiously put aside. A system that was originally framed by reference to the public good – it involved restrictions on the monopoly power of rights owners – has become a means of promoting private interests. What was once a system for ensuring public access to knowledge has now become a system, at least in the digital sphere, to prevent it – most obviously in the clauses making it illegal to attempt to circumvent electronic access controls even when accessing non-copyright material.[4] The 'burden' of copyright law has been transferred from rights owner to rights user: whereas once the rights holder had to persuade a court that an 'unauthorised' use of their work actually damaged them, now the 'illegal' user has to persuade a court that there is some specific reason to excuse their breach. Who would have thought ten years ago, when the first edition of this book came out, that in 2003 US music consumers would be being prosecuted for how they used their computers in the privacy of their own homes?[5]

The questions discussed in this book, then, are neither arcane nor irrelevant to everyday life, and it is particularly important to understand copyright in terms that are not simply derived from rights owners' property claims but also consider the broader effects of copyright on creativity and the social circulation of ideas. In the course of an extensive investigation of the present state of US copyright law for the *Atlantic Monthly*, Charles C. Mann came to the conclusion that "rampant musical piracy may hurt musicians less than they fear. The real threat – to listeners and, conceivably, democracy itself – is the music industry's reaction to it" (Mann 2000). Such a threat, as is described in later chapters in this book, has a number of components, but two seem paramount.

On the one hand, recent legislation seems to extend the notion of copyright from getting paid for usage to *controlling* usage, thus raising questions about copyright as a means of censorship, a restraint on creativity, a way of restricting the supply of music, and so on. While music industry lobbyists rhetorically involve artists in their anti-downloading campaigns, they cannot always disguise the tensions between composers and performers who want their works exposed as widely as possible (and who, like Janis Ian, see the Internet as a wonderful tool for promotion of their music) and record companies and publishers who want to keep tight control of their markets. In the words of Lawrence Lessig, copyright is 'not speaking for those who create, but those who hold massive amounts of copyright'.[6]

On the other hand, recent legislation seems to elevate the fact of copying above either the intentions of the copier or the effects of the copy. One of the recurring themes of this book (as of most criticism of recent copyright legislation) is that the notion of 'fair use' – once essential to the copyright attempt to balance the interests of the authors and users of a work – has been systematically marginalised. This is the context in which Siva Vaidhyanathan, one of the most prominent academic critics of the DMCA, wrote as follows:

> We make a grave mistake when we choose to engage in discussion of copyright in terms of 'property'. Copyright is not about 'property' as commonly understood. It

is a specific state-granted monopoly issued for particular policy reasons. While, technically, it describes real property as well, it also describes a more fundamental public good that precedes specific policy choices the state may make about the regulation and dispensation of property. But we can't win an argument as long as those who hold inordinate interest in copyright maximisation can cry 'theft!' at any mention of fair use or users' rights. (Vaidhyanathan 2002: 5)

Vaidhyanathan goes on to call for academics to play a more active part in encouraging public debate about copyright issues. But, alas, if this is a field where conceptual clarity is called for above all, it is also a field in which such clarity is very hard to attain.

What is copyright?

If there is one thing upon which copyright scholars can agree, it is that copyright is very complex, and it can seem particularly mysterious to those approaching it from a non-legal background. In this section, we will outline some of its most important characteristics. Our approach here is descriptive and does not offer justifications or criticisms; these will emerge in later chapters.[7] Indeed, it is perhaps advisable to read this section alongside the chapters in the first section of the book.

'Copyright' is a noun not a verb, a thing rather than an action: you cannot 'copyright something' (Litman 1991: 39). However, although copyright is a thing, its existence depends upon the existence of a work that is eligible for copyright. For this reason, copyright is said to *subsist* rather than exist. If a person writes a song (known in copyright law as a 'work', as are any other creations), then the song exists and the copyright of the song subsists in the song, but the copyright cannot exist without the song itself. It is extremely important to distinguish between the work and the copyright of the work – they are not the same thing. If you buy a CD, then you own the physical disc and the recordings of the musical works on it. You can listen to the works, lend the CD to your friends, write rude comments all over the sleeve notes or use it as a Frisbee. You own the thing as a material, physical object. You cannot, however, copy it because you do not own the copyright to the work. (And here is the first complication: these days you can, of course, copy it – 'burn' its content onto a blank CD – but this usage, unlike the others, has to be 'authorised'.)

Although we talk of copyright as a singular thing, it is actually generally understood in law as a *'bundle of rights'*. If a work is eligible for copyright, then the copyright owner is permitted to do a number of different things with the work which are not permitted to those who do not own the copyright (unless they have been licensed by the rights holder). The most obvious of these rights is the right to copy, but there are others. In general, copyright provides the rights holder with the exclusive rights to:

- copy the work
- make adaptations of the work (or prepare derivative works)[8]
- issue copies of the work to the public
- perform the work in public
- broadcast or send a cable transmission of the work.[9]

Exclusivity is extremely important to note here. No-one but the rights-holder is allowed to do these things without prior authorisation (not even the author if he is not the rights-holder). So far so straightforward. The complications begin with the nature of the 'work' at issue. Copyright was initially invented to protect literary works (the first copyright act – known as the Statute of Anne – became English law in 1710). Copyright protection for musical compositions developed later – in 1831 in the US and 1842 in the UK. When copyright was initially granted to music compositions, the definition of what counted as 'music' was fairly straightforward: it referred to the written score (that which can be printed). Following the invention of the phonograph, however, 'music' became more and more associated with the recorded song and copyright law has attempted to come to terms with this while still centring its focus on the composed work (this is discussed in more detail in Chapter 7). The chronological history of copyright remains the best framework for understanding the various rights that are now involved.

To begin with there is a song (or composition). The first owners of the copyright in a song are its creator, the people (or person) who wrote it.[10] Because they have the exclusive rights described above (by virtue of being the copyright owner, not by virtue of being the author), they also have the exclusive rights to permit other people to do these 'restricted' acts, and in most cases (because they want their works to be known to the public and to make money from them) authors and composers will turn to other people to help them exploit their rights.[11] They can either *assign* (usually by selling) their rights to a third party or *license* them to particular people to do specific restricted acts. There are numerous complications here simply in terms of the number of parties who may be involved – licensed or assigned, the rights to do different things to and with the work, in different territories, for different periods of time (the increasing range of uses to which music may be put is described further in Chapter 10). In practice, though, rights are often licensed collectively. In Britain composers thus assign their performance and broadcasting rights to a single agency, the Performing Right Society (PRS), which handles all the further negotiations involved in licensing the work's performances (collecting societies are discussed further in Chapter 6).

One right which can be assigned by the first copyright owner (following the development of sound recording) is the right to record the work, which is known as the *mechanical right*. In the UK composers usually assign their mechanical rights to the Mechanical Copyright Protection Society (MCPS) which, in its own words, 'negotiates agreements with those who wish to record music, collects the mechanical royalties (on record sales, for example) and then distributes them to the correct copyright owner'. Over the course of the twentieth century the recording of a work (rather than its publication in sheet music form) became the usual way in which a work reached the public and a composer's most valuable right (except, perhaps, for classical composers), but it also led to a new kind of exploitation, as first broadcasters, then film makers and juke box owners began to use records (rather than live musicians) for public entertainment. A new kind of musical copyright was created, a right related to the original composition but subsisting in the recording itself rather than the underlying musical work. This *neighbouring right* is usually owned not by the composer but by the company that organises and publishes the recording (in legal terms, known as the producer). The owner of this right has the exclusive rights to cause the recording to be heard in public, to broadcast the recording (by whatever means – including, now, the Internet), and to make another recording embodying this recording or any part of it (this is where the problem of sampling arises, but it also involves 'dubbing rights' and 'synchronisation rights', the use of recordings or extracts from recording on film soundtracks, advertisements, and so on). In Britain record companies usually assign these rights to Phonographic Performance Limited (PPL).

The distinction between copyright and neighbouring rights is an important one, not least because they are intended to benefit different parties (though in practice this may not be the case). They also last for different periods of time (offer different **terms** of protection in legal parlance): in most industrialised countries copyright lasts for seventy years after the death of the author; neighbouring rights last for a finite period from the date a recording is published which, though substantial (ninety-five years now in the USA), is still likely to be less than that of the copyrights involved.

One further type of right needs mentioning in this context: *performers' rights* (which can be distinguished from *performance rights*). Performance rights relate to the exclusive rights of a rights-owner to perform his song in public. Any kind of public performance by anyone except the rights-owner has to be licensed (these are the licenses administered in the UK by the Performing Right Society). Performers' rights refer to the rights all the musicians involved have in the performance itself. The UK has provided some form of performers' rights since 1925, though they were significantly strengthened by the 1988 Copyright Act (Sherrard 1992: 57). The US had no performers' rights at all until 1994, when a new act to prevent bootlegging was introduced (making it illegal to record a performance without the explicit permission of the performer) (Deas 1998). But the most significant extension to performers rights can be found in the EC Rental Directive that the UK government adopted at the end of 1996. This was designed to ensure that everyone involved in a recording (the session musicians as well as the 'featured' musicians) should benefit when that recording was licensed for broadcast use (on a soundtrack, for example). In effect this means that income previously distributed (by PPL) between record companies and the featured artists now has to be distributed between record companies, featured artists and non-featured performers, a change which makes little difference to a self-sustained band like U2 but involves a new and rather intricate division of the pie for, say, an orchestral recording. Whether or not this has actually benefitted the musicians now entitled to some sort of financial return from the broadcast of their work, given the administrative costs involved and the rewriting of employment contracts, is open to question (this is discussed further in Chapter 7).

There are quite significant differences between the ways in which the various rights described here are defined in different countries (traditionally, until the DMCA, the USA had a much more restricted definition of the neighbouring rights in a recording than the UK, for example) and these are discussed further in the next chapter, but one further right does need to be described here. In the civil law approach to copyright originating in France and the norm in continental Europe, authors and composers have a **moral right** (*droit moral*) in their work. (Moral rights only became a part of UK law in the 1988 Copyright Act, as an effect of its membership of the European Union, and are not recognised as such in US law.) Unlike other elements of copyright, moral rights are inalienable: they cannot be assigned to another party (though they can be waived). In Britain the moral rights available to an author include most significantly:

- The paternity right (*droit à la paternité*) – the right to be identified as the author of a work. (There is also a right not to have a work falsely attributed to oneself as an author.)

- The right of integrity (*droit à l'intégrité*) – the right to object to the 'derogatory' treatment of the work, to its alteration in any way which is 'a distortion or mutilation of the work or is otherwise prejudicial to the honour or reputation of the author'.

In continental law authors also have a publication right (*droit de divulgation*) – the right to determine when and whether a work shall be published; and a withdrawal right (*droit de retrait*) – the right to withdraw or modify a work already published.

Copyright Problems

We hope that this brief description of the types of rights existing under the general label of 'copyright' indicates both the complexity of the area and the significance of copyright for the institutional structure of the contemporary music industry. Take an average compilation CD as an example of how the system works. It includes the cover art (itself a copyrightable work), maybe some sleeve notes (a copyrightable literary work), a number of tracks written by different songwriters (some written by more than one person) and sung by different singers (some with a known band, some using session musicians). It is possible that this one disc has upwards of sixty different rights interests (and many more if samples are involved), something indicated by the ever-lengthening small print on the CD package.[12]

But in outlining here the basic terms involved in copyright we also need to draw attention to some of the conceptual problems that are taken for granted in copyright discussions but are not always explicitly acknowledged. It usually goes without saying, for example, that not all works are eligible for copyright. The most significant criterion for claiming copyright in the first place is that a work must be **original**. In copyright terms, original merely means that the work has not been copied from elsewhere (that is, that the author is the originator of the work) and does not refer to any intrinsic, aesthetic quality (even the most banal 'formulaic' songs are eligible for copyright as long as they have not been copied). Technically, this means that two individuals could independently write exactly the same song and both would qualify for copyright because both would be 'original'. Neither could be said to have copied the other; neither would be benefiting from the other's skill or labour. (Thus in many plagiarism cases the argument before the court is not whether song A sounds like song B but whether songwriter A had heard the work of songwriter B before writing his or her composition.)

The criteria for originality were initially devised to prevent publishers from claiming copyright in ancient works, and this is where the concept of **public domain** comes into play. A work is in the public domain when no-one can claim exclusive rights to its use. This will happen either when the term or period of protection has come to an end (more than seventy years have passed since its author's death) or when there is no author who can claim to be its originator (because it was composed anonymously, collectively, as part of a 'folk' process).[13] But the prominence of the idea of originality within copyright discourse also reflects particular conceptions of authorship that have developed in Western modernity (the conceptions that inform the idea of an author's moral right). This has created particular problems for traditional musicians, as discussed in Anthony Seeger's chapter (the issue here is not that a work is too old to copyright or even that composition is collective but that the continuing process of re-creation is not understood in terms of the Romantic artist). And even in the West the argument that copyright is a way of acknowledging the value of artistic creativity is not as straightforward as it may seem.[14] Encouraging authorship is one of the central justifications for copyright, but, on the other hand, authors are usually in a very weak position to exploit their own rights. As authors they may be the first owners of copyright in a work but they are almost entirely reliant on other agencies to publish, reproduce and distribute their work to the public, and their bargaining position with publishers and record labels is not strong. In order to get any financial return from their work, they have to cede many of their rights in it to management companies, publishers, and record labels. To put this another way, the history of music is a history of composers and artists, as well as their rights, being exploited.

A second issue that arises here is how best to discuss copyright as an overarching concept while simultaneously acknowledging the many differences between copyright regimes both legally and socially in different countries. The protection of literary works evolved relatively independently in many states in the eighteenth and nineteenth centuries (see Chapter 2) and different power relations and ideologies resulted in a great many local variations in who and what was protected and how (different countries had very different policies on the copyright protection to be afforded to foreign authors, for example). Similarly, popular music industries in different countries have developed their own idiosyncrasies. CD rental, for example, has a role in the Japanese industry that would not be legally possible elsewhere, while in the USA the strength of the radio lobby has always managed to prevent the development of the kinds of neighbouring rights in recordings long acknowledged in Europe.

Is it possible, then, to develop an analysis that uses both 'copyright' and 'the music industry' as general concepts while facilitating a nuanced understanding of local variations? Twenty years ago, the answer would probably have been no. Even in the first edition of this book, ten years ago, chapters were organised on a country by country basis. In this volume, though, we have asked authors to approach copyright thematically, taking evidence from more than one country while paying attention to the particularity of national situations. We believe, in fact, that today it would be difficult to analyse the copyright situation in any one country without reference to global developments, to the ways in which different national copyright systems are beginning to be 'harmonised'. Developments within media industries over the last twenty to thirty years have resulted in increasingly *transnational* legal structures; local actors now find themselves in very similar situations. Indeed, one purpose of this book is to draw attention to how such transnational developments in copyright law are affecting our everyday musical lives at the local level, for good or ill (see Chapters 4 and 6).

The music industry has always been an international industry, of course, and historically the main way that interested parties have sought to deal with local differences in copyright law has been through multinational treaties binding signatory countries to an agreed set of minimum standards of rights protection. The first such copyright treaty was the Berne Convention for the Protection of Literary and Artistic Works, which was established, mainly by authors and artists, in 1886, and which has been revised a number of times since. The Berne Convention concerned the protection of literary and artistic expressions that were fixed in a tangible form (such as books and sheet music—performances are not protected through this convention); protection was to be granted by member states for a minimum period of fifty years after the death of the author. Among other things the Convention also mandated moral rights for artists (which was the main reason for the USA not signing up to Berne until over 100 years after its inception).

Berne protected musical works, but not sound recordings and so in Rome in 1961 an additional agreement, The International Convention for the Protection of Performers, Producers of Phonograms and Broadcasting Organisations, was established to help prevent the international piracy of sound recordings. The Rome Convention, as it is known, protects sound recordings in signatory countries for a minimum of twenty years and offers some limited protection to performers. Again, however, the USA did not sign the agreement; this time because it did not recognise performers' rights. The slightly curious situation arose, therefore, that the world's largest exporter of copyrighted works, including sound recordings, was not a signatory to either of the major international treaties relevant to copyright in the music industry. If nothing else, this suggests that copyright may not be as necessary for music business activities as is often suggested.

This situation changed, anyway, in the 1990s as part of a dramatic paradigm shift in international copyright regulation which has seen copyright become embedded within a wider network of trade relations and not just subject to specific copyright conventions such as Berne and Rome. The most significant development in this context was the TRIPs agreement of 1993. TRIPs (an acronym for Trade Related Aspects of Intellectual Property) is part of GATT (General Agreement on Tariffs and Trade), the central plank of the global market economy, and the TRIPs agreement significantly strengthened protection for copyright by not only establishing minimum levels of protection, but also, perhaps even more importantly, establishing minimum levels of enforcement. TRIPs thus incorporates many of the substantive provisions of Berne and Rome (though increasing the minimum protection of sound recordings from twenty to fifty years) while making available new kinds of sanction against countries which do not sufficiently police copyright law. Crucially, by embedding copyright into a trade agreement, TRIPs makes it possible for net copyright exporters (such as the UK and US) to impose cross-sectoral trade sanctions on those countries which fail to enforce copyright protection (over the last ten years various countries – such as the Ukraine, India and China – have been threatened with such action). TRIPs also means that many more countries are now bound to protect copyright than were signatories to Berne or Rome. There are currently 146 members of the World Trade Organisation (WTO), the body established to liberalise trade, which binds members to GATT. Thus today national music industries with many different histories come under the same copyright regulations, and are threatened with similar international sanctions (such as export bans) if they do not enforce Western-style copyright protection in their own domains.

It would be easy to conclude from the sort of arguments we've been making here that copyright is (and has always been) the dynamic driving the music industry; that what the industry does (music publishing, record making, rights management and so on) is determined by what the law allows it to do. And it is certainly the case that lawyers have a prominent role in everyday music business and that the courts are routinely involved in adjudicating music industry disputes (rather more so than in other businesses – see Frith 2002 and Chapter 6 in this book). But this would be a misleading conclusion, nonetheless. As the chapters that follow explain, the legal concept of copyright has been shaped by music industry practice and, in particular, by the distribution of music industry power, as much as it has shaped them. If individual music companies have to ensure that what they do is lawful, the music industry devotes much of its energy as an industry to seeking to change the law – in ceaseless lobbying of Congress, the EU, the WTO and so on. In recent years, as we noted at the beginning of this chapter, it has been remarkably successful, which is to confirm our point that copyright has to be understood as a political construct as well as a legal principle. Or, perhaps it would be more accurate to say that as a legal principle copyright is a political construct – *with economic causes and consequences*.

One problem for academic studies of copyright (particularly for economists – see Chapter 3) is that while it is easy to explain why copyrights are valuable for the music industry in general terms, it is extremely difficult to document how much the different rights in a particular work are worth, or how the flow of income works. One can show clearly enough, that is to say, that the value of copyrights determines certain sorts of market decision (following the development of talkies, for example, it paid Hollywood studios to buy up music publishers in order to ensure a supply of musical content, just as it paid Sony to buy CBS fifty years later to ensure a supply of film and music and TV content for the new era of home entertainment). But it is all but impossible to discover the financial return to all the rights holders involved in licensing all the uses of the tracks on, say, Dido's *Life for Rent*, or to track where all the money made by these tracks goes. (Remember too, that they can go on earning income for at least another ninety-five years and possibly several decades longer.) Part of the problem here is that the industry is nowadays so structured that much of the flow of copyright income is internal to one company – in accounting terms, record company payments of mechanical rights fees to publishers, and television company payments of neighbouring right fees to record companies, may simply mean moving figures from one part of a corporate balance sheet to another. Indeed, one economic consequence of copyright seems to be to encourage, under certain technological conditions, the merger of content producing (or rights owning) and content (or rights) using companies (leading to the emergence of a rights oligopoly). The former companies are thus able to ensure not only exposure for their works but fee income; the latter are able to ensure a supply of content at a reasonable rate. Such synergy makes good sense to the companies concerned; it is less clear that it benefits either the consumer or the artist; and it is certain that it is impossible to get at the figures which would show who is really earning what from the copyright system.

The structure of this volume

As editors, what most surprised us about the following chapters was the recurring scepticism expressed about the benefits of copyright. We asked people to write about copyright using different disciplinary approaches and from the perspective of different positions in the industry; we were not trying to develop any specific kind of copyright 'line'. Yet many of the authors involved concluded that the current copyright regime was of limited benefit to the musical practitioners they describe. We hope that what follows illuminates the complexity and the interest of the issues involved, both in the range of questions covered and in the ways in which different chapters overlap. We haven't attempted to edit out some of the more obvious examples of repetition – the various discussions of 'fair use', for example. The cumulative effect is to clarify the issues involved and to draw attention to the most prominent arguments currently engaging popular music scholars.

We have divided these chapters into two sections. We feel that it is impossible to understand current copyright issues in the music industry without an understanding of the historical processes which have led us to where we are. The three chapters in Part I thus describe the conceptual and historical background to contemporary copyright discourse. Martin Kretschmer and Friedemann Kawohl provide a comprehensive guide to development of the idea of copyright as a kind of property, *intellectual property*, since its origins in eighteenth-century European political and legal thought. Ruth Towse examines in detail the economic arguments for (and against) copyright, again taking a broad historical overview, while Dave Laing focuses on the politics of copyright or, to be more specific, on the way in which the various music business interests have shaped (and been shaped by) the international copyright framework over the last 200 years. Between them, these three essays should help readers understand the legal structure in which everyday musical practices now take place but note the assumption being made here: we've organised this part of the book on the principle that law is best understood as an effect of philosophical and economic thought, the result of economic and political power struggles, rather than developing as a legal doctrine *sui generis*.

This should be borne in mind when reading the second part of the book, which collects together chapters on how copyright is experienced by different music business practitioners, for whom the law certainly is materially present, sometimes as a defence against exploitation, more often it seems as a constraint on what they can do, as producers or consumers. Firstly, Steve Greenfield and Guy Osborn describe the reasons why copyright disputes reach the courts, giving judges an unusual influence on record business practice, and also discuss how power relationships within the music industry affect the distribution of copyright rights. Roger Wallis considers the place of composers in 'the music industry value chain', and the dilemmas facing the national collecting societies established to administer their rights as the music industry is increasingly organised globally. Jason Toynbee and Paul Théberge reflect on the ways in which copyright provides a misleading account of musical creativity. Their arguments overlap, though Toynbee's derives from a historical sociological account of popular musical production, while Théberge's rests on an account of how digital technology has affected recent music-making practices in the studio. For both writers the problem of copyright law is that it assumes that music is a kind of object (a work, a score, a thing) that it long since ceased to be. Anthony Seeger looks at the way in which Western copyright law not only fails to make sense in other kinds of music culture but also denies traditional musicians moral or financial control of the use of their works by Western entrepreneurs. Finally, Simon Frith considers the ways in which copyright affects media uses of music and its casual consumption, and Lee Marshall 'is concerned with those people who ignore or disregard copyright in their daily lives'.

As we have already mentioned, all the writers here describe the ways in which the present copyright system restricts rather than encourages creativity; limits rather than supports musical activity. There is no consensus, though, on what should be done about this. Some of the authors imply that copyright law will just have to change because in its present shape it is becoming irrelevant. Others propose specific legal changes that need to be brought about by political campaigns. Others still seem more fatalistic, suggesting that the present system reflects political and economic realities that we, musicians and consumers alike, will have to live with. We return to the question of the future of copyright at the end of the book.

Notes

1. This was certainly an unanticipated consequence. Janis Ian remembers the head of Sony marketing explicitly enthusing that 'CDs were uncopyable' when persuading her to license her record, *Between the Lines*, in CD format (at a reduced royalty rate). See Janis Ian: 'A freedom that works: the upside

of download', available among other places on www.openDemocracy.net, downloaded 31 July, 2002.

2. We should also mention in this context the Sonny Bono Copyright Term Extension Act of 1998, which extended the term of copyright protection in the USA from fifty years after the death of the author to seventy years (as in Europe) and the term of copyright protection of the work of 'corporate creators' from seventy-five to ninety-five years.

3. This is not to say that corporate media content providers were the only lobbyists concerned. Media access providers such as Internet servers, computer equipment manufacturers and telecommunications companies had their own interest in increasing the consumer demand for downloading devices and in avoiding prosecution for the consumer 'misuse' of their equipment. But the lack of much media coverage of or political argument about the WIPO treaties or EU Directives or even Congressional hearings does suggest that digital copyright regulation has been shaped primarily by corporate argument.

4. On 27 October 2003, the *New York Times* reported that students at MIT were developing a version of peer-to-peer music sharing that would distribute tracks via the university's analog campus cable system. This would be legal as analog technology is not regulated as rigorously as digital technology is. (John Schwartz: 'With Cable TV at M.I.T., Who Needs Napster?' Thanks to Peter Meech for this reference.)

5. In its 20 August 2003 issue, the American satirical magazine, *The Onion*, published its response to the hype surrounding the iPod. Under the headline 'I Have An iPod – In My Mind!', Ted Lascowitcz wrote that 'I can call up any song I've ever heard, any time I want. And I never have to load software or change batteries. There are no firewire cords or docks to mess with. I just put my hands behind my head, lean back, and select a tune from the extensive music-library folder *inside my brain.*' After absorbing the endless anti-theft messages from the RIAA, it's impossible to read this without thinking immediately of the ways in which publishers will seek to do something about such an appallingly unregulated use of their properties. (Thanks to Alfred Archer for this reference.)

6. Quoted in Karlin Lillington, 'Sentries at the gate', *Guardian Online*, 20 December 2001, p. 3.

7. What follows is indebted to Carey and Verow (1997).

8. A derivative work is a new work that incorporates aspects of a pre-existing work. Translations, screenplays based on novels and abridgements are all examples of derivative works. A new artistic creation could also be a derivative work. For example, painting a moustache on an image of the Mona Lisa creates a new work but one that is derived from an earlier work, as is a rap record that utilises samples.

9. This list is taken from the 1988 Copyright Designs and Patents Act. As already discussed these provisions have now been extended to cover digital/ Internet transmission.

10. There are some exceptions to this. If a work is commissioned, then the copyright is vested in the person or company who did the commissioning; similarly if a work is produced as a normal part of employment then its copyright is vested with the employer. Arguments about who owns the copyright in such situations can be complicated (and will be affected by the nature of the contracts between the parties) – disputes about who owns the rights to advertising jingles regularly reach the courts, for example. In 1999, using this 'work for hire' principle the American recording industry attempted to amend US copyright act so that all recordings made under contract were classified as work for hire, but this did not succeed. Their model was the Hollywood studio system – as film studios initiate and fund films they own their copyright. Record companies argued that they were working in a similar way.

11. One feature of digital distribution is that it makes it easier for 'first owners' to reach a public without third party help.

12. Example taken from Cornish (2000: 11–12).

13. It is quite common in plagiarism cases for a defendant to claim that the plaintiffs did not in fact 'originate' the song at issue but simply lifted a melody from the public domain. They could therefore not claim any exclusive rights in it.

14. One further complication here is the nature of collective authorship or collaboration. How should rights premised on the author be assigned when the creation of a work was a group process?

References

Carey, P. and Verow, R. (1997), *Media and Entertainment Law*, Bristol: Jordans.

Cornish, G. (2000), *Understand Copyright in a Week*, London: Hodder and Stoughton.

Deas, S. (1998), 'Jazzing up the Copyright Act? Resolving the uncertainties of the United States anti-bootlegging law', *Hastings Communications and Entertainment Law Journal* 20 (3): 567–637.

Frith, S. (2002), 'Illegality and the music industry' in M. Talbot (ed.) *The Business of Music*, Liverpool: Liverpool University Press, 195–216.

Litman, J. (1991), 'Copyright as myth', paper presented to conference on 'Intellectual Property and the Construction of Authorship', Case Western Reserve University, 19–21 April.

McLeod, K. (2001), *Owning Culture. Authorship, Ownership, and Intellectual Property*, New York: Peter Lang.

Mann, C. C. (2000), 'The heavenly jukebox', *Atlantic Monthly*, September. http://the atlantic.com/issues/2000/og/mann.htm

Sherrard, B. (1992), 'Performer's protection: the evolution of a complete offence', *Entertainment Law Review* 3 (2): 57–63.

Vaidhyanathan, S. (2002), 'Copyright as cudgel', *Chronicle of Higher Education*, 2 August. http://chronicle.com/free/v48/i47/47b00701.htm

PART I
Conceptual Approaches

CHAPTER 2

The History and Philosophy of Copyright[1]

Martin Kretschmer and Friedemann Kawohl

Introduction

In modern legal parlance, copyright has become subsumed under a concept of intellectual property. This appears to evoke the justificatory package of individual property rights that has shaped Western societies since John Locke's *Second Treatise of Government* (1690). Legitimising private ownership in the wake of the Glorious Revolution of 1688, Locke proposed that by 'mixing' labour with previously common goods a new 'private dominion' would be created.

Characteristic of the property approach are exclusivity (that is, the right to deny use by third parties of the intellectual territory claimed) and transferability (that is, the right to transfer title of the intellectual territory freely to third parties).[2] Trespassing on intellectual territory (unauthorised copying) has been condemned with the property term 'piracy' since the eighteenth century.[3] The Eighth Commandment, 'Thou shalt not steal' is still cited as a 'sacred principle' behind the provisions of modern copyright law (Laddie 1997: 2).[4]

In this chapter, we suggest that the concept of property is not very helpful in determining the appropriate regulatory policy for the creation and distribution of culture. Property is that to which protection is afforded, not *vice versa*. In the case of copyright, it has been said that without the artificial scarcity introduced by property concepts, the costs of production of creative works will remain above the costs of copying. Creative production therefore would not take place.[5] However, this argument from the utility of property provisions is implausible for a copyright term that is calculated from the life of the author (plus fifty to seventy years), and for a copyright scope that prevents desirable cultural engagement, for example, in adaptation and sampling.

If there is another, independent (non-regulatory) moral argument for copyright, it is problematic. We shall argue that norms of authorship do not support claims to a private, exclusive, transferable domain of intellectual property; rather they justify an informational link between creator and creative products, and perhaps a claim to rewards from unauthorised exploitation of such products.

The chapter is structured around the key evolutionary phases of the modern copyright paradigm: (1) the proto-copyright of crown privileges and letter patents, responding to the invention of the printing press since the late 1400s; (2) the eighteenth-century Battle of the Booksellers, eventually asserting copyright as a limited incentive in the production and dissemination of cultural products; (3) the parallel development of author norm towards the end of the eighteenth century, associated primarily with the philosophers of German Idealism; (4) the nineteenth-century statutory construction of abstract works to which all acts of exploitations refer, fusing the property concept of utilitarian incentives with restrictions derived from the author (culminating in the Berne Convention).

The justificatory arguments for music copyright are generally similar to those for other literary or artistic creations. Initially copyright mechanisms evolved for the predominant technology of book printing, with music being denied statutory protection until 1777. This changed with the early nineteenth century, when music became a trend setter in defining abstract work identity through the newly restricted acts of public performance and adaptation. The focus of the chapter is on the four jurisdictions that have shaped modern copyright: Britain, Germany, France and the United States.

Proto-copyright: crown privileges and letter patents

During the period dubbed the Renaissance by historians in the nineteenth century, several factors combined to turn copyright into a legal issue. The first factor was the emergence of a sense of individualism (realised in the art of Italian painters and sculptors). The second factor was a period of rapid economic expansion carried by a new class of international merchants. Commerce became organised around annual trade fairs which created an efficient distribution structure for new ideas (Epstein 1998). In turn, the merchants themselves created a market of people with surplus income and demand for leisure goods. The third factor was the invention (around 1450) of a technology enabling the fast and efficient reproduction of ideas: Gutenberg's printing press. These elements were in place by the end of the fifteenth century, when an estimated 20 million books were circulating in Europe (Eisenstein 1979).

Reprints of popular books were soon pervasive, but the late medieval states had a ready-made device for controlling the dissemination of new ideas while solving the profitability problem of some printers: the Crown privilege. Awarding monopoly rights against a fee was the defining economic instrument of late feudalism (cf. North and Thomas 1973). Early printing privileges are documented in Venice (1469), Milan (1480s), Germany (1501) and France (1507) (Pohlmann 1962). In England, the first book printed with a privilege from the sovereign was published in 1518 (Patterson 1968). The earliest known privilege for exclusive rights to print and sell music was granted on 25 May 1498 by the Venetian signoria to Ottaviano dei Petrucci, for a term of twenty years (Püttlingen 2001: 141).

Typically, Crown privileges were issued to printers, either individually or collectively, mostly for a limited period of time, sometimes for specific books only. There are also many examples of privileges obtained by individual creators with court connections. The two systems operated in parallel.

In Germany, we find letters patent protecting the work of authors and composers on a common law basis from around 1500. The first known imperial patent to a composer was Maximilian's privilege for Arnold Schlick (1511). A prominent example was the protection afforded to Orlande de Lassus (1532–94) who collected privileges in various jurisdictions (France 1575; Germany 1581). Privileges were influential at the Frankfurt book fairs which took place under imperial legislation. Emperor Rudolf II even issued a *Mandat* (1596) that gave preference to the protection of authors over publishers. Injunctions and substantial penalties were regularly enforced through the courts, though this tradition disappeared with the religious wars in central Europe (1618–48) (Pohlmann 1962).

In London, the Stationers were a minor London guild of writers, illuminators, bookbinders and booksellers, established since 1403. With the arrival of the printing press, booksellers and printers became the two dominant groups. Stationers obtained the right to print a new book by stating their claim before the Stationers' Company Warden. Because of the monopolistic control of the London printers, this amounted to a safeguard of the right to copy, though the practice had its roots (as in France) in censorship: registering a book at Stationers' Hall was necessary to legalise publishing.[6] The Stationers' Company royal charter of 5 May 1557 was an attempt by the Catholic Queen Mary to control the spread of heretical material:

No person within this our realm of England or the dominions of the same shall practise or exercise by himself, or by his ministers, his servants or by any other person the art or mistery of printing any book or any thing for sale or traffic within this our realm of England or the dominions of the same, unless the same person at the time of his foresaid printing is or shall be one of the community of the foresaid mistery or art of Stationary of the foresaid City, or has therefore license of us or the heirs or successors of us the foresaid Queen by the letters patent of us or the heirs or successors of us the foresaid Queen. (Patterson 1968: 32)

In Saxony, central to the German book trade because of the annual Leipzig trade fair, a *Bücherkommission* governed by the Lutheran Church formally controlled the trade after 1687. Like the London Stationers, the Leipzig Books Commission had to provide a body for both censorship and regulation of reprint. It was composed of a councillor, a professor, a books inspector (i.e. a policeman), and a clerk all working under surveillance of the *Kirchenrat*, the local Lutheran Church board. The Books Commission had the power to order bans, confiscations or further investigations (Curtius 1831: 204ff. §1,505; cited in Kawohl 2002a: 276).

Until the end of the eighteenth century, authors (and composers) typically handed over their manuscripts against one single payment. John Dowland's wife, for example, received £20 from George Eastland for ownership of the manuscript and half the dedication reward of Dowland's *Second Booke of Songs or Ayres* (1600) (Dowling 1932). The Stationers' *Hall Book* or Leipzig's *Eintragsrolle* provided a safeguard for publishers against other publishers; it provided no institutional recognition of authors' rights. In fact, when selling on manuscripts (which was soon commonplace: a significant trade had developed by 1700), publishers were utterly unconcerned about the authors.

A few exceptions are documented where authors began to assert themselves. They came to some written agreement, such as Thomas Ford who, upon registration of *Musicke of Sundrie Kindes* (13 March 1607), obtained the right 'that this copye shall never hereafter be printed agayne without the consent of master fford the Aucthor' (Hunter 1986: 271). Alternatively, authors with access to the Crown could obtain a letter patent of monopoly protection, much like the earlier imperial practices of central Europe. In 1575, Elizabeth I granted twenty-one-year monopolies to Thomas Tallis (1505–85) and his pupil William Byrd (1543–1623) which coincided with the publication of their celebrated collection of thirty-four *Cantiones Sacrae* in the same year. Crown privileges sometimes conflicted with the interests of publishers, as in the case of George Wither who, after obtaining a letter patent for his *Hymns and Songs of the Church* (1623), took the Stationers' Company to court (Carlson 1966). Prominent beneficiaries of English Crown privileges include Handel, J. C. Bach and Thomas Arne. While some composers succeeded in exploiting these early institutional mechanisms, others remained firmly locked into restrictive relationships. Joseph Haydn's contract of employment with Prince Esterházy in 1761 still contained a clause forbidding the publication of his works (Tschmuck 2002: 214).

The old system of printing privileges and letters patent has been identified as a progenitor of modern copyright (Pohlmann 1962; Patterson 1968; Feather 1994). There are indeed striking similarities between privileges and copyright: both are granted by the legislator and serve as a means to protect printers, and sometimes authors, against competitors or unauthorised exploitation. However, there are important differences in practice, as well as in underlying rationale: unlike copyrights, privileges were not automatic and could be revoked; they could be granted both to printers of original books and to reprinters; and privileges would not extend past a state's border (cf. Dölemeyer and Klippel 1991: 191).

Apart from their role in censorship and raising revenue, Crown privileges were also an aspect of protectionist economic policies. While occasionally recognising individual creativity, they remained part of an absolutist and mercantilist framework. Thus their legitimation waned with the decline of these economic and political systems: in England at the end of the 1600s; on the European continent half a century later.

From the Statute of Anne to the US Constitution

In 1690, John Locke proposed what would become known as the 'labour theory' of property. For our purposes Locke's theory may be summarised thus: in a state of nature, goods are held in common through a grant from God. 'Being given for the use of men, there must of necessity be a means to appropriate them some way or other, before they can be of any use or at all beneficial.' Every man has property in his own person: 'this nobody has a right to but himself. The "labour" of his body and "work" of his hands, we may say, is properly his.' If a person 'mixe[s] his labour' with a common good, it is converted into an exclusive 'private dominion'. Private appropriation, however, is limited by some provisos: one may only take as long as 'enough and as good' is left for others, and one may not appropriate so much that goods 'waste or spoil'. The first condition is akin to an equal opportunities provision; the second condition condemns waste as a diminution of the common stock of potential property.[7]

Lockean property thoughts have become part of the fabric of Western political expression. There are obvious resonances with contemporary corporate lobbying for intellectual property protection. We are familiar with the argument that 'creative effort' and/or 'investments' justify 'exclusive control' of the 'value added'. Natural rights are supposed to function as a constraint on political decision-making because they cannot be overruled or amended to achieve desirable social outcomes. Intellectual property as a Lockean right may remain outside the scope of regulation.

It is therefore remarkable that the first statutory copyright law conceived in a Lockean environment expressly refused to grant copyright as a natural right. The so-called Statute of Anne came into force on 10 April 1710 and protected 'Books and Other Writings' against reprints for fourteen years from first publication, renewable once.[8]

Politically, the Statute of Anne was a response to the lapse on 3 May 1695 of the Licensing Act of 1662, a censorship law introduced by the Restoration king, Charles II. The Licensing Act had been announced as 'An Act for Preventing Abuses in Printing Seditious, Treasonable and Unlicensed Books and Pamphlets, and for Regulating of Printing and Printing Presses', granting the Stationers' Company the power to seize, destroy and levy fines with the effect of consolidating the monopoly of the London Stationers as the only legitimate publisher of printed materials. By the 1690s, Parliament had noticed that stationers 'are impowered to hinder the printing [of] all innocent and useful Books', and that scholars were forced to buy classics and foreign books from the stationers 'at the extravagant Price they demand, but must content with their ill and incorrect Editions' (XI H. C. Jour.: 305–6, quoted in Patterson 1968: 139ff).

Table 1: Statute of Anne (1709/10) for the Encouragement of Learning

Protected Subject Matter	Owner	Criteria for Protection	Exclusive Rights	Term	Registration
'Books and other Writings' (s.1)	'Authors or Purchasers' (preamble & s.1)	silent; s.1 suggests (emphasis added): 'for the Encouragement of learned Men to compose and write *useful* Books'	'print, reprint, or import, or cause to be printed, reprinted or imported' sell, publish or expose to Sale' (s.1)	14 years from publication date (s.1) after expiry 'sole Right of printing or disposing of Copies' returns to author for second term of 14 years (s.11)	'Register Book of the Company of Stationers' kept at Stationers' Hall (s.2)

The Statute of Anne replaced the Stationers' Company's perpetual prerogative with a statutory but limited monopoly open to all 'Authors or Purchasers'. The Act was constructed as a regulation of the book trade for the public interest, and the original Lockean preamble, referring to 'the undoubted property' that authors had in their books as 'the product of their learning and labour' was scrapped during parliamentary reading (Rose 1993: 45). The new preamble suggests 'An Act for the Encouragement of Learning'. 'Learned Men' would now be encouraged to 'compose and write useful Books' because the consent of 'Authors or Proprietors' would be required for the printing, reprinting, sale and publication of their work (s. 1). The wording remains ambiguous as to where the incentive should bite precisely: at the point of creation (author) or investment in publication and distribution (proprietor).

Music was not thought to be protected under the Statute of Anne but although unauthorised publication of a composer's work was therefore not illegal, accusations of piracy still flew between music publishers. For example, three editions of Corelli's *Twelve Sonatas Op. 5* were available in London around 1700: the Rome edition imported by Banister and King, Roger's Amsterdam edition sold by Francis Vaillant, and Walsh's, copied from the Rome edition. Roger and Walsh tried to compete on authenticity, citing corrections by various Italian musicians associated with Corelli. The composer would not have seen any financial benefits from these activities (Hunter 1986; Rasch 2002). Interestingly, eighteenth-century music publishers, unlike their book selling colleagues, did not lobby for statutory protection. 'For music publishers, the maintenance of copyright protection over 14 or 28 years was unnecessary, as most musical works would not remain in fashion that long' (Hunter 1986: 276). It appears that the control of distribution channels and predatory pricing against new entrants was as effective a means of market dominance as statutory protection. Copyright law cannot be evaluated independently of economic behaviour.[9]

The two most important copyright cases of the eighteenth century were the King's Bench decision in *Millar v. Taylor* (1769), in which an author's perpetual right in common law was asserted on the basis of Lockean arguments; and *Donaldson v. Becket* (1774), in which the House of Lords upheld the public interest aims of the Statute of Anne. Overturning *Millar v. Taylor, Donaldson v. Becket* exposed copyright as created and limited by statute. These cases influenced the development of both American and European copyright law, articulating many of the concepts in which copyright is still discussed today. They warrant a closer look.

In *Millar v. Taylor* (1769; also Burrow 1773), Robert Taylor, a printer from Berwick, had published an edition of *The Seasons* by James Thomson which Andrew Millar, a London bookseller, had purchased from the author in 1729. Thomson died in 1748, and it was evident that the (once renewable) fourteen year term of the Statute of Anne must have expired when the case was brought in 1767. Millar argued that there existed a perpetual author right under common law, independently of the statutory provisions of the Statute of Anne. The King's Bench court, dominated by the eminent jurist William Murray (Lord Mansfield) who was involved in many of the early copyright cases, supported Millar's claim from first principles of property:

> Because it is just, that an author should reap the pecuniary profits of his own ingenuity and labour. It is just, that another should not use his name, without his consent. It is fit, that he should judge when to publish, or whether he ever will publish. It is fit he should not only choose the time, but the manner of publication; how many; what volume; what print. It is fit, he should choose to whose care he will trust the accuracy and correctness of the impression; in whose honesty he will confide, not to foist in additions; with other reasonings of the same effect.' (98 *English Reports*: 252)

Strangely, the court did not even consider why such an author right should be structured as property, transferable to a London bookseller in perpetuity. After all, Mansfield appears to argue for two kinds of author rights: (1) reward for labour; and (2) the right to protect an author's reputation by preserving the integrity and source of a work. These rights could have been provided independently of property interests (see final section below). Patterson has argued that Lord Mansfield's opinion in *Millar v. Taylor* prevented the development of a doctrine of author rights under common law independently of a publisher's exclusive property control. (1968, ch. 8; see also Patterson 1987). In doing so, Mansfield sowed the seeds for the modern misery of copyright, *pace* the Lords' decision in *Donaldson*.

Donaldson v. Becket (1774 also Burrow, 1774) is probably the most celebrated of all copyright cases. Reasserting the fourteen year term of the Statute of Anne, and perhaps abolishing the author's common law copyright, the case was eventually decided by a simple vote in the House of Lords. 'Thus the peers gave an answer to the literary-property question, but they did not provide a rationale.' (Rose 1993: 103). Unsurprisingly, *Donaldson v. Becket* has been interpreted and reinterpreted ever since. Debate is still raging today about which Lord/Judge/Act meant what (cf. Deazley 2003). The case was uniquely dramatic, enthralling the contemporary literary scene. People queued for admittance to the final hearing.

Alexander Donaldson was an Edinburgh bookseller who specialised in reprints of literary standards. In 1763, he had set up a shop in London where he sold his books at 30–50 per cent less than London prices (Rose

1993: 93). In 1768, Donaldson deliberately and provocatively brought out another edition of Thomson's *The Seasons* (the subject of the litigation in *Miller v. Taylor*). Upon Andrew Millar's death in 1768, Thomas Becket and fourteen stationers purchased the copyrights of Millar's estate at auction for £505 (13 June 1769). Donaldson was excluded from the sale. In November 1772, Becket and his partners obtained an injunction against Donaldson who was said to have sold several thousand copies of *The Seasons* printed in Edinburgh. Donaldson appealed to the House of Lords where the case was heard on 22 February 1774. Five questions were directed to the Lord Judges (98 *English Reports* 257–8) who answered as indicated below, though there remains, as already mentioned, considerable confusion as to the exact legal significance of these votes.[10]

1. Whether an author of a book or literary composition had at common law 'the sole right of first printing and publishing the same for sale,' and a right of action against a person printing, publishing, and selling without his consent. Held, yes by a vote of 10 to 1.
2. If the author had such a right, did the law take it away upon his publishing the book or literary composition; and might any person thereafter be free to reprint and sell the work? Held, no by a vote of 7 to 4.
3. Assuming the right of common law, was it taken away by the Statute of Anne, and is an author limited to the terms and conditions of that statute for his remedy? Held, yes by a vote 6 to 5.
4. Whether an author of any literary composition and his assigns have the sole right of printing and publishing the same in perpetuity by the common law? Held, yes by a vote of 7 to 4.
5. Whether this right was restrained or taken away by the Statute of Anne? Held, yes by a vote of 6 to 5.

The first three questions refer to the rights of the author, the latter two were phrased in terms of 'the author and his assigns', the language of the Statute of Anne and, in practice, the rights of the booksellers. Following the decision in *Donaldson*, copyright was again a right created and limited by statute, not a source of income for the London stationers under the veil of perpetual author interests exercised by assigned proprietors.

The notion of copyright as a regulation for the benefit of the public, incentivising creative production, was most emphatically adopted by the United States. The US Constitutional Convention convened from May until September 1787. On 5 September, the copyright clause was agreed without debate. Congress should be empowered 'To promote the Progress of Science and the useful Arts, by securing for limited Times, to Authors and Inventors, the exclusive Right to their respective Writings and Discoveries' (Art. I, s. 8, cl. 8).

The first federal Copyright Act was passed in 1790: 'An act for the encouragement of learning, by securing the copies of maps, charts, and books, to the authors and proprietors of such copies, during the times therein mentioned.' It was closely modelled on the Statute of Anne in its utilitarian rationale, limited fourteen-year term (renewable once), registration requirement, and the restriction of specified acts of 'printing, reprinting, publishing and vending'.[11] Particularly interesting is section 5 which encourages pirating of foreign works as:

> nothing in this act shall be construed to extend to prohibit the importation or vending, reprinting, or publishing within the United States, of any map, chart, book or books, written, printed, or published by any person not a citizen of the United States, in foreign parts or places without the jurisdiction of the United States.

The public interest is clearly articulated as the national interest of a young nation, benefiting from the quick and cheap dissemination of the latest foreign advances in scientific and cultural thinking. The 1831 Copyright Act extends this prescription: one may import from abroad any kind of work without exception.

In *Wheaton v. Peters* (1832), the leading case of early American copyright law, the US Supreme Court denied that there was any author's right in common law (after publication) independent of the copyright statute. In the language of the court, copyright is a limited statutory grant of a monopoly which benefits the author in order to satisfy the public interest in learning. US copyright law remained steadfastly utilitarian until well into the twentieth century. The Congress Report accompanying the 1909 Copyright Act still argues that the legislation 'is not based upon any natural right that the author has in his writings . . . but upon the ground that the welfare of the public will be served'.[12]

Most contemporary observers believed that the House of Lords in *Donaldson* had taken away the author's common law right upon publication, and replaced it with a limited copyright granted by statute for the public's benefit. As we shall see, though, it was later thought that *Donaldson* did admit an underlying natural common law right (cf. Rose 1993; Deazley 2003). Copyright's utilitarian rationale was thus replaced with a broader concept, whose term and scope was derived from arguments about the author. The following section argues that this nineteenth-century reinterpretation owes much to philosophical developments in German Idealism.

Kant – Fichte – Hegel: The author arrives

Early print regulations – the statutes of booksellers' guilds, Crown privileges – were underpinned by collective structures. Copyright, on the other hand, is based on claims of individuals. Within eighteenth- and nineteenth-century discussions, those individual claims were most easily justified via the concept of property. As an English pamphlet of 1747 claimed:

> For that the Product of the *Mind* is as well capable of becoming Property, as that of the *Hand*, is evident from hence, that it hath in it those two essential Conditions, which, by the allowance of all Writers of Law, make things susceptible of Property; namely common *Utility*, and a Capacity of having its Possession *ascertained.*' (William Warburton, *A Letter from an Author to a Member of Parliament Concerning Literary Property*, quoted in Rose 1993: 72)

Despite Warburton's optimism, it was not straightforward to support copyright as a form of property under the then prevailing Roman law tradition of absolute ownership of land and movable things. The Roman law obsession with occupancy as the source of all property claims is still reflected in Locke's approach where the undoubted possession of one's own labour is converted into individual ownership of previously common goods.

In France, Denis Diderot experimented with a non-labour, genius-based theory of literary creation, ironically in a pamphlet commissioned by the Paris Guild which – in the Stationers' tradition – sought to establish a property title for printers via contracts with authors (1763, *Lettre historique et politique adressée à un magistrat sur le commerce de la librairies*). Diderot (who had translated some of John Locke's writings) rejected the Lockean notion that intellectual territory could be appropriated like land. For Diderot, an author's bond with a work is inviolable not because of the conversion of common into private goods but because of an act of first creation: 'what form of wealth could belong to a man, if not a work of the mind . . . if not his own thoughts . . . the most precious part of him, that will never perish, that will immortalize him' (quoted in Marshall 2001: 24).

Immanuel Kant's 1781 discussion *Von der Unrechtmäßigkeit des Büchernachdrucks* (of the illegality of reprinting) similarly derives copyright from the natural right of self-expression rather than from a property right of authors or publishers. According to Kant: 'in a book, conceived as a writing, the author speaks to his reader'. Thus the book as a physical entity is a mere 'tool to transfer a speech to the audience'. Following Kant, the Idealist philosopher, Johann Gottlieb Fichte, advanced what he deemed to be a proof that ascertaining intellectual possession was in fact possible via the concept of form. In his 1792 article *Beweis von der Unrechtmäßigkeit des Büchernachdrucks* ('proof of the illegality of reprinting') Fichte identified the permanent feature of a book as 'the form of the thoughts', the result of a twofold abstraction: the intellectual part is abstracted from the physical part ('printed paper'); and within the intellectual part 'the form of the thoughts' is abstracted from the ideas. Hence there are three types of property in a book. The physical book as full property is completely at the owner's disposal. The ideas after being shared with the readers become a common property of the author and his readers. But the abstracted form necessarily remains the author's property, because it is 'physically impossible' to be appropriated by another person.

There is a tension in Fichte's theory between form as a property (*proprium*) of the work from which it is abstracted, and form referring to the process of formation rather than its result. This was addressed by Georg Wilhelm Friedrich Hegel. Property for Hegel connects a person to his freedom; it is 'the manifestation of a personality' ('*das Dasein der Persönlichkeit*', Hegel 1828, s. 51). Property becomes the foundation of a Philosophy of Right since, without property, a person is not conceivable at all. Hegel employed a twin concept of form (on the objective side) and formation (on the subjective side). Neither mere physical seizure nor mere symbolic marking of the property is an appropriate way to acquire property, but 'formation' is. Thus formation has in Hegel's theory a similar function to labour in Locke's. With respect to intellectual property, Hegel distinguishes between disposable things of 'external nature' and inalienable 'inner' capabilities. An author may sell the right to use a 'single production' of his intellectual capabilities for a 'restricted period'. After buying and reading a book, its ideas are indeed the property of the buyer. The buyer is in possession of the 'capability to express himself in exactly this way'. But this capability can never be his *property*, since it remains with the author.

The perpetual bond between an author and his work in Fichte's and Hegel's theories was combined with the Kantian 'right of expression' in Eduard Gans' justification of performance rights. Gans, a Hegel follower and professor of law at Berlin University, was referring to theatre plays when he wrote in 1832:

> In performances the author exposes himself to the risk of disapproval and thus the dramatic author should be able to decide every time anew to which public he presents his work. The opinion according to which a play once published may be performed on every stage, is wrong for two reasons, first, it allows someone to enrich oneself at another's expense and, secondly, it exposes someone to a danger, to which he possibly does not want to be exposed. (Gans 1832: 381)

Since that time, to use a work means not only to accept the authorship of a dramatist or a composer but also to recognise that *everything* ever done with the work is associated with the author's personality. Copyright concepts in German Idealism thus deviate from property concepts in the exclusive, transferable sense that Anglo-American liberalism derived via Locke from Roman law. Kant's concept of copyright was based on a person's right to express himself. In Fichte's and Hegel's theories, while an author's ownership of his intellectual creation provides the justification for copyright, this property is inalienable and thus, in an Anglo-American legal sense, not property at all.

Abstract works: The road from Paris to Berne

We have so far identified the main justificatory avenues for individual copyrights developed during the eighteenth century: (1) the labour theory of property initiated by John Locke, expressed in the debates around the author's common law rights; (2) the utilitarian incentive to creative production, implicit in the Statute of Anne, reasserted in *Donaldson v. Becket*, and canonised in the Constitution of the United States; (3) the personality theory advanced within German Idealism.

The early nineteenth century saw a paradigm shift towards the concepts that characterise modern copyright law. Three features appear in seminal legislation such as the French revolutionary laws of 1791 and 1793; the Prussian Law of 1837; and Talfourd's Act (1842) in the UK:

1. The author becomes the source of protection. The term calculation shifted from the date of publication to the life of the author (including a *post mortem* allowance to cover the author's dependants).
2. Protected subject matter extends beyond printed books to literary and artistic creations in a wide sense (including music). A threshold criterion of merit (i.e. originality) is introduced.
3. Restricted acts refer to an abstract work identity rather than printed matter. Performing rights are introduced for dramatic and musical works; adaptations, such as excerpts or instrumental arrangements, and transcriptions of sermons and lectures become restricted as unauthorised derivatives.

This new conception of copyright has been recognised by many academic commentators as a crucial moment. Sherman and Bentley (1999: 2–6) date the transformation within the British tradition from what they call a 'pre-modern' to a 'modern' intellectual property law to 'the middle period of the 19th Century'. Authors within critical literary theory (Woodmansee 1984; Woodmansee and Jaszi 1994; Boyle 1996) and the sociology of copyright (Marshall 2001) have associated this transformation with the emerging Romantic conception of the author around the turn of the nineteenth century. We offer a different account, emphasising a process of abstraction that has an important source in Idealist philosophical thought which fused in the early nineteenth century with the exclusive, transferable property concept that had developed in the liberal tradition (drawing on both on labour and utilitarian justifications).[13]

The first copyright statutes that take their lead (in term and scope) from the author are the French revolutionary Acts of 1791 (regarding performances of theatre and musical drama) and 1793 (regarding the sale and dissemination of artistic works of any genre) which replaced the old system of publishers' rights. The Act of 19 January 1791 introduces for the first time a *post mortem* ownership of five years, while the famous decree of 19 July 1793 ('Declaration of the Rights of Genius') grants a general transferable life of author term (plus ten years). The philosophical basis of the French laws, however, is somewhat uncertain. On the one hand, we have expression-related justifications. As Le Chapelier put it in his famous speech introducing the decree (quoted in Davies 2002: 137): 'The most sacred, the most legislate, the most unassailable . . . the most personal of properties, is a work which is the fruit of the imagination of a writer.' On the other hand, there is a strong public interest undercurrent suspicious of exclusive control. Condorcét had argued in the 1776 pamphlet *Fragments sur la liberté de la presse* that literary property was not a natural individual right but 'founded in society itself' (quoted in Hesse 1991: 103). According to Hesse, the revolutionary laws represented copyright as a reward to the author as public servant, not as the Lockean property right of liberal individualism. Ginsburg (1990) suggests that early French copyright was indeed very similar to the Anglo-American tradition, with the courts regularly balancing the rights of the authors with the needs of the public.[14]

In the context of the argument advanced in this chapter, these early French author laws contain the first signs of rights granted without formalities (all privileges were abolished), and of rights granted for public performance. The imminent paradigm shift toward the protection of *all* instantiations of abstract works can be nicely illustrated with the changing protection afforded to music.

The Statute of Anne did not cater specifically for music, though case law developed classifying sheet music as 'writings' within the meaning of the Act. In the wake of *Millar v. Taylor* and *Donaldson v. Becket*, a test case was launched by Johann Christian Bach (the youngest son of J. S. Bach) and Carl Friedrich Abel, then at the height of their fame as organisers of a popular London concert series. The dispute concerned an unauthorised edition of a Bach exercise and sonata published by Long-man & Lukey. On 18 March 1773, the case was brought in Chancery but it was only in 1777 that it was finally heard, again before Lord Chief Justice Mansfield. Cowper reported it thus (Small 1985):

> Lord Mansfield called on Mr. Wood [attorney for the defendant] to begin; and without hearing Mr. Robinson [attorney for the plaintiff] in answer, said, the case was so clear and the arguments such, that it was difficult to speak seriously upon it. The words of the Act of Parliament are very large: 'books and other writings.' It is not confined to language or letters. Music is a science; it may be written; and the mode of conveying the ideas, is by signs and marks. A person may use the copy by playing it, but he has no right to rob the author of the profit, by multiplying copies and disposing of them for his own use. If the narrow interpretation contended for in the argument were to hold, it would equally apply to algebra, mathematics, arithmetic, hieroglyphics. All these are conveyed by signs and figures. There is no colour for saying that music is not within the Act. Afterwards, on Monday, June 16th, the Court certified in these words, 'Having heard counsel and considered the case, we are of the opinion, that a musical composition is a writing within the Statute of the 8th of Queen Anne'.

Note that protection was expressly confirmed only against 'multiplying copies' of printed material, while any 'person may use the copy by playing it'. There was thus no protection for the work itself whose identity was still uncertain![15]

A favourite argument of publishers remained that they had acquired a copy legitimately. They thus denied that a musical work could be owned independently of what they were actually selling (that is, a copy of a manuscript of ostentatiously 'uncertain' authorship obtained from a third party). In J. C. Bach's second law suit (also filed in 1773, but probably settled out of court), the defendants Longman & Lukey admitted 'that the said three symphonys entitled as follows: Three symphonies in 8 parts for Violins Hoboys Horns Tenor and Bass were purchased from The Hague by [Dutch publisher] Hummell', this being a 'constant, uniform and well known custom and practice' (Allen-Russell 2002: 27).

The emerging modern regime of copyright (as epitomised by the Berne Convention) employs a new concept of an *abstract* authored work to which all acts of exploitation are related, be they publication, engraving, reprinting, recital, translation or arrangement. Previously, each of these activities was subject to its own separate regulation (or non-regulation) according to specific policy circumstances. We can trace the formation of the new regime in two important statutes of the early nineteenth century.

Legal historians consider the Prussian Act of 1837 as the most influential copyright Act in nineteenth-century Germany, integrating for the first time the various regulations of the publishing industries into a comprehensive *Gesetz zum Schutze des Eigenthums an Werken der*

Wissenschaft und der Kunst gegen Nachdruck und Nachbildung ('law for the protection of property in works of science and the arts from reprint and imitation'). The Prussian Act came into force on 11 June 1837, and was the first copyright law in Germany to employ an extensive concept of art including literature, music and the fine arts. It figured as the model for Germany's evolving federal laws.

Significantly, the drafters of the Prussian Copyright Act included the term 'property' in the title, referring to Fichte's concept (albeit without citing his name):

> The buyer of a book gets by the purchase the physical property in his copy and the right to use and to process the expressed thoughts in his particular manner. What inviolably remains the author's and can be identified as the real intellectual property [*das eigentliche Geistes-Eigenthum*], is the particular form, in which he has expressed his thoughts. These principles are not new, they already have been laid down in the 90s of the last century by learned men who made an effort, to develop the particular matter of reprint out of its own nature. (Philipsborn, preliminary paper to the Act, quoted in Wadle 1988: 65)

The Act was influenced by a sustained campaign led by Adolph Martin Schlesinger, Carl Maria von Weber's publisher and a leading figure in Prussia's musical establishment. Schlesinger resented unauthorised arrangements, in particular of Weber's blockbuster operas *Der Freischütz* (1821) and *Oberon* (1826), which were of great commercial value.[16]

In 1822, Schlesinger filed a complaint at the Berlin town court against a *Freischütz* piano arrangement of Viennese provenance that had been sold in Berlin book shops. The judge commissioned an expert opinion from the famous poet and composer E. T. A. Hoffmann. Hoffmann, a lawyer by training and a former Prussian civil servant, was asked whether the Viennese piano score was 'arranged along' Schlesinger's piano score. The Prussian statute book of 1794 (*Allgemeines Landrecht*) explicitly had included 'musical compositions' under the subjects protected against reprinting. However, Hoffmann argued that the specific sections for arrangements should not be applied to musical composition, because:

> it is impossible to extract musical compositions in the same way, as it can be done with books. Reprint of a composition would only take place when an original would be 'reengraved' [*nachgestochen*] and reprinted identically with the original. (Kawohl 2002a: 269)

According to Hoffmann, Schlesinger's copyright did not involve the rights to an abstract work *Der Freischütz*; it was confined to the singular piano score version that he had published. The subject matter of copyright was a work of print – a copper engraving. Hoffmann drew a comparison to works of art. A copper engraving showing a painting was not infringing a copyright in this painting. Another engraving of the same painting was an infringing copy of the first copper plate only if it was a counterdraw, but not if it was modelled on the original painting.

The key point of Hoffmann's argument was its denial of the abstraction which would soon be pervasive in European laws. Schlesinger's claim for damages was refused. Between 1821 and 1837, Schlesinger filed at least six complaints in Prussian courts and made repeated applications for an amendment of the arrangement rules of the *Allgemeines Landrecht*. He eventually saw success with the new copyright law of 1837. Here is a summary of its provisions.

Table 2: Prussian Act (1837) for the Protection of Property in Works of Scholarship and the Arts from Reprint and Reproduction

Protected Subject Matter	Owner	Criteria for Protection	Exclusive Rights	Term	Registration
'works of scholarship and art' (preamble) writings (s.1) incl. books, yet unprinted manuscripts, lectures and sermons (s. 3) geographical topographical scientific and architectural drawings (s. 18) musical compositions (s. 19) works of art (ss 21–3)	author and 'those who derive their authority from the author' (s. 1, e.g. heir, publisher) transferable wholly or in part (s. 9)	*eigenthümlich* (original) as criterion for non-infringing derivative works (s. 20 and s. 23) determined by committee of experts (s. 17)	reprinting (s. 2) publication, distribution (s. 9) public performance prior to publication of dramatic and musical works (s. 32) publication of transcribed lectures and sermons, (s. 3) adaptation of musical compositions, (s. 20) reproduction (*Nachbildung*) of copper engravings, lithographs (of works of art, s. 29)	*post mortem auctoris* life plus 30 years (ss 5 and 6) works of arts 10 years *pma* (s. 27) public performance 10 years *pma,* (s. 32)	no formalities for works of literature and music works of art registered at the Ministry for Cultural Affairs (s. 27) for translations: notice on title page for claim to produce within 2 years (s. 4)

In Britain, the key legislation fusing author and property norms is the Copyright Act of 1842. By the early 1800s, the utilitarian rationale implicit in English copyright law since the Statute of Anne (1710), and sustained in the case of *Donaldson v. Becket* (1774) had become diluted. The House of Lords ruling in *Donaldson* was increasingly seen as a compromise between those who denied authors' rights altogether and those who asserted a perpetual property in the produce of labour. It was argued that even if perpetual copyright had been rejected, the author still had a natural right to his work. In this reading, the natural or common law right of the author and the statute became merged. In 1814, a revised statute extended the copyright term for the first time to life of the author (or twenty-eight years, whichever was longer).[17]

In 1837, the year of the new Prussian Act, a campaign was launched by Thomas Noon Talfourd, a member of parliament, lawyer, author and friend of leading figures of the Romantic literary scene. Several draft bills were submitted to Parliament supported by letters and petitions from William Wordsworth, Robert Southey, Thomas Carlyle and Hartley Coleridge. Their main aim was an extension of the copyright term to author's lifetime plus sixty years (while existing copyrights would revert to the author after twenty-eight years). The theoretical bases were new concepts of Romantic theory as well as the more traditional Lockean labour arguments. As Talfourd put it in a speech to Parliament: why should literary property not 'last as long as the works which contain truth and beauty live?' (Talfourd 1837: 8; quoted in Rose 1993: 111). Talfourd's disciple J. J. Lowndes wrote, in a supporting treatise:

> For the object of the Bill is not to give greater value to the light and trivial productions of the day, which either reap a sufficient and quick reward from their admirers, or fall with well merited contempt into oblivion; but to secure to authors of genius and learning – whose works, although they become the classics of the country, often make their way but slowly into public favour – some slight pecuniary advantage, by extending their Copyright for a further period, at the very time it has commenced to be valuable, and to repay them for their long and unceasing labours. (Lowndes 1840: 101)

Talfourd's Bill reached the committee stage but not a final vote before the general election of 1841 in which Talfourd did not stand. A revised copyright Bill was passed early in the next Parliament, compromising on the *post mortem* term (now seven years *pma*) while preserving Talfourd's structure. The Act of 1842 concentrates on books, but extends the right of 'representation or performance' to 'dramatic pieces' and 'musical compositions'. The abstraction of authored works of art remains tentative, as reflected in ambiguous wordings about abridgements, anthologies, translations and dramatisations. All rights were subject to entry in the Book of Registry at Stationers' Hall, revealing a tension in the law: if the new rationale of copyright derived from the character of abstract, original, authored works (as opposed to the earlier incentive to the creation or dissemination of useful products), then its legal protection should coincide with the moment of creation not publication (Kawohl and Kretschmer 2003: 221).

Table 3: United Kingdom Copyright Act (1842)

Protected Subject Matter	Owner	Criteria for Protection	Exclusive Rights	Term	Registration
'books', incl. 'every volume, part or division of a volume, pamphlet, sheet of letterpress, sheet of music, map, chart, or plan separately published' (s. 2) dramatic pieces and musical compositions, incl. 'every tragedy, comedy, play, opera, farce, or other scenic, musical or dramatic entertainment' (s. 2)	author or 'assigns' as personal property whether 'derived from such author before or after the publication of any book', by 'sale, gift, bequest, or by operation of law' (s. 2) publisher (if 'projector' or 'conductor' of 'encyclopaedia, review, magazine, periodical work') (s. 18)	[silent, preamble suggests (emphasis added) 'literary works of *lasting benefit* to the world']	'print or cause to be printed, either for sale or exportation' 'import for sale or hire' 'sell, publish, or expose to sale or hire, or cause to be sold, published, or expose to sale or hire, or shall have in his possession, for sale or hire' (s. 15) representing or performing musical and dramatic pieces (s. 20)	*post mortem auctoris* life plus 7 years, but at least 42 years from publication (s. 3)	'Book of Registry' kept at Stationers' Hall (s. 11) 'proprietorship in the copyright of books, and assignments thereof, and dramatic and musical pieces, whether in manuscript or otherwise, and licences affecting such copyright' for dramatic and musical pieces in manuscript: registration only of title, name and place of author, name and place of proprietor, and time and place of first performance (s. 20)

The formation of modern copyright law was completed with the Berne Convention of 1886, elevating an international regime that took its term and scope from the creator, regardless of subsequent ownership or public policy implications. Led by Victor Hugo, a preliminary Congress on Literary and Artistic Property was held in Brussels in 1858 and adopted the following principles (quoted from Petri 2002: 116):

> the author's ownership rights to his works of art and literature should be expressed in the laws of 'all civilised peoples';

> all countries should recognise the same rights of non-nationals to their works as they do to works of their own citizens [the principle of national treatment];

> copyright legislation in all countries should rest on a common foundation.

At the diplomatic conference in Berne in 1886, the principle of national treatment was established, but the minimum standards that applied regardless of national traditions remained quite weak.[18] Not until the Berlin conference of 1908 was it agreed that the rights granted under Berne should not be contingent on national formalities. The structure of the Berlin conference is still the bedrock of modern international copyright law. The US, for so long reluctant to follow the route to a *droit d'auteur*, eventually acceded to Berne in 1989 when the export interests of its copyright industries in Hollywood and Redmond became paramount. In 1994, the TRIPs Agreement (Trade Related Aspects of Intellectual Property Rights: Article 9.1) incorporated the Berne standards into the World Trade Organisation (WTO). Any country that wishes to participate in global trade (by the latest count, the WTO has more than 140 members) must now enact exclusive transferable copyrights for more than a generation.

The minimum term of Berne has remained at author's life plus fifty years while Europe (with the 1993 Directive on harmonising the term of copyright protection) and the United States (with the 1998 Sonny Bono Copyright Extension Act) have adopted an extended term of seventy years *post mortem auctoris*. At the insistence of the US, the *droit moral* introduced with the Rome revisions (1928) of the Berne Convention was omitted from TRIPs: Article 6*bis* of the Rome revisions provided for the right to claim first authorship of a work (paternity right) and the right to object to any distortion, mutilation or other modification which would be prejudicial to the honour or reputation of the author (integrity right). The *droit moral* is distinct from copyright as an economic property right in that it cannot be transferred or waived. We shall argue in the next section that this distinction may be the way forward.

Below is a table summarising the structure of rights under Berne:

Table 4: Berne Convention (1886), Berlin revision (1908) for the
Protection of Literary and Artistic Works

Protected Subject Matter	Owner	Criteria for Protection	Exclusive Rights	Term	Registration
literary and artistic works, including 'every production in the literary, scientific and artistic domain' Art. 2)	Author (Art.1) [silent on successor in title]	original intellectual creation (not 'news of the day' and 'miscellaneous information' Art. 9)	translation (Art. 8) reproduction (Art. 9) public performance (Art. 11) indirect appropriations, incl. 'adaptations, musical arrangements, novelisations, dramatisations' (Art. 12)	*post mortem auctoris* life plus 50 years (Art. 7)	the enjoyment and exercise of rights in respect of works 'shall not be subject to any formality' (Art. 4)

Whither now?

Ever since the eighteenth century Battle of the Booksellers, when
Stationers evoked an absolute author's right that they had acquired
(so they argued) via contract, the justifications for copyright have been
extremely confused. Samuel Johnson's comments in 1773 (as reported by
Boswell) neatly illustrate the different arguments:

> There seems (he said) to be in authours a stronger right of property than that by
> occupancy; a metaphysical right, a right, as it were, of creation, which should from
> its nature be perpetual; but the consent of nations is against it, and indeed reason
> and the interests of learning are against it; for were it to be perpetual, no book,
> however useful, could be universally diffused amongst mankind, should the
> proprietor take it into his head to restrain circulation.[19]

The decision in *Donaldson v. Becket* (1774) did little to stem the tide that
was transforming a sensible investment incentive into a generation-long
burden on cultural activity, ostensibly under the guise of the author's
original expression.

Private property can be defined negatively as the right to exclude. Access
to property becomes conditional on the discretionary decision of the owner.
Property entails the right to say no. It is widely accepted in (utilitarian)

economic theory that property rights are justified if they prevent a so-called 'tragedy of the commons' (Hardin 1968). For example, fish stocks held in common are liable to deplete because there is no individual owner who has an incentive in their preservation. (For further discussion of this argument see Chapter 3.) From a public interest perspective, though, property rights should not be more far-reaching than needed to achieve this welfare purpose. In the case of intellectual property, in particular, they should not encroach on others' 'freedom of expression' more than is necessary to give an incentive to creative expression and dissemination in the first place. Historically, however, this utilitarian perspective has been superseded by a second family of property justifications, stemming from John Locke's notion of men's 'natural' entitlement to the fruit of their labour, and from the Hegelian notion of rights as the 'manifestation of a personality'. The form and scope of acceptable rights under these premises is somewhat elusive. In particular, it is not clear how far other people's expression can be justifiably limited by such property claims.[20]

In this section, we shall finally unbundle the concepts of creator and investor which, as we have seen, have formed an unholy alliance in the formation of modern copyright law. The argument is presented from premises that attempt to capture widely held views in modern societies (which echo some of the justificatory strategies discussed earlier).

Proposition 1: There is no unified category of right owners, covering creators (authors) and investors (producers).

Creators have four main interests:

1. to see their work widely reproduced and distributed
2. to receive credit for it
3. to earn a financial reward relative to the commercial value of the work
4. to be able to engage creatively with other works (in adaptation, comment, sampling etc.).

Regarding the structure of author rights, this leads to three conclusions:

1. The creator has little to gain from exclusivity (it prevents widest distribution; it prevents access to other works; it does not ensure financial reward)
2. The creator has little to gain from transferability (under normal contractual practices, particularly in the media, the creator will be bought out in a one-off commercial transaction)
3. The creator has a lot to gain from the so-called *droit moral* (a kind of creative trade mark, ensuring integrity of origin).

In the past, authors' interests could only be met with considerable economic inefficiencies (mainly caused by the costs of administrating rights). Digital technology offers new possibilities of tracing use and rewarding the creator. Transforming collecting societies into regulatory bodies answering to society at large (not only to rights owners) may be the best way forward (cf. Kretschmer 2002).

Proposition 2: Investors want exclusive and transferable property rights, to extract maximum returns from their investments. Exclusive rights, however, come at a cost to society.

1. Useful works become more expensive than they would have been (this is a direct consumer loss)
2. Works become available for creative engagement only on the terms of the right holder (this means in practice a loss of cultural diversity, innovation and critique)
3. Automatic returns from a back catalogue of works subsidise existing large right holders, creating an entry barrier to the creative industries (this is an anti-competitive effect).

Regarding the structure of copyright as a property right, this leads to one conclusion:

1. Investors should be granted exclusive terms of protection only as a response to market failure: that is, where without the incentive of exclusivity, a work in the 'useful arts' would not be produced and distributed at all.

The normal exploitation cycle of cultural products suggests that a short exclusive term would be sufficient. If the first statutory copyright, the Statute of Anne, granted a term of fourteen years (renewable once), the faster dissemination and exploitation environment of digital technologies would suggest an even shorter term. An extreme example of that rationale is the UK's first design copyright, the 1787 'Act for the Encouragement of Designing and Printing of Linens, Cottons, Calicos and Muslins'. It provided a producer head start of less than one season by granting an exclusive right to print and reprint for two months; in 1794, the term was extended to three months (Sherman and Bently 1999: 63).

Star creators

Many creators have demanded control over their artistic output which, they say, can only be ensured through exclusive rights. In commercial practice, however, artistic control is only available to a few star creators whose bargaining power is sufficient to benefit from the exclusivity and transferability of rights (see Chapter 4). Only the interests of star creators are similar to investor interests. They benefit disproportionately from the current copyright system.

Figures provided in the 1996 UK Monopolies and Mergers Commission Report on the British Performing Right Society (PRS) show that 80 per cent of author members earned less than £1000 from performance royalties for 1993; and that 10 per cent of authors received 90 per cent of the total distribution. Similarly, according to German music copyright society GEMA's yearbook for 1996–7, 5 per cent of members received 60 per cent of the total distribution. We have calculated that in both Germany and the UK between 500 and 1,500 composers can live substantially off copyright royalties. There are indications that such winner-take-all markets are prevalent in most cultural industries. For the US, Tebbel claimed in a 1976 study that only 300 self-employed writers could live off the copyright system (Tebbel 1976). For 90 per cent of authors, the copyright system did not provide a sufficient reward. The creative base of a modern society is supported by other means.

Early in their careers, many creators wish to become known by all available means, including being copied without permission. Piracy is welcome if source credits are given. Once creators have become famous, they typically perform a U-turn. Their monetary interests suddenly compete with investors' interests, aligning both in their defence of exclusive rights. 'Take a stand for creativity. Take a stand for copyright.' implored a petition to the European Parliament signed by 400 recording artists in 1999. 'We make our living through our music. The music that we create touches the lives of millions of people all over the world. Our creativity and our success depend on strong copyright protection. We now need your help.'[21] This dubious harmony of interests remains the official industry line in its piracy campaign: 'Ultimately, if creators do not get paid, you will not get music' (John Kennedy, president and chief operating officer, Universal Music International, Letter to the *Financial Times*, 23 January 2003).[22]

We believe that despite such rhetoric we are reaching the end of the period of copyright expansion traced in this chapter. Within a generation, copyright laws will be unrecognisable, abandoning the Berne paradigm. The history of copyright supports arguments for a system in which short terms of exclusivity, encouraging fast exploitation, are followed by a remuneration right for the lifetime of the creator. As the following chapters in this book demonstrate, copyright *practice* is already changing, as, in their various ways, bootleggers, DJs, samplers, consumers and performance artists invent new forms of cultural engagement. Copyright law must eventually follow.

Notes

1. This chapter draws on the following previously published research: Kretschmer (2000); Kawohl (2001); Kawohl (2002a); Kawohl and Kretschmer (2003); and Kretschmer (2003).
2. In the law and economics literature (Maughan 2001), two further features of property rights are identified: universality (that is, a complete set of property relationships between all parties is specified) and enforceability (that is, the rights are stable and can be reliably asserted).
3. 'Piracy' in its literal meaning asserts extraterritorial jurisdiction over robbery on the sea. The *Oxford English Dictionary* traces this use back to 1552. Piracy as 'infringement of right conferred by a patent or copyright' is first referenced in 1771. An early example of its use in court with reference to music is in *D'Almaine v. Boosey* (1834): 'To publish, in the form of quadrilles and waltzes, the airs of an opera of which there exists an exclusive copyright, is an act of piracy' (quoted in McFarlane 1986).
4. It should be noted that the prescription that you should not appropriate what is not yours does *not* presuppose a conception of copyright as individual exclusive property. Unauthorised non-commercial use that acknowledges its source may be consistent with the Eighth Commandment.
5. The orthodox expression of this argument is in Landes and Posner (1989).
6. The first systematic regime of printing privileges as a means of censorship was installed in France in 1521. Under the 1723 *Code de la Librarie*, the book trade was still regulated via the Paris Guild, supporting perpetual monopolies (Hesse 1991).
7. The authoritative text of Locke's *Two Treatises of Government* is the third edition of 1698. The quotes are all from Chapter 5. In recent political philosophy, there has been much debate about the interpretation and scope of the Lockean proviso. For good discussions in the context of intellectual property, see Hughes (1988); Hettinger (1989); Drahos (1996); Shiffrin (2001); Fisher (2001).
8. In the literature, the Statute of Anne is variously cited with the years 1709 (the year it was enacted: this is today the usual way of citing Statutes) and 1710 (the year it came into force). Note that English legislation at the time referred to the year of reign of the monarch ('The Statute of the 8th of Queen Anne'), which does not coincide with the modern calendar year.
9. A graphic illustration of the competitive practices of eighteenth-century music publishing in England is provided in the autobiography (1803) of Charles Dibdin (1745–1814), a composer of highly successful popular songs. When Dibdin resorted to self-publishing in 1790 in order to increase the lowly returns offered by the established publishing houses, 'the music-shops discouraged their sale . . . [and I] began, as usual, to feel their power, and my own incapacity to struggle against it . . . I had scarcely opened my shop, when the clamours, among the music-sellers, became universal . . . Some of

these crotchet-mongers made an open declaration that they would not sell any article in my catalogue' (quoted in Hunter 1986: 243). Avoiding London's publishing oligopoly, Charles Dibdin toured the country with his music and survived. Here are contrasting figures of Dibdin's payments, before and after he opened his own business. In 1768, he received £45 for the music of *The Padlock*, the vocal score alone selling 10,000 copies in thirteen years. Another group of songs which Dibdin claims to have sold for £60, made the publisher £500. As a self-publisher, Dibdin sold 10,750 copies of the song *Greenwich Pensioner*, yielding profits of more than £400.

In Germany, Georg Philipp Telemann (1681–1767) was the archetypal eighteenth-century musical entrepreneur. At the outset of his career, he was still forced into a feudal contract (1717), preventing the communication of new compositions beyond his court employer. From 1721, as music director of the independent merchant city of Hamburg, he pioneered many new exploitation techniques. Since it was unseemly to charge for church concerts, he 'ordered guards to the doors who prevented anybody from entering who had no printed copy of the Passion [performed]' (from Telemann's Autobiography in Mattheson 1740). In order to prevent unauthorised reprints of his works, Telemann invented a music magazine, serialising his compositions, publishing one movement at a time (Schleuning 1984).

10. The law lords' vote was advisory and did not determine the outcome of the case. The decision for Donaldson was the result of (probably) a voice vote by *all* peers, which was supposedly quite conclusively in *favour* of a statutory right. The likelihood seems to be that the law lords voted just about in favour of a perpetual right, but this was ignored by the peers. There remains much controversy about whether the law lords definitively decided for a statutory right or whether this was a result of misreporting – an early example of how quickly copyright decisions get confused!

11. Not suprisingly 'maps' are mentioned in a prominent position. Unlike novels and scholarly books which were easily reprinted from imported English originals, maps of, say, West Virginia had to be supplied by domestic engravers and printers. In England maps had qualified as copyrightable subject matter not many years earlier, in the Engraving Copyright Act 1766. Since maps and sea charts necessarily resemble one another in form, the more so as they accurately represent the reality, a threshold of originality could not easily be defined. Lord Mansfield in *Sayre v. Moore* (1785) admitted, 'whoever has it in his intention to publish a chart may take advantage of all prior publications', but acknowledged the claimant's correction of some soundings and (new) application of the Mercator principle. Copyright in maps could only be justified within a utilitarian rather than a natural author's rights framework. Thus the turn from a utilitarian towards a author's right based copyright can be identified in a 'shift of categories': As Lord Justice Sir W. M. James, clarified in *Stannard v. Lee* (1871): 'Formerly maps had been considered artistic works, now they

were to be brought into their proper place as literary works. And rightly so, in my opinion, for maps are intended to give information in the same way as a book does' (see Kawohl 2002b).

12. By the late twentieth century, the utilitarian rationale of US copyright had succumbed to the lobbying efforts of increasingly powerful multinational right holders, most dramatically with the 1998 Sonny Bono Act, which extended the US copyright term by twenty years to life plus seventy years (or ninety-five years for works 'for hire'). The bill was sponsored by Congressmen who received significant campaign contributions from Disney. In the Supreme Court challenge of the Act (2003), an *amici curiae* brief by a group of economists, including five Nobel laureates, suggested that a copyright term of life plus seventy years provided 99.99 per cent of the value of protection in perpetuity; that is, virtually perpetual copyright economically speaking. It is evident that a *retrospective* extension to the term of copyright restricts public access whilst not providing any additional incentive to cultural production. Still, the majority of judges (7:2 votes) refused to rule against the extension on the grounds that the court could not challenge the powers of Congress in a matter of policy. One of the two dissenting judges advanced a more principled constitutional analysis: 'This statute will cause serious expression-related harm. It will likely restrict traditional dissemination of copyrighted works. It will likely inhibit new forms of dissemination through the use of new technology. It threatens to interfere with efforts to preserve our Nation's historical and cultural heritage and efforts to use that heritage, say, to educate our Nation's children. It is easy to understand how the statute might benefit the private financial interests of corporations or heirs who own existing copyrights. But I cannot find any constitutionally legitimate, copyright-related way in which the statute will benefit the public' (Breyer, J., dissenting, at 26). See also Breyer 1970.

13. For modern 'rule-utilitarians', the inviolability of property rights may itself be justified from the outcomes of such a system. This line of thinking goes back to Jeremy Bentham who remarked that: 'a state cannot grow rich except by an inviolate respect for property' (quoted in Drahos 1996, ch. 9).

14. Compare Louis XVI's letter to his government (1776): 'Every effort should be made to deal, as soon as possible, with the requests of the Parisian and provincial publishing houses regarding ownership rights to works and the duration of privileges. A large number of authors have made representations to me to this effect, and I realize the matter is one close to the heart of scholars . . . to an author, a privilege is the fruits of his labour, to a publisher a guarantee against costs . . . The author should be given precedence, and assuming the publisher's share stands in proportion to his expenses and he is able to return a reasonable profit, he should have no cause to complain' (Dock 1963: 127; quoted in Petri 2002: 62ff). The king's intervention led to a rejection of publisher's rights beyond the lifetime of the author.

15. The Prussian *Allgemeines Landrecht* (1794, 1.11§ 997) had listed musical compositions alongside maps and copper engravings (Wadle 1998: 176), and a publishers' petition (Duncker 1834) to the federal assembly (*Bundesversammlung*) mentions musical compositions after mathematical schedules but before maps. The official commentary on the copyright Act of the German state of Saxony still stated in 1844: 'Musical compositions do not belong to the category of products of literature because the means of representation are symbols, not script. They belong to the products of art, of the fine arts. The law is intended to protect works of fine art in addition to the products of literature' (Meinert 1844: 16).

Composers probably formed the concept of a performing right as early as they conceived of publishing rights. In 1664, the German composer Heinrich Schütz stated in the preface to the printed edition of his *Christmas Oratorio* that performances could only take place with the author's consent (*mit des Authoris Bewilligung*). As a practical solution, he offered the orchestral parts separately against an additional fee (MGG 1966: 1,168). During the seventeenth century, a performance royalty system became common practice at the Paris theatres where monitoring constituted no serious problem. In 1791, Pierre-Augustin Beaumarchais instigated a bureau for collecting royalties for writers and composers of *dramatic* work (in 1829, this became the *Société des Auteurs et Compositeurs Dramatiques*, still active today). It was not until the early nineteenth century that the right to public performance became an indicator of the emerging concept of an abstract authored work.

Publishers immediately took advantage of the ruling in *Bach v. Longman*, registering music at the Stationers' Company. Between 1770 and 1779, thirty-five scores were registered; during the last decade of the eighteenth century the figures reached 1,828 (from the transcription of the register of the Worshipful Company of Stationers, analysed by Krummel 1975, quoted from Hunter 1986: 281). Yet, Hunter argues, composers seem not to have won an immediate improvement in earnings. Litigation was generally conducted between publishers (see Coover 1985).

Note that despite the nascent provisions of music copyright, composers continued to use entrepreneurial, non-copyright strategies to make a living. Until well into the nineteenth century, the most important sources of income for successful, independent composers were not publishing revenues but commissions, dedications and performances of new compositions. Handel and Mozart made their (changeable) fortunes through organising the performance of their own works, a commercial route closed to many lesser composers. Not much of the fortunes accumulated by publishers such as the Ballard dynasty in Paris, Breitkopf & Härtel in Leipzig, Artaria in Vienna, or London's father and son Walsh, reached the composers. John Walsh senior published Handel's first set of sonatas under a false Amsterdam imprint to avoid payments to the composer. After business relations were established, Handel received £20–£30 per opera or oratorio (Rasch 2002). John Walsh senior's estate amounted to £30,000 in 1736; his son left £40,000 thirty years later (Hunter 1986: 75).

16. Within two years of its first performance at the Berlin Royal Opera House, *Der Freischütz* had been performed for the fiftieth time. Apparently, 9,000 copies of his piano version were sold in only one year (Berlin had no more than 200,000 inhabitants at the time).

17. For a lucid discussion of this subsequent reinterpretation of *Donaldson v Becket*, see Rose 1993: 107ff.

18. First signatories were Germany, Belgium, Spain, France, Britain, Haiti, Liberia, Switzerland and Tunisia.

19. James Boswell, *Life of Johnson*, 1791; quoted in Rose 1993: 85. Johnson argued in favour of a term between sixty and 100 years (20 July 1763).

20. The tension is present in the Universal Declaration of Human Rights (1948) which recognised in Article 27.(1) that 'Everyone has the right freely to participate in the cultural life of the community, to enjoy the arts and to share in scientific advancement and its benefits.' But Article 27.(2) reads: 'Everyone has the right to the protection of the moral and material interests resulting from any scientific, literary or artistic production of which he is the author.' For discussion, see Drahos (1999).

21. Petition 'Artists Unite for Strong Copyright', led by Jean Michel Jarre with the assistance of IFPI (19 January 1999), signed by among others Boyzone, the Corrs, Robbie Williams, Tom Jones, Eros Ramazotti, Mstislav Rostropovich, Barbara Hendricks, Die Fantastischen Vier, Aqua and Roxette. Note that Robbie Williams later declared that Internet music file sharing is 'great' (MIDEM music trade fair, Cannes, January 2003).

22. The German publishers' campaign against the copyright exception for teaching and scientific research (s. 52a) argued: 'If copies of books are free, nobody will buy originals. If nobody buys originals, nobody will publish books or journals. The result: If nobody publishes, Germany's thinkers will soon have to look for a different employment' (Advert *Frankfurter Allgemeine Zeitung*, 31 March 2003).

References

Allen-Russell, A. von (2002), ' "For instruments not intended": The second J. C. Bach lawsuit', *Music & Letters* 83 (1): 3–29.

Boyle, J. (1996), *Shamans, Software, and Spleens: Law and the Construction of the Information Society*, Cambridge, MA: Harvard University Press.

Breyer, S. (1970), 'The uneasy case for copyright', *Harvard Law Review* 84: 281–351.

Burrow, J. (1773), *The Question Concerning Literary Property, Determined by the Court of King's Bench on 20th April, 1769, in the Cause Between Andrew Millar and Robert Taylor*, London (reprinted in *The Literary Property Debate: Six Tracts 1764–1774*, ed. S. Parks, New York: Garland 1975).

Burrow, J. (1774), *The Cases of the Appellants and Respondents in the Cause of Literary Property, Before the House of Lords*, London (reprinted in *The Literary Property Debate: Six Tracts 1764–1774*, ed. S. Parks, New York: Garland 1975).

Carlson, N. E. (1966), 'Wither and the Stationers', *Studies in Bibliography* xix: 210–15.

Coover, J. (ed.) (1985), *Music Publishing, Copyright and Piracy in Victorian England*, London: Mansell.

Curtius, K. F. (1831), *Handbuch des im Königreiche Sachsen geltenden Civilrechts*, vol. 4, 2nd edn, Leipzig: E. B. Schwickert.

Davies, G. (2002), *Copyright and the Public Interest* (2nd edn), London: Sweet & Maxwell.

Deazley, R. (2003), 'The myth of copyright at common law', *Cambridge Law Journal* 62 (1): 106–33.

Dock, M.-C. (1963), *Étude sur le droit d'auteur*, Paris: LGDJ.

Dölemeyer, B. and Klippel, D. (1991), 'Der Beitrag der deutschen Rechtswissenschaft zur Theorie des gewerblichen Rechtsschutzes und Urheberrechts', in *Gewerblicher Rechtsschutz und Urheberrecht in Deutschland. Festschrift zum Hundertjährigen Bestehen der Deutschen Vereinigung für Gewerblichen Rechtsschutz und Urheberrechtund ihrer Zeitschrift*, vol. 2, F.-K. Beier, A. Kraft, G. Schricker and E. Wadle (eds), Weinheim, 185–240.

Donaldson v. Becket (1774), 2 *Brown's Prerogative Cases* 129, 1 *English Reports* 837.

Dowling, M. (1932), 'The Printing of John Dowland's *Second Booke of Songs or Ayres*', *The Library* xii (4th series): 365–80.

Drahos, P. (1996), *A Philosophy of Intellectual Property*, Aldershot: Dartmouth.

Drahos, P. (1999), 'The universality of intellectual property rights: origins and developments', Geneva: WIPO.

Duncker, F. W. et al. (1834), *Vorschläge zur Feststellung des literarischen Rechtszustandes in den Staaten des deutschen Bundes*, in *Acta des justizministeriums betreffend: das Nachdrucken der Bücher u.d.m. bis 1838*, Geheimes Staatsarchiv Preußischer Kulturbesitz, HA.l, Rep 84 ll 2 N, Nr.1, Bd.1, Bl.106.

Eisenstein, E. (1979), *The Printing Press as an Agent of Change: Communications and Cultural Transformations in Early-Modern Europe*, Cambridge: Cambridge University Press.

Feather, J. (1994), *Publishing, Piracy and Politics: A Historical Study of Copyright in Britain*, London: Mansell.

Fichte, J. G. (1792), 'Beweis von der Unrechtmäßigkeit des Büchernachdrucks. Ein Räsonnement und eine Fabel', *Berliner Monatsschrift* 21: 443–483; also in: I. H. Fichte (ed.), *Fichte. Vermischte Schriften und Aufsätze*, Berlin 1845/46, reprint Berlin 1971, 223–44.

Fisher, W. (2001), 'Theories of intellectual property', in S. R. Munzer (ed.), *New Essays in the Legal and Political Theory of Property*, Cambridge: Cambridge University Press, 168–99.

Gans, E. (1832), 'Ueber das Recht zur Aufführung gedruckter Theaterstücke', in *Beiträge zur Revision der Preußischen Gesetzgebung*, ed. E. Gans, Berlin: Duncker and Humblot.

Ginsburg, J. C. (1990), 'A tale of two copyrights: literary property in revolutionary France and America', *Tulane Law Review* 64: 991–1,031.

Hardin, G. (1968), 'The tragedy of the commons', *Science* 162: 1,243–8.

Hegel, G. W. F. (1821–33), *Grundlinien der Philosophie des Rechts*, Berlin.

Hesse, C. (1991), *Publishing and Cultural Politics in Revolutionary Paris, 1789–1810*, Berkeley: University of California Press

Hettinger, E. C. (1989), 'Justifying intellectual property', *Philosophy and Public Affairs*, 18(1): 31–52.

Hughes, J. (1988), 'The Philosophy of intellectual property', *Georgetown Law Journal* 77: 287–366.

Hunter, D. (1986), 'Music copyright in Britain to 1800', *Music and Letters* 269–82.

Kant, I. (1785), 'Von der Unrechtmäßigkeit des Büchernachdrucks', *Berliner Monatszeitschrift*: 403–17; reprinted in UFITA (Archiv für Urheber-, Film-, Funk-, und Theaterrecht) 106 (1987): 137–44.

Kawohl, F. (2001), 'Examining a paradigm shift in intellectual property: music copyright around 1800', paper presented at symposium *A New Feudalism of Ideas?*, Centre for Intellectual Property Policy and Management, Bournemouth University (proceedings available at www.cippm.org.uk/symposium2001).

Kawohl, F. (2002a), *Urheberrecht der Musik in Preußen 1820–1840*, Tutzing: Hans Schneider

Kawohl, F. (2002b), 'Maps and sheet music: hybrids between artistic and literary copyright', paper presented at conference *Legal Frameworks: Intellectual Property and the Visual Arts*, 3 October 2002, University of Copenhagen.

Kawohl, F. and Kretschmer, M. (2003), 'Abstraction and registration: conceptual innovations and supply effects in Prussian and British copyright (1820–50), *Intellectual Property Quarterly* 2: 209–28.

Kretschmer, M. (2000), 'Intellectual property in music: a historical analysis of rhetoric and institutional practices', special issue: 'Cultural Industry' (ed. P. Jeffcutt), *Studies in Cultures, Organizations and Societies* 6: 197–223.

Kretschmer, M. (2002), 'The failure of property rules in collective administration: rethinking copyright societies as regulatory instruments', *European Intellectual Property Review* (EIPR) 24/3: 126–37.

Kretschmer, M. (2003), 'Digital copyright: the end of an era', *European Intellectual Property Review* (EIPR) 25/8: 333–41.

Laddie, H. (1997), 'Copyright: over-strength, over-regulated, over-rated?', in 'Innovation, incentive and reward: intellectual property law and policy', *David Hume Papers on Public Policy* 5(1): 1–16.

Landes, N. and Posner, R. (1989), 'An economic analysis of copyright law', *Journal of Legal Studies* 18: 325–66.

Locke, J. (1690), *Two Treatises of Government*, London.

Lowndes, J. J. (1840), *An Historical Sketch of the Law of Copyright*, London: Saunders and Benning.

Maughan, C. W. (2001), 'Property and intellectual property: foundations in law and economics', paper presented at symposium *A New Feudalism of Ideas?*, 26 June 2001, Centre for Intellectual Property Policy and Management, Bournemouth University (proceedings available at www.cippm.org.uk/symposium2001).

Marshall, L. (2001), *Losing One's Mind: Bootlegging and the Sociology of Copyright*, PhD thesis, University of Warwick.

Mattheson, J. (1740), *Grundlage einer musicalischen Ehrenpforte*, Hamburg.

McFarlane, G. (1986), *Copyright through the Cases*, London: Waterlow.

Meinert, F. W. (1844), *Das Königlich Sächsische Gesetz vom 22. Februar 1844 zum Schutze der Rechte an litterarischen Erzeugnissen und Werken der Kunst*, Leipzig.

MGG (1949–68), *Musik in Geschichte und Gegenwart* (music encylopaedia), Kassel: *Bärenreiter*.

Millar V. Taylor (1769), 98 *English Reports* 92.

Munro, J. H. A. (2001), 'The "New Institutional Economics" and the changing fortunes of fairs in medieval and early modern Europe', *Vierteljahrschrift für Soziat und Wirtschaftsgeschichte* 88 (1): 1–47.

North, D. C. and Thomas, R. (1973), *The Rise of the Western World: A New Economic History*, Cambridge: Cambridge University Press.

Patterson, L. R. (1968), *Copyright in Historical Perspective*, Nashville: Vanderbilt University Press.

Patterson, L. R. (1987), 'Free speech, copyright, and fair use', *Vanderbilt Law Review* 40: 1–66.

Petri, G. (2002), *The Composer's Right*, Stockholm: Atlantis.

Pohlmann, H. (1962), *Die Frühgeschichte des Musikalischen Urheberrechts (ca. 1400–1800) Neue Materialien zur Entwicklung des Urheberrechtsbewußtseins der Komponisten*, Kassel: Bärenreiter.

Püttlingen, J. V. von (1864), *Das musikalische Autorrecht*, Wilhelm Braunmüller, Vienna; reprinted in UFITA (Archiv für Urheber-, Film, Funk-, und Theaterrecht) (2001): 137–277

Rasch, R. A. (2002), *Music Publishing in Europe 1600–1900* (ch. 1 'Basic Concepts'; ch. 6 'Publishers and Publishers'), Strasbourg: European Science Foundation (available at www.let.uu.nl/ ~ Rasch/personal/Musicpublishing.htm).

Rose, M. (1993), *Authors and Owners: The Invention of Copyright*, Cambridge, MA: Harvard University Press.

Sayre v. Moore (1795), 1 East 351, K.B.

Sherman, B. and Bently, L. (1999), *The Making of Modern Intellectual Property Law, The British Experience, 1760–1911*, Cambridge: Cambridge University Press.

Schleuning, P. (1984), *Das 18. Jahrhundert: Der Bürger erhebt sich*, Reinbek/Hamburg: Rowohlt.

Shiffrin, S. V. (2001), 'Lockean arguments for private intellectual property', in S. R. Munzer (ed.), *New Essays in the Legal and Political Theory of Property*, Cambridge: Cambridge University Press, 138–67.

Small, J. (1985) 'J. C. Bach goes to law', *Musical Times* cxxvi: 526–9.

Stannard v. Lee (1871), 6 Ch App 346, 21, 22 March.

Talfourd, Th. N. (1837), *A Speech Delivered by Thomas Noon Talfourd, Sergeant at Law, in the House of Commons*, London.

Tebbel, J. (1976), 'The book business in the USA', in David Daiches and Anthony Thorlby (eds), *The Modern World: Reactions*, vol. 3, London: Aldus Books.

Tschmuck, P. (2002), 'Creativity without copyright: music production in Vienna in the late eighteenth century', in Towse, R. (ed.) *Copyright in the Cultural Industries*, Cheltenham: Edward Elgar, 210–20.

Wadle, E. (1988), 'Das preußische Urheberrechtsgesetz von 1837 im Spiegel seiner Vorgeschichte,' in R. Dittrich (ed.), *Woher Kommt das Urheberrecht und wohin geht es?*, Vienna, pp. 55–98.

Wadle, E. (1998), 'Preußische Privilegien für Werke der Musik: ein Kapital aus der Frühzeit des Urheberrechts 1794–837', in M. J. M. Chiner and H. Schäffer (eds), *Musik und Recht: Symposium aus Anlaß des 60. Geburtstags von Prof. DDr. Detlev Merten*, Berlin.

Wadle, E. (1999), 'Privilegienpraxis in Preußen', in: B. Dölemeyer und H. Mohnhaupt (eds), *Das Privilegium im europäischen Vergleich*, Vol. 2, Frankfurt a. M., pp. 335–62.

Wheaton v. Peters (1832), 29 Fed. Cas. 863.

Woodmansee, M. (1984), 'The genius and the copyright: economic and legal conditions of the emergence of the 'author'', *Eighteenth-Century Studies* 17: 425–48.

Woodmansee, M. and Jaszi, P. (eds) (1994), *The Construction of Authorship: Textual Appropriation in Law and Literature*, Durham: Duke University Press.

Woodmansee, M. (1994), *The Author, Art, and the Market: Rereading the History of Aesthetics*, New York: Columbia University Press.

CHAPTER 3

Copyright and Economics

Ruth Towse

Introduction

There has been a long debate in economics on the justification of copyright and patent law. The so-called 'patent debate' lasted throughout the nineteenth century without, however, reaching a definite conclusion as to whether patents are the spur to innovation and economic growth. The debate on copyright was less prominent but, even so, the question attracted the attention of several notable economists, among them Adam Smith, Jeremy Bentham and John Stuart Mill. Most of them opposed copyright law as unnecessary and damaging to competition and claimed that there were other ways to stimulate creativity and artistic innovation. That view was still being expressed in the 1960s by the few economists writing on the subject. However, the growth of cultural industries and copying technologies of an unprecedented speed and scope, on the one hand, and the development of the academic study of information goods and the discipline of law and economics, on the other, have combined to increase economists' awareness of the importance of copyright for economic and cultural development.

The economic analysis of copyright takes several approaches: there is what can be called the economics of copying; there is the fast-growing field in law and economics of the study of property rights, as well as the economic analysis of legal doctrines of copyright; and there is the macroeconomic approach that looks at the economic value of the creative industries in which copyright law is held to be a defining factor. In this chapter, each of these approaches is discussed with particular reference to the music industry. The music industry has been more affected to date than the other cultural industries by digitalisation, Internet downloading and illegal behaviours and it is important to investigate the economic effect of these changes on the music industry.

Some historical perspective is also useful. Paul David (1993) has argued

that all countries throughout history have copied the ideas and technologies of more developed countries and only introduced patent and
copyright laws when they believed they had more to gain thereby.
The US during its own period of industrialisation and cultural development protected its own patents and copyrights but not those of other
countries, and engaged in wholesale *reprinting* of English authors. The
history of music is full of examples of copying and unauthorised use;
music piracy is not a new phenomenon – Haydn and Beethoven suffered
from it in the eighteenth century and Rossini in the nineteenth before
copyright law was established and, even after authors' rights had been
introduced in Italy, Verdi took endless unsuccessful precautions to
prevent unauthorised copying of his works. Yet these composers managed
to earn well from their compositions anyway (Rossini was rich enough to
retire at the age of 37). Of course, they might have been even richer with
better protection but would they have written more or better music? The
advocates of copyright law believe the answer is yes.

A brief history of economic thought on copyright

Copyright law is a development of market economies which gradually
replaced the medieval guild system. The 1709 Statute of Anne was
passed in England to establish property rights – copyrights – for the
publishers in the Stationers' Company whose seemingly perpetual rights
in their 'copy' – the original manuscript of the work – had been revoked
by the demise of Crown grants of monopoly, and the new law replicated
the convention the guild had adopted for conducting its business. The
publisher paid the author for the right to publish his work and the
Stationers' Company recognised that 'right' as excluding its publication
by other publishers.[1] The limited duration of the copyright was in line
with the limitation of other monopolies and, as for patents, was set at
fourteen years, twice the length of the guild apprenticeship, which
enabled the apprentice to become a master of his craft, and then protected
the master from the subsequent competition of the new entrant. In
economic terms, the new copyright law was concerned with the incentive
to supply and with conditions of production for publishers rather than
with authors' protection. However, it gave authors one advantage: the
term of the copyright was made renewable for a further fourteen years, at
which point authors had the right to control renewal. Thus the system
was a mixed one of authors' and publishers' rights, reflecting earlier
customs that did not necessarily accord with the needs of a competitive
market economy.

This was the economy that Adam Smith analysed in his great book *Wealth of Nations*, published in 1776. Smith's belief in the 'invisible hand' of the price mechanism followed his rejection of the system of monopolies, protectionism and prices administered by the state. Smith believed that, without them, the market economy would spontaneously coordinate the production and distribution of goods. The incentive to produce a good can rely on market prices to signal demand and supply conditions to entrepreneurs and does not require state promotion; the duties of the state are to establish and defend property rights so that entrepreneurs can reap the benefits of their investment and effort. Economic growth comes about because the desire to make profits stimulates production and innovation and this leads to specialisation that reduces costs. Lower costs result in lower prices to consumers, whose incomes grow from higher wages and greater productivity, and so welfare is improved. The greater good of society is served by producers and consumers pursuing their own interests in an economy that is self-regulating.

Smith did recognise that there were economic conditions under which competitive markets would not develop without some state intervention. One problem is when the risk of an undertaking is too great to be borne privately; another is that production techniques for some goods necessitate a large investment, which acts as a barrier to other entrepreneurs entering the industry and competing with incumbent producers. These 'economies of scale' naturally encourage the development of large firms – monopolies or oligopolies. High risk and uncertainty (a feature of the present-day music industry, as discussed below) can also lead to what modern economists call 'market failure', by which is meant the failure of the market economy to yield the best outcomes of growth and welfare. Smith also recognised another aspect of market failure that is important in the modern economic analysis of copyright – the problem created by the existence of 'public goods' – which he applied to the case of literary works (and we nowadays apply to all 'information' goods – see the discussion of this issue in the next section). Whatever the problems, though, Smith still believed that the advantage of being 'first to market' was great enough to make unnecessary state intervention in the form of copyright creation.

Copyright, with its historical connection to the corrupt and anti-competitive Crown monopolies, was tainted in Smith's view and therefore open to suspicion. Subsequent economists shared this suspicion but also accepted that authors created value to society and should receive a reward to encourage their intellectual labour. They were thus in two

minds about copyright law, something that was well expressed by
Macaulay in 1841:

> Copyright is a monopoly and produces all the effects which the general voice of
> mankind attributes to monopoly . . . the effect of a monopoly is to make articles
> scarce, to make them dear, and to make them bad . . . It is good that authors be
> remunerated; and the least exceptional way of remunerating them is by a monopoly.
> Yet monopoly is an evil; for the sake of good, we must submit to evil; but the evil
> ought not to last a day longer than is necessary for the purpose of securing the good.

And, in one of the most famous comments on the subject, Macaulay
concluded: 'The principle of copyright is this. It is a tax on readers for the
purpose of giving a bounty to writers . . . I admit, however, the necessity
of giving a bounty to genius and learning.'[2] Here we have a clear
expression of the trade-off in copyright law between the cost of monopoly
(higher prices) and its benefits (the incentive to create and publish works
of literature, art and music). This understanding has been the chief
hallmark of the economic analysis of copyright.

The economic justification of copyright is that it provides an incentive
to authors and publishers to create and publish literary, artistic and
musical works by enabling them to control exploitation and thus to recoup
the outlays involved. Once a work is published, it becomes vulnerable to
being copied and the copier does not have to put up the costs of
production (only the costs of reproduction). Moreover, a copier does
not take the risk of the work's first publisher because he only copies works
that are successful on the market. Therefore the copier can supply the
work at a much lower price than the first publisher, who will not be able to
compete and cover his production costs. On the other hand, the monopoly
that copyright law gives the publisher enables him to set a price for the
work above the competitive price and therefore consumers have to pay
more for it, thus reducing demand, and production. That is a cost to
society. There is a dual cost and benefit of copyright: without it, some
works would not be published, and with it, the price is higher. Copyright
protection thus involves a trade-off between costs and benefits.

Before the advent of modern home copying machines, copying had to
be done by industrial processes. So, for example, in the days when
printing used type-setting, a copier had to set up the type to print a book
and this meant making a considerable outlay and it therefore took time
before copies could be sold on the market. The same was true of music
printing and sound recording; it took time for a publisher or record
company to reproduce copies copied from the first publisher. Early
economists like Smith thought that the 'lead time' of being first to

market was sufficient to give publishers the competitive advantage over copiers. However, now that that lead time has been reduced to minutes, even seconds, by photocopying, CD burners and digital delivery, this argument may not be so persuasive, though many still believe that copyright protection is excessive and that it acts as a deterrent to finding new business models.

Economics of information goods

The advent of digitalisation has extended the application of the economics of innovation and research and development (R&D) to the methods of production of what have come to be called information goods. Any material – music, film, data – that is compressed into digital form can be viewed as information or 'content' that can be supplied by electronic means and become a good or service in the hands of the end user. Many of these goods are produced in the so-called creative industries, and they may be thought of as the 'package' in which the copyright content is delivered. A CD packages musical composition and performance, which are copyrighted information; a book is the package in which an author's creation is delivered to a reader. The essential difference that digital delivery of music has made for the consumer is that she can now provide (or 'write') her own copy rather than buying it in a shop. But from the producer's point of view, this has meant that cheap and easy copying can now be done with equipment that is becoming standard in homes in the developed world and, as a consequence, composers, performers and sound recording makers are no longer sole suppliers.

In economic terms, music, like other information goods, is a 'public good'. Public goods have the characteristics of being both 'non-excludable' and 'non-rival' (the fact that one person has 'consumed' or read a book does not mean that someone else can't also read it; one listener's enjoyment of a piece of music has no consequence for someone else's enjoyment of it). Public goods are not used up by consumers, in contrast to private goods (like food and clothes), which when consumed by one person are no longer available to others. At the same time, public goods are subject to what is called 'free-riding', that is to say that consumers may benefit from the goods without actually having paid for them (by reading a friend's magazine, for example, or burning a friend's CD). The producers of such goods therefore cannot capture all the returns that might be due to them.

The creation and enforcement of private property rights, such as copyright, can overcome free-riding. Indeed, economic analysis of property rights provides the economic rationale for the institution of private property on the grounds that it provides incentives to a more efficient use of resources and results in greater economic welfare. The so-called 'tragedy of the commons' is when land or other goods (for example, fish) are held in common so that all users have free access, over-use results – over-grazing on common land, over-fishing, and so on – and this leads to under-investment in improving the quality of the land or stocks of fish. The 'tragedy' is that human nature and self-interested economic behaviour (free-riding) lead to a reduction in welfare for all. This can be corrected by 'privatisation' through enclosure that asserts private property rights and allows the owner to fence the land and exclude grazers who do not value the land enough to pay for its use. Information goods differ in one respect from land, though, because, as we have already noted, they are 'non-rival'. To listen to music is not to diminish its value; it remains audible by someone. This is unlike the use of land or the consumption of fish, which are 'rival': the more one person has, the less there is for another. For this reason, the economic rationale for privatising information goods through property rights such as patents and copyrights is somewhat different from the argument for property rights in land (this is one reason why copyright is limited in duration and not perpetual, as are property rights in land). Nevertheless, the main point remains: unless property rights are fully established and defended, at least for a period of time, under-investment in production will take place and welfare will be reduced by free-riding.

Writers on copyright often use the term 'intellectual commons' to describe the application of this reasoning to copyright. They also use another term that is revealing: 'anti-commons', which describes the situation when property rights are so split up, the owners so dispersed, that no use can be made of the land or other goods because the 'transaction costs' of tracing all rights-owners and obtaining all the necessary consent outweigh the value of the property. The notion of transaction costs has become very important in modern economics, with the recognition that there are costs of using markets, such as making contracts and finding out about prices. Transaction costs can arise in other ways too, in fencing to enclose common land, for example. Economists would assume that if the cost of fencing to exclude unauthorised (non-paying) users or free-riders is greater than the net revenues from the property, it will remain as common property.

It is easy to see how this theory applies to the case of music. Composers, lyricists, music publishers, performers and record companies all need rights in their works in order to exploit them and prevent others from free-riding. However, proliferating rights by extensions of copyright risks creating 'anti-commons' problems that raise the cost of exploitation, and unless there is some way for all rights-holders to assert their rights and collect payment for the use of them (which they currently do through collecting societies as discussed in Chapters 5 and 6), the situation can become unmanageable. To return to the digital situation, the cost of excluding unauthorised downloading of music on the Internet by 'fencing' devices may be prohibitive, in which case it will lead to under-investment in music by record companies and over-use of music by free-riders. The challenge for record companies (and economists) is to develop business models that overcome the problem. Copyright law is necessary to establish intellectual property rights but ultimately it is the benefits of the rights (net of the costs) as valued by the market for the information goods that determine its success as an economic incentive.

The music industry, along with other information goods industries, has some particular economic characteristics. The initial set-up costs for creating the content – the musical composition, the performance, the master copy – are high in relation to the low (or even negligible) marginal costs of delivery.[3] These economies of scale are the classic economic characteristics of 'natural monopolies', and they help to explain an oligopolistic industrial structure in which a few large firms are dominant. Oligopolies have sufficient market power to raise prices above the minimum needed for covering costs and they may practise price fixing and collusion. A second economic feature of the music industry, as of other creative industries, is uncertain demand on the part of consumers and the incessant search for novelty, making production in the creative industries highly risky. In the music industry, this has led oligopolies to tolerate the presence of small independent companies, which seem to be necessary to the big corporations as a source of artistic R&D. Large, bureaucratic organisations, it seems, lack the right kind of organisation for spotting new talent.

The effect of this market structure is another economic dilemma: copyrights are needed as an incentive to create music and deliver it to consumers, but the ownership of copyrights is likely to be concentrated in enterprises with excessive market power. It was argued earlier that copyright law overcomes the market's failure to provide sufficient en-trepreneurial incentive but also causes market failure by raising prices; now it is argued that on top of that, the economics of information goods industries point to a tendency to market concentration, which can raise prices further. Yet it is precisely the presence of high fixed costs and risk that make the deterrence of free-riding – the incentive provided by copyright law – so important.

The law and economics approach to copyright

Law and economics is a relatively new discipline in which the law and legal doctrines are analysed using the tools of economics. It has grown very quickly over the last forty years or so since the important work of Ronald Coase gave it impetus.[4] Coase's analysis, which developed into what is now called the 'Coase Theorem', began with a problem in welfare economics. Welfare economics considers how the welfare of the whole society may be maximised while recognising that most actions that would increase the welfare of some members of the society would impose costs on others. How should such clashes of interest be resolved? By the government, through regulation and taxes, or through the private market via the price mechanism? Before Coase, most economists would have said the government should intervene to correct market failure by introducing corrective taxes or subsidies. So, for example, if a power station generating electricity is emitting noxious gases, the government should control pollution by rules limiting emission, punishing the power company if it fails to comply; the power company now has to install air-cleaning equipment which raises its costs and ultimately its prices, so that the users of electricity now pay for the pollution. On the other hand, people living in the area who previously had to suffer from the pollution are now better off. Government regulation thus shifts the costs of the pollution from the people living nearby the power company to its customers.

Coase maintained that government action in such a case is not necessary as long as property rights are fully established, because the market could allocate costs and benefits voluntarily (and probably more efficiently). Markets can deal with such problems by letting the price mechanism place a value on the strength of people's preferences. People in the neighbourhood could organise to contract with the power company to clean up its emissions. They would be willing to pay an amount less than or equal to the cost they already are paying for the pollution. House and land prices in the neighbourhood will reflect the strength of people's aversion or indifference to the emissions and Coase argued that the initial distribution of property rights (who owned what) does not matter as long as there is a free market, because rights will be traded so they end up with the person or firm that places the highest values on them. But there are two very important provisos: one, that the transaction costs of making the side-payment arrangements be zero (or very low) and two, that there is no significant difference in the wealth of the two sides of the bargain. Therein lie the problems, however, since such actions are likely to have positive transaction costs and electricity companies are likely to be much wealthier than the surrounding householders.

The contribution of Coase to the economic analysis of property rights, then, was to show that the problem of using the market to solve welfare dilemmas lay in transaction costs and wealth inequalities. We will see later, for example, that transaction costs are important in the administration of copyright and need to be considered when assessing the benefits of legal change. Markets may fail to develop if transaction costs exceed the value of copies to individual users (possibly the case with online music delivery). Moreover, in a free market for intellectual property, authors are likely to be much less well off than their publishers.

Despite these caveats, Coase's arguments have given rise to the application of economics to a wide range of property rights and legal doctrines, and copyright law is one area in which it has been applied fruitfully (see, in particular, Landes and Posner (1989)). Take the doctrine of 'fair use', which is particularly important in the music industry. The economic rationale for fair use lies in balancing the benefit of the incentive to create with that of the cost of restricting users' access to the works that are created. The exclusive right of authorisation is therefore limited in copyright statutes and exceptions are made for certain types of 'fair use' (or 'fair dealing', the term in UK law). In these cases the use of copyrighted material without the rights-owners' consent and without payment is not regarded as an infringement of copyright law. Fair use doctrine also recognises that most new works are derived from existing material in some way or another, through inspiration, reference, imitation, shared language and cultural values, and so on. Copyright law therefore also has to find a way of giving creators of new works access to protected extant work without excessive transaction costs and royalty payments, while still protecting the intellectual property rights that provide the incentive to create. A too-strong copyright regime, tolerating little fair use, raises transaction costs and copyright-based earnings, transferring the gains to artists from users, but it also raises the costs of creation. A too-weak regime, on the other hand, provides insufficient incentives to look for means of charging for the use of copyright, and so reduces artists' earnings while making easier what Landes and Posner call the 'productive' (as against 'reproductive') fair use, the use of copyright material for creating new works (so benefiting consumers).

Wendy Gordon (1982) has also analysed the role of transaction costs in relation to fair use. She recognises that markets may fail to develop when transaction costs exceed the value of copies to individual users and suggests a 'three part test' for determining what should therefore be considered as fair use. First, fair use is an acceptable defence against copyright infringement when there is market failure; secondly, use is fair when transferring control to the 'infringer' is in the public interest; and thirdly, use is fair when the incentives to the copyright owner are not substantially altered by the use. The second point suggests that the public interest may be served in some cases by allowing free use of new technology, since the adoption of new technology promotes economic growth. Fragile markets in new technology must be encouraged, not nipped in the bud, and fair use doctrine can achieve this by encouraging widespread free take-up. Such an argument could have been used in the early days of downloading music on the Internet to justify Napster-type operations: they were helping form a market that would then operate legally.[5] Gordon's third test – does a use affect rights-holders' incentives? – is also relevant to downloading of music files. Record company anti-downloading campaigns depend on the argument that it is reducing record sales and thereby the incentive to invest in new talent.

Collecting music royalties

We can identify two markets for the use of copyright material: the primary market of sales (sales of sheet music and sound recordings) and the secondary market in which recorded works are used in broadcasts and in public performances in discos, shops, pubs and all the other venues in which music is now played. In the primary market, royalties based on the price of the item are paid to composers and performers for the use of their work by the publisher or record company, in accordance with the contract between the parties concerned.

Royalties are the usual means by which publishers pay authors and the royalty contract is the typical contract in the publishing and music industries (see Caves 2000). Under the terms of the standard contract, the publisher pays the author an agreed percentage of the value of the sales of the work on a six-monthly or annual basis. From the economic point of view, this contract ties the author into sharing the risk with the publisher without necessarily rewarding the author sufficiently for taking the risk. Some economists have questioned the use of the royalty contract and argued that it is not a favourable arrangement for a composer or performer in the music industry (see Watt 2000).

A royalty deal may not yield more over the duration of the copyright than a flat fee that buys out future exploitation of rights. Moreover, few individual artists are in a position to bargain with publishers or record companies. They have to accept the terms offered or quit the deal; only the few superstars have the bargaining power to improve their terms. In addition, it is questionable whether the 'typical' artist earns much from copyright at all. Copyright is said to 'reward' creators but how much reward they reap in practice depends upon the market valuation of their work and that may be very low. Copyright generates more rhetoric than money for the majority of composers and performers in the music industry.

In the secondary market, special arrangements are necessary for collecting and distributing remuneration from copyright because individual copyright owners cannot contract with all the users or check up on all uses, as the transaction costs would be far too high. These problems are solved by collecting societies. Copyright collecting societies are membership collectives that administer specific rights accorded to authors and publishers under copyright law, by licensing users and distributing the revenues to their members (in the case of the music industry, to composers, publishers, performers and record companies). Collecting societies are set up in different ways in different countries. In the UK, they are private, non-profit organisations which set their tariffs in deals with users represented by their trade associations. Disputes between the parties are settled by the Copyright Tribunal. In European countries and Japan, collecting societies are usually set up by grant of monopoly, and rates (both the licence tariffs and the administrative charge) may be determined by the government. In the US and Canada, the collecting societies are regulated by a Copyright Board, which must approve agreed tariffs or set them in case of dispute.

Collecting societies operate by issuing a blanket licence to users for the repertoire of all the works of their members, which allows the user unlimited use of the whole repertoire assigned to (or licensed by) the collecting society for the duration of the licence. Collecting societies worldwide form a network of cross-national agreements for licensing each others' members' works and thus form an international mutual network that vastly reduces costs of international copyright transactions. They therefore pool transaction costs for rights-owners that would otherwise be prohibitively expensive for individuals and, at the same time, reduce costs for licensees, who would otherwise have to trace and contract with a multitude of rights-owners worldwide. Though the licence is across the board, revenues are distributed to individual members in accordance with the use made of their works on a 'pay-per-use' basis. That requires information from licensees as to their use of individual works, for example, the play time on the radio of a particular track and the size of the audience it is deemed to have reached. This information is logged by the user and transferred to the collecting society, which then pays the rights-owner according to the appropriate tariff. The database of the collecting society enables it to provide its service to its members and it is the main reason why a collecting society is a natural monopoly.

With the use of electronic databases, collecting societies are finding it worthwhile to share information in order to reduce costs (Gramex in the Scandinavian countries has done this for some time; the Performing Right Society and the Mechanical Copyright Protection Society now share a database in the UK). Digital rights management (DRM) is also developing but that requires the implant of data, for example, using an ISRC code, which can be done for new sound recordings but does not solve the problem of managing rights for earlier works.[6] It has been suggested that DRM could lead to international mergers of collecting societies, creating a formidable monopoly (that could confront multinational corporations in the media industries).

The revenues of collecting societies around the world are in the millions of pounds, indicating the value of copyrights to their owners and providing some evidence of the benefits to authors and publishers of having copyright protection. The other side of the coin, though, as we have seen, is that consumers pay for the authors' and publishers' 'bounty', as Macaulay termed it, in the price of the goods that deliver the copyrighted works.

Valuing musical copyrights and the economic contribution of the music industry

The overwhelming problem of valuing copyrights is that they are sold in a bundle of different rights making it impossible to assign an individual value to one right or another. What, for example, is the separate value-added of the performers' and record company's contribution to the final CD price? We can find out the studio fees for non-featured performers and know that featured artists typically get 10 to 15 per cent royalty on sales,[7] but do such figures tell us their market value or, indeed, their earnings? Information periodically appears about superstar income but it is also well-known from studies of performers' earnings that the distribution is very uneven: returns to the 'typical' performer are modest if not very low.[8]

The revenue from music and record sales provides the size of the 'pie' that is divided between featured performers, songwriters, composers, publishers and the sound recording maker. The division is highly complex and it is not necessary to go into it here (Passman 1998). What is an issue, though, is whether the award of new rights under copyright law to one group is at the expense of others. That must be the case but it was obscured for quite some time by the continuous growth of sales revenues. Another issue is whether the introduction of remuneration schemes in the secondary market (as for example, the European Rental Directive, which requires that musicians taking part in a recording receive a fee when it is used in, say, a television broadcast) will lead to a reduction in the payments to performers under the terms of their original contracts. Are record labels reducing royalty and studio payments on the grounds that performers will now be getting additional compensation for their work?[9]

How the value of the recording right to sound recording makers should be measured – by profits, sales revenues, or a calculation of the value of copyright assets over fifty years– is an issue that has received little attention from economists. Figures on the value of copyright assets periodically appear: 'Happy Birthday to You', for example, was report-edly bought by Warner Communications for $28m in 1988.[10] Moreover, the record industry itself appears to assess value in terms of sales; for instance, it uses sales figures to estimate losses from piracy. It could be argued, however, that profit rates are a more telling measure of value.

The contribution of copyright in the music industry to the national economy is also difficult to value. It is only recently that attempts have been made to quantify the size of the creative industries in general, and the task is difficult because national income statistics do not refer to the creative industries as such. There is no standard listing of the relevant industries and while most economists agree on the 'core' copyright industries, the definition of what else to include as 'copyright-dependent' or 'partial copyright' industries is open to debate. All economists do concur, though, that the correct way to value the contribution of these industries is in terms of value-added. Studies of the copyright-based industries in Australia, Canada, Finland, the Netherlands, Norway and the USA have all shown that they constitute a relatively large sector of the economy – 4.3 per cent of Gross Domestic Product (GDP) in the USA, 5.5 per cent in the Netherlands – and, perhaps more importantly, that these industries are growing more or less twice as fast as other sectors such as manufacturing and services.

The music industry forms part of this sector of the economy. It may be said to consist of composition, live performance, music publishing, and sound recording. The last two sectors are globalised and are owned by transnational corporations. Around 80 per cent of the world market in sound recording is controlled by five record companies – EMI, BMG,

The Warner Music Group, Sony Music Entertainment and Universal/ Polygram – which also dominate music publishing. These companies are in turn owned by large multinational conglomerates (see Bettig (1996). World revenues from music publishing were US$6.9 bn (thousand million) in 2000. Sound recording was estimated to have worldwide sales of $37 bn in 2000. The USA had 38 per cent of world sales of sound recordings, Japan 18 per cent and the UK 8 per cent. The proportion of domestic recordings sold in the USA was 92 per cent, 78 per cent in Japan, 51 per cent in the UK.[11] It is very difficult to use such figures (the standard industry statistics) to calculate the contribution to GDP of, say, live performance in each country or to avoid 'double-counting' (counting the value added by each activity more than once).

Conclusion

Throughout its 300-year history, copyright law has adapted to techno-logical change while retaining essentially the same legal and economic principles. Until digitalisation, however, copies of most products, espe-cially musical ones, were inferior to the 'original' (as evident in the quality of bootleg recordings, home-taped cassettes, and so on). The copy was clearly an inadequate substitute for the original, even though it cost less, and most economists thus rejected the case for copyright law as a necessary protection against unauthorised copying. Arguments against copyright also emphasised lead time and the competitive advantage of being first to market with a new good like a musical composition or sound recording. The current debate about copyright law, however, is not whether or not it should exist but if, in the digital era, it can possibly work. This is a debate to which economists can make a valuable contribution: copyright is, after all, not only a matter of legal principle but also one of economic pragmatism.

Part of that pragmatism is measuring the economic contribution of the music industry, along with that of the other creative industries, to the economy. Although difficult, this is a far easier task than measuring the value of copyright to the music industry or, indeed to the economy at large, a Holy Grail currently being sought by the World Intellectual Property Organisation (WIPO). Some economists, as we have seen, believe that the economic role of copyright is overrated and that copyright law errs on the side of over-protecting firms in the creative industries at the expense of both authors and of consumers.

Piracy and downloading of music from the Internet – the flouting of copyright law – are claimed to have had a negative impact on the music industry, which has recently experienced falling sales, which in turn reduce royalty earnings of composers and performers (though it could be argued, given the present market value of music publishing companies, that these losses are compensated for by increasing returns from secondary markets – see Chapter 6). This may be a short-term phenomenon, however, and one could certainly point to other causes of the downturn in record sales (these are discussed in Chapter 11). Unfortunately, most of the information on the effects of unauthorised copying come from the music industry's own high profile anti-piracy campaign, and economists need independent verification of its claims before pronouncing further. Whatever the facts of the matter, the industry is now beginning to look to new pricing strategies, such as earning revenues from merchandising and concert tours, and to new types of licensing deals for legal downloading, rather than relying solely on record sales revenues. These are the kinds of strategy to which economists, going back all the way to Adam Smith, have always looked. To survive in the digital era the music industry must look to market-based incentives for the creation and publication of new work and not simply place its faith in increasing the strength of copyright protection.

Notes

1. For more details, see Hadfield (1992).
2. Quoted in Hadfield (1992: 29–30).
3. See Shapiro and Varian (1999) and Acheson and Maule (1999).
4. No single reference to Coase's publications conveys the full impact of his ideas. For a short non-technical overview of his work see the entry on Ronald Coase in J. Eatwell, P. Newman and M. Milgate (eds) (1987), *The New Palgrave: A Dictionary of Economics*, London: Macmillan.
5. Gordon's analysis of the Betamax case (concerning the time-shifting of TV programmes by means of VCRs) was indeed used in the Napster case.
6. For details, see Einhorn (2002) and Matsumoto (2002).
7. This is often only on 85 per cent of sales revenue, however.
8. See Towse (2001) and Matsumoto (2002).
9. See Acheson and Maule (1999); also Towse (2001), Chapter 5.
10. Reported in Caves (2000: 311). The copyright was due to expire in 2010 but that may now be prolonged since in the USA company-owned copyrights have been extended to last ninety-five years, a clear windfall gain for music publishers in this case.
11. Figures taken from Throsby (2002: 10).

References

Acheson, K. and Maule, C. (1999), *Much Ado about Culture. North American Trade Disputes*, Ann Arbour: University of Michigan Press.

Bettig, R. (1996), *Copyrighting Culture*, Boulder: Westview Press.

Caves, R. (2000), *Economics of the Creative Industries*, Cambridge: Harvard University Press.

David, P. (1993), 'Intellectual property transactions and the panda's thumb: patents, copyrights and trade secrets in economic theory and history', in M. Mogee and R. Schwen (eds) *Global Dimensions of Intellectual Property Rights in Science and Technology*, Washington: National Academy Press, 19–61. Reprinted in Towse R. and Holzhauer, R. (eds) (2002), *The Economics of Intellectual Property*, Cheltenham and Northampton: Edward Elgar, 242–84.

Einhorn, M. (2002), 'Musical licensing in the digital age', in R. Towse (ed.) *Copyright in the Cultural Industries*, Cheltenham and Northampton: Edward Elgar, 165–77.

Gordon, W. (1982), 'Fair use as market failure: a structural and economic analysis of the *Betamax* case and its predecessors', *Columbia Law Review* 82 (8): 600–57.

Hadfield, G. (1992), 'The economics of copyright: an historical perspective', *Copyright Law Symposium*: 38, 1–46. Reprinted in R. Towse and R. Holzhauer (eds) (2002) *The Economics of Intellectual Property*, Cheltenham and Northampton: Edward Elgar, 129–74.

Landes,W. and Posner, R. (1989), 'An economic analysis of copyright law', *Journal of Legal Studies* 18: 325–66.

Matsumoto, S. (2002), 'Performers in the digital era, in R. Towse (ed.) *Copyright in the Cultural Industries*, Cheltenham and Northampton: Edward Elgar, 196–209.

Passman, D. (1998), *All You Need to Know about the Music Business*, New York: Prentice Hall.

Shapiro, C. and Varian, H. (1999), *Information Rules*, Boston: Harvard Business School Press.

Throsby, D. (2002), *The Music Industry in the New Millennium: Global and Local Perspectives*, Paris: Division of Arts and Cultural Enterprise, UNESCO.

Towse, R. (2001), *Creativity, Incentive and Reward: an Economic Analysis of Copyright and Culture in the Information Age*, Cheltenham: Edward Elgar.

Watt, R. (2000), *Copyright and Economic Theory. Friends or Foes?* Cheltenham: Edward Elgar.

CHAPTER 4

Copyright, Politics and the International Music Industry

Dave Laing

Introduction

This chapter is concerned primarily with the development of an international copyright framework designed to facilitate the activities of the European and North American music industry. It is therefore about copyright policy and politics rather than the conceptual basis or juridical origins of copyright.

The need for such a framework was evident in the early nineteenth century, as the system of patronage that had supported European art music was superseded by a market economy in music centred mainly on sales of printed scores for parlour pianos and domestic singing. This economy was heavily internationalised and, to ensure that income was received from abroad, composers and their publishers were obliged to licence their work to foreign publishers who, it was hoped, would both market the songs, sonatas, symphonies and opera and use national copyright protection to safeguard them from pirate editions.

However, reliance on national copyright laws to protect foreign music frequently proved to be insufficient. In the mid-1840s, the Milanese publisher Ricordi licensed Bellini's opera *La Sonnambula* to the London publisher Boosey & Son. Its subsequent popularity led three other London publishers to print copies of arias from the opera. Relying on the UK's 1838 International Copyright Act, Boosey sued for infringement of copyright only to lose the case at the highest court of appeal, the House of Lords (Barnes 1974: 162–72).

This case was not unique and by the last decade of the nineteenth century, the growth of the music industry and other culture industries in Europe and North America was such that the pressure for international copyright regulation to protect cultural exports became irresistible. The activities of the international music industry in this sphere since that time can be divided into three phases:

1. From the 1880s to the 1930s the process of copyright reform was dominated by the interests of composers and songwriters together with those of literary and dramatic writers. The principal vehicle for the international recognition of the rights of these groups as authors was the Berne Convention for the Protection of Literary and Artistic Works (1886).

2. The growth in importance of mechanical and electrical media such as the cinema, phonograph and wireless triggered the second phase in which 'neighbouring rights' were given an international dimension. These rights derived from the role played in cultural production of such interest groups as performing musicians, singers and actors, recording companies, film studios and radio and television broadcasters.

3. US computer software, film and music interests have played a commanding role in the third phase of the international copyright process that gathered momentum in the 1980s. This phase has been characterised by an emphasis on the commercial and trading role of the cultural industries, and on the contribution of copyright protection (or the lack of it) in direct governmental intervention to establish a 'level playing field' for the global trade in films, music and audiovisual programming. While the protagonists of phases one and two concentrated much of their efforts on establishing and strengthening international copyright conventions, phase three is focused more closely on bilateral relations between governments (notably concerning piracy) and on international trading agreements, above all the Trade-Related Aspects of Intellectual Property Rights, Including Trade in Counterfeit Goods (TRIPs) chapter of the 1993 World Trade Organisation (WTO) treaty.

The Rights of the Author

In 1849, several composers were drinking in a Paris café when they recognised their tunes in the repertoire of the café orchestra. Enraged at receiving no payment for this use, they refused to pay their bill and brought a court case against the café proprietor (Attali 1985: 77–8). The ruling in the composers' favour confirmed the existence of a 'performing right' for music authors and established the legal principle that they should be paid whenever their compositions were performed in public.

As a direct consequence of the court's decision, the first national organisation devoted to the assertion of the rights of songwriters and composers was founded in France in 1853. This was the Société des Auteurs, Compositeurs et Editeurs de Musique (SACEM). The role of SACEM was to act on behalf of all its members in collecting fees whenever their compositions were performed. SACEM was necessary because it would have been impossible for each composer individually to discover when and where his works were being performed and to negotiate a fee for each performance.

SACEM embodied the principle of the 'collective management' of authors' rights, a business practice that has become central to the operation of the music industry, and tolerated by anti-monopoly agencies because the existence of a single music rights organisation in each country (except for the US and Brazil) greatly simplifies the business dealings of music users such as broadcasters, café owners and concert promoters who can obtain a single licence permitting them to use virtually any musical work. Currently the global market in performing rights for musical works is worth over US$3 bn (NMPA 2003).

Similar authors' societies developed slowly elsewhere in Europe during the second half of the nineteenth century and early part of the twentieth. Only seven were formed before 1914 although the present day total is over 100. The initial reluctance to establish national organisations was due to different attitudes within the music industry towards the importance of receiving payment for the performance of music. While SACEM regarded this of equal significance to the sale of printed copies of songs, in Britain music publishers for many years refrained from charging singers or music hall owners because they believed the main purpose of public performance was to publicise songs in order to generate sales of sheet music. This argument was later to be echoed in debates over the airplay of pop records, the televising of music videos and even the downloading of tracks from the Internet through unlicensed 'peer-to-peer' networks.

The divergence between the approach of SACEM and that of the British publishers caused a dispute in 1890 when SACEM appointed a UK representative to charge fees for the public performance of works by French composers. The lack of cooperation from the British music industry was such that SACEM contemplated reporting the UK to the committee responsible for administering the 1886 Berne Convention, of which both France and Britain were signatories (Ehrlich 1989: 6–7).

Nine countries signed the original Berne text, seven of them European. By 2003, there were over 130 signatories. Since 1886, the Berne Convention has been amended six times, mainly to enable authors' rights to keep pace with new uses of their work made possible by technological change. The 1908 meeting in Berlin revised the Convention to incorporate references to photography, the cinema film and sound recording. The Rome Act of the Convention in 1928 extended authors' control of their works to sound broadcasting while television was brought within the scope of the Convention at Brussels in 1948. The concept of an author's 'moral right' was first included in 1928. Later revisions in Stockholm

(1967) and Paris (1971) concentrated on such issues as the 'compulsory licensing' of films (I discuss compulsory licensing later) and possible exemptions from parts of the Berne Convention for less developed countries. The most recent revision is the 1996 WIPO (World Intellectual Property Organisation) Copyright Treaty that has the status of a 'special agreement' under Article 20 of the Berne Convention. The 1996 Treaty provides additional protection for authors when their works are made available on the Internet or elsewhere 'by wire or wireless means, in such a way that members of the public may access them from a place and at a time individually chosen by them'.

By acceding to the Convention each signatory state agrees to incorporate its provisions into national law. But there are significant limits to this process and to the type of protection a Berne signatory can choose to provide for works created by citizens of other Berne states. Additionally, the Convention includes only minimum standards of protection that may be increased in national law, and several of the Convention's provisions are optional.

Within the Berne Convention rules, the protection of the works of foreign authors can take two different forms. 'National treatment' for foreign authors means simply that these copyright owners will receive the same level of protection as domestic authors. But a Berne Convention member can instead decide to grant 'reciprocal treatment'. This means that foreign authors will get only the level of protection that is granted in their own country. The most prominent current examples of reciprocal treatment are the private copying or 'home taping' levies that exist in many European countries. The only foreign composers entitled to share in the distribution of these levies are those from countries that also have a private copying levy system.

An important optional aspect of Berne is the granting of moral rights such as the right of an author to be properly identified and to insist that any editing of a work preserve its integrity. When the United States finally joined the Berne Convention in 1989, pressure from film industry interests ensured that the country opted out of the moral rights part of the treaty.

Another potential opt-out for governments was introduced when authors' rights were extended to broadcasting. The general right of authors granted in the Convention gives them the power to 'authorise or prohibit' any use of their work. By the late 1920s the radio industry had become a powerful force in Europe and music was one of the most important forms of programme material. When the issue of broadcasting rights for composers and songwriters was considered by the Berne

Convention nations, the pro-radio lobby argued for a 'compulsory licence' to be preferred to the 'authorise or prohibit' approach. Under such a licence, copyright owners cannot prevent the broadcasting of their works but broadcasters are required by law to pay for any copyright music they use. The compulsory licence system ensures a constant supply of broadcast music even when there is a dispute over royalty payments. In return, the broadcasters are committed to the payment of 'equitable remuneration' to copyright owners. To be equitable the level of such payments must either be agreed between broadcasters and authors' societies or be imposed by the decision of a government-appointed tribunal or special court. The compulsory licence lobby was strong enough to ensure that the Berne Convention member states decided to allow each national government the option of introducing the licence.

The definition of authorship itself came into question in 1928 in the context of cinematographic works. Prior to this, the Convention had assumed that an author of a book, play or song was a single individual or partnership of named individuals. The author had a separate existence from a publisher whose role was to put the work into circulation but who had no separate legal right (though the author did have moral rights). But filmmaking was a complex collaborative activity that made it difficult to locate an author or partnership of authors. Further, the production or creation of a movie was generally controlled by companies (the 'studios') rather than individuals. The committee dealing with the incorporation of cinematographic works into the Berne Convention was deadlocked over whether the Convention should accept the idea of corporate authorship. As a result it was again decided to take the optional approach: the definition of the author of a film was to be decided at national level, by the government of each Convention member state.

Disputes over the definition of authorship, including the authorship of broadcasts as well as films, have been interpreted by some commentators as a direct reflection of two conflicting legal philosophies. One of these legal discourses prevailed in the Latin countries of continental Europe and their former colonies and the other in the Anglo–American group of nations plus countries formerly colonised by the British. For instance, Vincent Porter writes that: 'the Roman Catholic countries of France, Italy, Spain and to a lesser extent Germany, saw the author's right as a human right with almost mystical overtones . . . In some countries, this mystic right stretched beyond the grave into eternity' (Porter 1991: 2). This emphasis on the right of the author as the fundamental and primary right in creative work can be found in the Berne Convention itself. The text deals solely with authorship and does not acknowledge the interests of other contributors to the creative process.] In the terminology of Latin jurisprudence, they possess 'neighbouring rights' (*droits voisins*), a secondary level of legal right. The contrasting approach, deriving from English common law, is described by Porter, somewhat disingenuously, as the 'public interest approach' (Porter 1991: 3). While this definition recognises that the Anglo-American notion of copyright gives greater weight to the interests of users of copyright works, it underplays the extent to which United States and United Kingdom copyright law was framed to accommodate the interests of the corporate owners and distributors of cultural products, through the granting of primary copyright status to 'producers' of film, television and music products.

This analysis also overstates the extent to which, in practice, the two legal philosophies are opposed. The American copyright expert Paul Edward Geller, who defines the two positions as norms of 'authorship' and 'marketplace', has argued that 'marketplace and authorship norms often lead to much the same results' in copyright disputes (Geller 1994: 159).

The Neighbouring Rights Era

When the Berne Convention was drawn up the music industry was on the eve of a technological and commercial revolution. In 1886 the only means of exploitation of music were by live performances and by the sale of printed music. Twenty years later, sound recordings were already becoming a powerful new means of communication with audiences, and twenty years after that, radio was to supplant records as the principal user of musical works. Not only did the Berne Convention have to contend with these new uses, but the recording and radio industries claimed to have their own copyright interests in music and other content.

In the United Kingdom, the 1911 Copyright Act acknowledged the ownership of sound recordings by 'record producers' (for the historical background to this development see Laing 2002: 185–7). Similar rights were introduced into other national laws. Although today the term 'producer' is generally employed to refer to a category of specialists who supervise studio recordings, its legal reference is to those who get rights in recordings because they provide the facilities/money for the recording session. In most cases these are record companies that contract performers, finance recording sessions and issue copies of the recordings to the public. The 1988 UK law defines the record or film producer succinctly as: 'the person by whom the arrangements necessary for the making of the recording or film are undertaken' (Dworkin and Taylor 1989: 46).

The 1911 Act gave the producers a single right, that of reproduction (manufacturing copies of their sound recordings on disc or cylinder). But the arrival of radio and, especially, the advent of electrical recording in 1925 meant that:

> commercial recordings became eminently suitable for many kinds of public musical entertainment . . . Could the industry contemplate, without misgiving, the ever-increasing use of its products for the benefit and profit of others in the form of public performance in theatres, cinemas, restaurants, cafes, fairgrounds, pleasure arcades, exhibitions, sports grounds and so on? (Bramall 1959: 96, 97–8)

The answer to this rhetorical question, posed by a leading recording industry official, was clearly 'No' because in the early 1930s several successful test cases were brought in European countries and new 'collective management' organisations were set up to administer this right by issuing licences and collecting payments from restaurateurs, broadcasters and other users of recorded music.

These decisions coincided with the formation of an international organisation to represent the interests of the record industry. This was the International Federation of the Phonographic Industry (IFPI) whose first congress in Rome in 1933 was attended by industry leaders from Germany, France, Italy and the UK. Subsequently IFPI was to become an energetic lobbyist for copyright reform at the international level, being granted consultative status with the International Labour Organisation, UNESCO, the World Intellectual Property Organisation and the European Commission.

One of its aims was to achieve a treaty for record producers and other owners of neighbouring rights, similar to the Berne Convention. It was almost thirty years before the adoption of the 1961 Rome Convention for the Protection of Performers, Producers of Phonograms and Broadcasting Organisations, mainly because of conflicts of interest between different categories of neighbouring rights' owners.

The Rome Convention confirmed that both performers and record producers should have the legal right to control the reproduction of their work and its public performance. It also set a minimum twenty-year period of copyright protection for sound recordings and broadcasts.

It followed Berne by permitting governments to introduce the compulsory licensing of broadcasts of sound recordings although signatories to the Rome Convention could opt out of granting broadcasting rights in sound recordings altogether. This option was taken by Monaco and Luxembourg, two small European states with powerful music radio stations broadcasting to nearby countries (because of its obligations as a European Union member, Luxembourg has since 'opted in' and introduced the broadcasting right).

The Rome Convention failed to determine how performance royalties for sound recordings should be divided between performers and record producers. Instead, the issue was left to national legislation or to a voluntary agreement that had been made between IFPI and the two international unions of performers – the International Federation of Musicians (FIM) and the International Federation of Actors (FIA). In the European Union a directive of 1993 that ruled that the royalties be equally divided between recording artists and record companies clarified the issue.

Like the Berne Convention, the Rome Convention permitted both national and reciprocal treatment of foreign works. Like Berne, Rome stated that national treatment must apply to performers, producers and broadcasters of other countries that were signatories to the Convention. Countries could also use reciprocal treatment rules in order to avoid sharing performance royalties with performers and record producers from countries that had not joined the Convention. This opt-out is particularly important as the United States, where many of the most popular and most played recordings originate, was, and is still not a member of the Rome Convention.

By 2003, seventy-six countries had joined the Rome Convention, slightly more than one-third of the membership of the Berne Convention. However, by then Rome had been supplemented by the 1996 WIPO Performances and Phonograms Treaty (WPPT) that had been drafted alongside the WIPO Copyright Treaty.

The WPPT provides new minimum standards of copyright protection in the era of digital media and the Internet. The new author's right relating to Internet distribution mentioned above is paralleled by a similar right for performers and record companies. Other elements of the 1996 treaties include the outlawing of devices designed to circumvent electronic protection systems linked to digital recordings, stronger protection against illegal copying and confirmation that Berne Convention and Rome Convention provisions on the reproduction of works or recordings are valid in the digital domain.

The WPPT also raises the Rome Convention's minimum twenty-year protection period for recordings to fifty years. By 1996, many countries had already introduced a fifty-year rule and under the 1998 Sonny Bono Copyright Term Extension Act (CTEA), the US Congress greatly extended the protection period for recorded music, films and broadcasts to ninety-five years. This was widely thought to have been the result of

...ollywood studios led by Disney which feared the loss of ...early Mickey Mouse movies.

...nal legality of the CTEA was challenged in 2003 in a ...urt hearing (*Eldred v. Ashcroft*). The complainants ...xtended terms of copyright contravened the Copyright ...Constitution that gave Congress the power 'To Promote the Progress of Science and useful Arts by securing for limited Times to Authors and Inventors the exclusive Right to their respective Writings and Discoveries'. The Supreme Court rejected the case by a majority vote on the narrow ground that the CTEA: 'reflects judgements of the kind Congress typically makes' but added that 'It does take a lot of things out of the public domain . . . in terms of policy this flies directly in the face of what the Framers [of the Constitution] had in mind' (*Music & Copyright* 2003).

Since the 1970s the copyright strategy of the international record industry has given a lower priority to performance rights than to piracy and various forms of 'private copying' such as home taping, CD-burning and Internet downloading. While it included broad protection against the infringement of copyright, the 1961 Rome Convention was drafted at a period when the piracy of sound recordings was a relatively minor problem for the music industry. The widespread piracy of printed music in Britain had been resolved by the 1906 Copyright Act (Coover 1985: 136–44) and although unauthorised copies of vinyl discs had been produced in earlier decades, it was the arrival of the compact tape cassette that (inadvertently) provided the technology to enable music piracy to become big business.

Cassette-tape technology was smaller in scale than the heavy industrial plant required for the manufacture of vinyl records. Tape duplication equipment was soon far cheaper to purchase than the heavy-duty presses needed for seven-inch, ten-inch and twelve-inch vinyl products. Apart from its cumbersome reel-to-reel predecessor, the compact cassette was the first mass-produced pre-recorded music technology that could also be used to make recordings.

By the end of the 1960s, it was clear that the piracy and counterfeiting of pre-recorded cassettes was becoming endemic in many parts of the world. As well as trying to galvanise police forces to combat piracy, IFPI decided to press governments for a new international treaty aimed specifically at the control and punishment of piracy. The result was the 1971 Convention for the Protection of Producers of Phonograms against the Unauthorised Reproduction of their Phonograms, known more briefly as the Phonograms Convention. This treaty added new import and distribution rights to those already embodied in the Rome Convention. Record producers could now stop illegal imports (so-called 'parallel imports') and take action against wholesalers and retailers as well as manufacturers of illegal copies.

The Phonograms Convention had gained the adherence of thirty-six countries by 1983 and seventy-two by 2003. After its passing, the international record industry devised a three-stage global strategy to control piracy. In 1983, IFPI's Stephen Stewart commented:

> Stage I was protecting the major markets; Stage II protecting minor markets in the record-producing countries and thus throwing a *cordon sanitaire* around 90% of the world's production. Stage III was clearing the countries that were very largely piratical and are mainly, but not entirely, situated in the developing world.

Stewart added that Stages I and II had largely been achieved but: 'Stage III has merely begun' (Stewart 1983: 17).

In the two decades since that judgement, new forms of piracy based on Compact Disc and MP3 technologies have to some extent undermined Stewart's optimistic prognosis about the success of Stages I and II, while progress in achieving Stage III has been much slower than had been expected. According to IFPI, piracy was rising rather than falling nearly two decades after Stewart's pronouncement. It estimated that the value of pirate sales in 2002 was US$4.6 bn, 7 per cent higher than in 2001, and the number of units sold on the pirate market was 14 per cent higher at 1.1 billion CDs and cassettes (IFPI 2003).

In addition, the size and character of the private copying of copyright recordings – defined by IFPI officials in 1993 as 'the non-commercial copying of sound recordings and audio-visual recordings for personal, domestic use' (Davies and Hung 1993: 1) – has changed in ways that could not have been predicted in the era of 'home taping'.

That phrase took hold in the late 1960s and early 1970s as a description of the copying of discs to tape or the recording from radio to tape practised not by commercially-minded pirates but by private citizens. Subsequently, newer technologies have enabled private copying to be conducted by 'burning' recordings onto blank CDs or by downloading music from Internet sites (these are discussed in Chapter 11).

Since the 1970s, sections of the music industry have adopted several different responses to the various forms of private copying. These have included educational and media campaigns such as the use of the widely-derided slogan 'Home Taping is Killing Music'; the so-far-unsuccessful introduction of 'spoiler' signals such as the Philips SCMS designed to block or interfere with copying; lawsuits against companies like Napster and Aimster that facilitated unlawful private copying and against individuals identified as using Napster-like Internet sites; and private copying levies on copying hardware and software. Only the last of these seems likely to furnish a long-term solution for the music industry since it implies acceptance of the fact that private copying cannot be stemmed by technological or judicial measures but that it can be made financially to compensate the industry.

The Era of Economic Interests

Since the 1980s, the reliance by the music industry on the system of international copyright conventions to assert its rights has been superseded by a different kind of lobbying. The new strategy harnesses the economic and political weight of the most powerful nation states and trading blocs to demand anti-piracy action by governments in the developing world. For this type of lobbying, an emphasis on the commercial importance of music, film and other copyright-based businesses as export industries has been much more effective than the simple assertion of the legal rights of copyright owners.

The rise of cassette piracy and home taping had been preceded by a globalisation of popular music and the record industry. The success of Elvis Presley, The Beatles and many others in the 1960s had significantly increased the share of world record sales taken by Anglo-American performers and songwriters. Based on data from IFPI and its national affiliates, one business publication estimated that by the late 1990s 'international repertoire' (mainly United States-originated recordings) accounted for 41 per cent of global sales outside the US itself (*Financial Times Music & Copyright* 1997). In 2001, the proportion of sales of international repertoire in national music markets ranged from 24 per cent in Japan to 89 per cent in Switzerland where the foreign music sold came from Germany, France and Italy as well as Anglophone countries (IFPI 2002: 170–1).

The growing cultural and commercial impact of American music internationally encouraged United States-owned record companies to take on an expanded international role in the 1960s and 1970s. US firms that had been content to license their music to local companies in Europe and Latin America set up foreign branches to take direct responsibility for selling their music to foreign consumers. This process gathered momentum in the 1980s and 1990s when take-overs and mergers produced an oligopoly of five major international record companies responsible for 70–80 per cent of global sales.

These developments brought about an increased awareness of the importance of foreign markets for US copyright music and recordings. A survey of US copyright industries estimated that 'core copyright industries' were responsible for export earnings of US$89bn in 2001(IIPA 2002). This was greater than the exports of both the chemical and motor vehicle industries. Of the US$89bn, music accounted for US$9.5bn and film, television and video for US$14.7bn, while computer software accounted for more than two-thirds. The 2001 total was almost three times the US$34bn copyright exports reported in 1990.

The focus on world markets led to special scrutiny of those countries believed by the US copyright industries to maintain trade barriers against exports of American films, music and television shows. In some cases the barriers took the form of quotas, restricting the amount of broadcasting time available for foreign programmes, but the exclusion of US copyright owners from home taping royalty payments in countries such as France and Germany was also included. Some nations had currency export regulations or corporate ownership rules that made it difficult for US companies to set up local branches or joint venture operations. But the main 'trade barrier' faced by the US was and remains weak copyright laws and even weaker enforcement of them – the Stage III situation of Stewart's strategic analysis.

In order to influence government policy, the US copyright industries formed the International Intellectual Property Alliance (IIPA). Its member organisations include the Recording Industry Association of America (RIAA), the National Music Publishers Association (NMPA) and the Motion Picture Association of America (MPAA). IIPA's first breakthrough came during the presidency of the former actor Ronald Reagan. In 1988 the Reagan administration introduced the Omnibus Trade and Competitiveness Act and its so-called 'Special 301' provision. Special 301 permitted the United States Trade Representative (USTR) to nominate 'Priority Foreign Countries' whose trading practices, especially relating to imports of intellectual property, were alleged to be harmful to US copyright industries, notably music, films, books and computer software. Once designated as Priority Foreign Countries, nations could be subject to trade sanctions if they failed to improve their commercial and trading practices.

The first Priority Foreign Countries, announced in 1991, were Thailand, China and India. An intensive six-month period of investigation and negotiation followed. Afterwards, the governments of China and India announced plans to improve copyright protection. China joined the Berne Convention in 1992 while the Indian government agreed to ease restrictions on the activities of foreign companies.

The announcement of a Special 301 list by the USTR is now an annual event, preceded by the publication by IIPA of an advisory report that recommends which countries should be the target of threatened sanctions. By 2000, the USTR list comprised fifty-nine countries, eighteen of which were in the most serious category, the Priority Watch List. Among the later were Israel (because of its production of illegal CDs), Malaysia (where there was a backlog of copyright cases in the courts) and India, again. On this occasion, India was accused of permitting cable television piracy and the illegal importation of CDs from other Asian countries.

The use of Special 301 by the US government to pressurise individual countries has been attacked by a European Commission report that pointed out that 'the unique feature of the "301" family of legislation is that it permits unilateral determinations and action, or threats thereof, inconsistent with, and in clear contradiction with, the multilateral trading system' (Services of the European Commission 1993: 14). More directly, in 2003, the justice minister of Taiwan accused the US of 'bullying' his country with Special 301.

The efficacy of the Special 301 strategy has been called into question by the continuing inability or unwillingness of the Chinese authorities to make good their promises to end the manufacture of pirate CD and CD-ROM software in factories based on the Chinese mainland. Despite the fact that China remains one of IFPI's ten priority countries for piracy, China was allowed to join the WTO in 2001 and the US government clearly decided to prioritise maintaining friendly relations with China over its Special 301 obligations.

The WTO treaty is the latest version of what the EC called 'the multilateral trading system', having superseded the GATT agreement, first negotiated in 1948 to promote and police free trade on a world-wide basis. The 1993 WTO treaty included trade in intellectual property for the first time in its chapter on Trade Related Aspects of Intellectual Property Rights, Including Trade in Counterfeit Goods (TRIPs).

The treaty was the result of the so-called Uruguay Round renegotiation of the GATT treaty that began in 1986 and the talks on the TRIPs element were marked by fierce disagreements between exporting countries, led by the US and EC and the group of seventy-seven developing countries with a negative balance of trade in intellectual property led by Brazil and India (see May 2000; Samuelson 1999; Shiva 1998).

Summarising many criticisms, Christopher May writes: 'The net effect of the TRIPs agreement is actually to critically reduce the area of public knowledge, especially in areas where new technologies and processes are important or even vital to socio-economic development' (May 2000: 77).

The most significant of these have been pharmaceutical patents, agricultural patents and computer software copyrights where multinational companies from the industrialised North have been accused of promoting TRIPs in order to impose their products on the South and increase the outflow of funds from the developing world (Houtart 2003: 146–7). The free trade in music and films encouraged by TRIPs is seldom mentioned in these critiques.

The final version of the TRIPs chapter of the WTO treaty has seventy-three clauses. Many reiterate the fundamental rights of authors, performers and producers already enshrined in the Berne and Rome Conventions. TRIPs additionally includes detailed instructions on the role of customs services and courts in dealing with piracy. There is also provision for the settlement of intellectual property disputes between members of the WTO.

The US was adjudged to be guilty in the first copyright dispute to be dealt with by the WTO. The complaint was brought by the European Union supported by several developing countries. It concerned a change to the US copyright law that exempted bars, restaurants and stores from paying to use copyright music when the music was sourced from radio or television programmes. In 2001, a WTO disputes panel agreed with the EU that this was a breach of the obligations of the US as a Berne Convention member. The panel ordered the payment of compensation by the US government. Congress voted through the payment of US$3.3 m as a sub-clause of the 2003 Wartime Supplemental Appropriations Act!

Developing countries were permitted to phase in TRIPs provisions over five or ten years. However, TRIPs broadly favoured Western copyright owners by opening up the markets of less developed states in a more comprehensive way than before. The only subsequent revision of this process has been the exception made for the manufacture of generic drugs to treat the AIDS epidemic in developing countries whose governments could not afford the prices charged by multinational companies that hold the patents on these drugs (Corrêa 2003).

The incorporation of copyright issues into the framework of international trade agreements also took place at the regional level. In the late 1980s and early 1990s free trade programmes were introduced in Europe and in North America. As part of its 1992 Single European Market project, the EU set out to harmonise the copyright regimes of its member countries in a series of directives dealing with the duration of copyright protection, rental of videos and CDs and transborder aspects of cable and satellite broadcasting. Countries applying to join the European Union were required to harmonise their copyright laws with those of existing EU members. Trade barriers between the US, Mexico and Canada were dismantled by the North American Free Trade Agreement (NAFTA). Under NAFTA the three countries give national treatment to each other's copyright owners.

Conclusion

The new global emphasis on the export value of intellectual property exemplified by TRIPs and the relentless rise in the quantity of commercial piracy and private copying of music have coincided with a lengthy slump in the sales of recorded music. Between 1996 and 2002 the retail value of global sales fell from US$39.8 bn to US$31 bn and the average annual decrease was 3.5 per cent. Most experts expect the fall in sales to continue until at least 2005 not least because of the almost total failure of record companies to organise an online market for their products.

The system of legislation that supports the copyright industries has also been the target of numerous attacks and critiques over the past decade, culminating in the *Eldred v. Ashcroft* case. Against these features that could be seen as weakening the copyright industries must be set the failure of that case to redress the excesses of US copyright law and the almost unanimous acceptance by national and international legal regimes that the Internet can be subsumed into the existing intellectual property power structure (even if enforcement of copyright law in cyberspace remains exceptionally weak).

This unprecedented concatenation of factors makes it extremely difficult to predict the next phase of development (or decline) of the international music copyright framework. One point that is often overlooked, however, is that the music industry as such is no longer a significant autonomous force in the international industrial landscape. Within the copyright sector, its sales and exports are dwarfed by those of the film and television industry and above all by the computer software industry. Equally, all but one of the major international record companies is but a small division of a large transnational media or consumer electronics conglomerate. On a global basis, the future direction of music as a copyright industry is dependent on the decisions and actions of others.

References

Attali, J. (1985), *Noise. The Political Economy of Music*, Manchester: Manchester University Press.

Barnes, J. J. (1974), *Authors, Publishers and Politicians: The Quest for an Anglo-American Copyright Agreement (1815–1854)*, London: Routledge.

Coover, J. (1985), *Music Publishing Copyright and Piracy in Victorian England*, London and New York: Mansell.

Corrêa, S. (2003), 'Medicine, health, AIDS', in *Another World is Possible. Popular Alternatives to Globalization at the World Social Forum*, W. F. Fisher and T. Ponniah (eds), London: Zed Books: 150–60.

Davies, G. and Hung, M. (1993), *Music and Video Private Copying. An International Survey of the Problem and the Law*, London: Sweet & Maxwell.

Dworkin, G. and Taylor, R. D. (1989), *Blackstone's Guide to the Copyright, Designs and Patents Act 1988*, London: Blackstone Press.

Ehrlich, C. (1989), *Harmonious Alliance. A History of the Performing Right Society*, Oxford: Oxford University Press.

Eldred v. Ashcroft (2003), 537 U.S.

Financial Times Music & Copyright (1997), 'Local repertoire grew to 54% of sales outside the US in 1996', 23 April: 1.

Geller, P. E. (1994), 'Must copyright for ever be caught between marketplace and authorship norms?' in, *Of Authors and Origins*, Brad Sherman and Alain Strowel (eds), Oxford: Clarendon Press.

Houtart, F. (2003), 'Knowledge, copyright and patents', in *Another World is Possible. Popular Alternatives to Globalization at the World Social Forum*, W. F. Fisher and T. Ponniah (eds), London: Zed Books: 144–9.

IFPI (2002), *The Recording Industry in Numbers*, London: IFPI.

IFPI (2003), *Commercial Music Piracy 2003*, London: IFPI.

IIPA (2002), *Copyright Industries in the US Economy*, New York: IIPA.

Laing, D. (2002), 'Copyright as a component of the music business', in *The Business of Music*, Michael Talbot (ed.), Liverpool: Liverpool University Press: 171–94.

May, C. (2000), *A Global Political Economy of Intellectual Property Rights: The New Enclosures?*, London: Routledge.

Music & Copyright (2003), 'US Supreme Court rules that the 1998 Sony Bono Copyright Term Extension Act is constitutional', 5 February: 14

NMPA (National Music Publishers Association) (2003), *International Survey of Music Publishing Revenues*, New York: NMPA.

Porter, V. (1991), *Beyond the Berne Convention*, London: John Libbey.

Samuelson, P. (1999), 'Implications of the Agreement on Trade Related Aspects of Intellectual Property Rights for cultural dimensions of national copyright laws', *Journal of Cultural Economics* 23: 95–107.

Services of the European Commission (1993), *Report on United States Trade and Investment Barriers. Problems of Doing Business with the US*, Brussels: European Commission.

Shiva, V. (1998), *Biopiracy. The Plunder of Nature and Knowledge*, Dartington: Green Books.

Stewart, S. (1983), 'The years 1963 to 1979', in J. Borwick (ed.), *IFPI, The First Fifty Years*, London: IFPI: 13–21.

PART II
Copyright and Everyday Life

CHAPTER 5

Copyright Law and Power in the Music Industry

Steve Greenfield and Guy Osborn

Introduction

This chapter is concerned with the implications of copyright law for the music industry. In particular, some fundamental questions relating to the ownership and control of music will be raised via the issue of sound sampling, but in addition the interrelated area of music business contracts, insofar as copyright law impacts upon this, will be considered. As is apparent from other chapters in this book and elsewhere (Greenfield and Osborn 1998 and 2000), copyright is the vehicle that drives the music business; essentially the value of the industry can be measured in copyright terms. The crucial role of copyright law can be demonstrated by its key part in attempts to restrict peer-to-peer file sharing (Carey and Wall 2001) and the dissemination of music via the Internet more generally. But well-publicised contractual disputes, focused on attempts by artists to free themselves from restrictive management, publishing or recording contracts, are also essentially about who has the right to exploit intellectual property and, more specifically, copyright. (Disputed management agreements are the exception here although it could be argued that even they deal with intellectual property tangentially.)

Of course, the changing technological landscape is responsible for much of contemporary music business litigation. While technology creates exciting new possibilities of production, dissemination and consumption, a perhaps unwelcome byproduct is that a raft of new legal problems now needs to be considered. Indeed, it is the ability to use musical material in different ways with a far greater degree of accessibility that is leading to many of the disputes. Perhaps the key issue for the music business and for legal scholars is whether copyright remains a functional tool to deal with these new problems, but for artists currently within the music industry the immediate question is a more practical one: how can they best use copyright and contract law to protect their musical output and retain their freedom of musical expression?

Copyright issues in the music industry

Copyright provides its owner with a bundle of exclusive rights that only he or she may exercise. Any attempt to use their work without permission may amount to an infringement. That is not to say, however, that copyright provides a complete monopoly over the use of the work. The law also recognises the need to ensure that a work can circulate and be commented upon, critically or otherwise, that it can be used for research, that it should be available in certain respects in the public interest.

To this end copyright works may be reproduced, without infringement, for the purpose of 'fair use' or 'fair dealing'. This permits limited free use of copyright material. For example, it is difficult to critique or review a work without copying at least part of it in some shape or form, and this is a legitimate defence of what would ordinarily, or technically, amount to a breach of copyright. The terminology employed within the Copright Act 1988 suggests limited use is permissible if it is 'fair' – this may involve consideration of the amount of copyright work reproduced or the rationale behind the reproduction. This latter point may be crucial particularly in that context of sampling. A comparable example of the application of the fair use doctrine in a United States sampling case is provided by *Campbell v. Acuff-Rose Music, Inc* (1994).

This case concerned the rap group 2 Live Crew, who utilised the composition 'Oh, Pretty Woman', the work of William Dees and Roy Orbison, as the basis for their own composition entitled 'Pretty Woman'. 2 Live Crew took the distinctive bass line and adapted the lyrics so that they were more in keeping with their own distinctive style. Effectively this took the song into the cachet of parody. The question for the court was whether this was indeed an infringement of copyright. On the face of it a strongly arguable case could be made that a substantial part of the work had been taken (see below for a discussion of the meaning of 'substantial part'). Could the defence of fair use nevertheless be applied? Four issues needed to be considered in applying the fair use defence under US copyright provisions:

1. the purpose of the use, including whether the use was commercial or for educational purposes;
2. the nature of the original copyright work;
3. the amount of work taken in relation to the work as a whole;
4. the effect of this upon the potential market for the original work (see Bernstein 1994).

The upshot of the decision (in 2 Live Crew's favour) was that in US law judgement of fair use involves a balancing act that takes account issues of creativity (of new work) and protection (of existing work):

> Long after the particular outcome of 2 Live Crew's fair use defence is decided on remand, *Campbell v. Acuff-Rose* will be remembered for a more fundamental reason: a balanced approach to copyright has been reaffirmed by the Supreme Court. As Kennedy J. recognised in his concurring opinion, underprotection and overprotection of copyright both disserve the constitutional purpose. The struggle is always to find the appropriate level of protection which will promote rather than stifle creativity, recognising the need to protect original works without inhibiting the creation of new or transformative ones. It will be interesting to see how the district courts balance these competing considerations in the cases to come. (Bernstein 1994: 97)

Within the context of fair use and sampling it is interesting to examine the issue of 'substantial part' that is at the root of arguments about copyright infringement where the whole work is not taken. Historically, copyright disputes in the music industry have focused upon the copying of another's song, and where this was not explicit (if the work was a cover version there could be little debate) this centred around whether the work was indeed recognisably a copy and, if so, whether what was copied was a significant part of the work. This issue of significance, or substantiality is key here. Section 16 of the UK Copyright Designs and Patent Act 1988 (CDPA 1988) provides the framework as to what counts as an infringement of copyright once ownership of copyright has been established. The copyright owner has the exclusive right to: copy the work; issue copies to the public; rent or lend the work; perform, show, play or broadcast the work; adapt the work. Disputes arise not only when someone uses a work to which they do not have title, but also when it seems they are claiming ownership of someone else's work, when the song in which they claim copyright seems 'substantially' the same as someone else's or, to put this another way, when their song seems to take a 'substantial amount' from someone else's copyrighted work. There are a series of guidelines British courts follow as to what substantial means here:

> Traditionally, the courts have looked at a number of factors when determining whether there has been a substantial taking. Amongst these are the quality and quantity of that which is taken, the intention of the user, and whether or not the two parties are in competition . . . it is difficult to predict with any certainty whether or not and how these factors will be applied to 'sampling' as a category. The reason for this is that the decision as to whether any instance of sampling constitutes an infringement will depend very much upon the facts of the case and these may vary considerably. (Bently and Sherman 1992: 159)

Traditionally, then, copyright disputes in British courts have primarily concerned plagiarism, the examination of similarities between different songs' music or lyrics, as in *Francis Day Hunter v. Bron* (1963). Here the particular slant was that the defendant professed never to have heard the original composition, 'In a Little Spanish Town', although his own composition, 'Why', produced some thirty years later, had a significant degree of similarity to the work. As Wilmer LJ put it: 'There is an undoubted degree of similarity between the two songs, the only question being what adjective to put before the word "degree"' (at 614). To constitute infringement two criteria need to be fulfilled, firstly objective similarity between the works in question and, secondly, that the copyright work must be the source from which the alleged infringing work is derived. As Upjohn LJ noted: 'If it is an independent work, then, though identical in every way, there is no infringement' (at 617). As in this case, the contention can be made that the defendant has not knowingly heard the original but has copied the work *subconsciously*. Here, both at first instance and on appeal, it was held that no infringement had taken place. (By contrast, an American judge ruled in 1976 that George Harrison's 'My Sweet Lord' was the same song as 'He's So Fine' and therefore under the law an infringement of copyright and 'no less so even though it may have been subconsciously accomplished' – quoted in Bronson 1985: 286.)

Other legal considerations in such cases include the 'recognisability' and the 'importance' of what has been taken from the old work to the new one. In *Hawkes v. Paramount* (1934) it was argued that even though the length of the 'sample' was fairly short within the context of the piece as a whole; 'anyone hearing it would know that it was the march called "Colonel Bogey", and though it may be that it was not very prolonged in its reproduction, it is clearly . . . a substantial, a vital, an essential part which is there reproduced.' In other words, in legal terms 'substantial part' involves qualitative as well as quantitative measures.

Such traditional legal disputes about musical theft and plagiarism continue. See, for example, *Ludlow Music v. Williams* (2001), in which Ludlow Music was awarded damages from Robbie Williams, his co-writer, Guy Chambers, and publishers EMI Music and BMG Music, for the 'substantial' copying of Loudon Wainwright's 'I Am the Way' in Williams' song, 'Jesus in a Camper Van'. But the same new technology that has given us new ways of consuming music, via the Internet and MP3 (Carey and Wall 2001), has also provided new ways of producing music. Whilst music, like all knowledge in fact, might be thought of as inherently derivative on one level, digital technological advances have allowed work to be produced that is more overtly derivative in that it relies explicitly not only upon 'original' musical and literary works of other creators, but also on sound recordings owned by someone else. One effect of this, as already described, has been the attempt by the rights-owners of recorded works (i.e. record companies) to protect their rights legally. The problem, in the light of previous plagiarism cases, has been to establish new principles of what is substantial and recognisable (where the 'taking' of original sounds is so direct the defence of subconscious copying no longer arises). As Bently and Sherman note, the rise of sound sampling as a creative technique makes the evaluative process in copying cases more contentious. Sampling as a process allows sound to be reduced to digital bytes that can then be saved and utilised elsewhere (Tackaberry 1990). The effect and potential of this was noted by Goodwin:

> These technological shifts go hand in hand (although sometimes just in parallel) with pop's changing attitude to its history. As old texts have become new again (through new media forms like music video and the increased use of pop as a film soundtrack, as well as CD reissues), pop has plundered its archives with truly postmodern relish, in an orgy of pastiche. The degree to which pop music in the 1980s has become self-referential is now so developed that some songs sound like copies of parodies. (Goodwin 1988: 260)

In short, the technology both allowed new methods of creation and also called forth a new pop aesthetic in which 'copying' became the creative act (for further discussion see Chapter 8 in this volume). Given that the law attempts to regulate most areas of commercial life, we might have expected a plethora of legal challenges as this practice developed, but, in fact, the legal cases on sampling are few and far between. This is largely because it is in the interests of parties involved in sampling cases to settle out of court, for reasons of costs and because of the potential restricting effects a court decision might have on future conduct (in its role as a precedent for future legal interpretation). Because of this, even cases that are not settled before litigation takes place are usually settled before a definite judgement is handed down, which has created difficulties – there is presently a lack of legal certainty and clarity about what is and isn't legitimate in sampling terms. The few cases that have come before the courts tell us little about sampling in terms of legal principle as to what constitutes infringement, but do reveal the differing approaches to this phenomenon and some of the legal difficulties caused by this magpie form.

An example of this can be seen in *Hyperion Records Ltd v. Warner Music* (1991). In this case, the group The Beloved had constructed a piece of work entitled 'Sun Arising' which utilised a section of the work 'O

Euchari' (from *A Feather on the Breath of God*). The composition involved was out of copyright (having been written in 1179 by Abbess Hildegard of Bingen!), but the copyright in the sound recording was still owned by Hyperion. The Beloved sampled eight notes of 'O Euchari' which were then looped to repeat throughout a large part of their own composition, 'Sun Arising'. No permission was sought to do this and so Hyperion brought an action against the owners of the sound recording of 'Sun Arising', WEA, claiming damages accruing from this alleged breach of copyright. WEA argued for the action to be struck out on the basis that there was no arguable claim. Hugh Laddie QC in the High Court (sitting as deputy judge) rejected WEA's application on the basis that there was a reasonably arguable case that the eight notes could be considered a substantial part of the Hyperion sound recording of 'O Euchari':

> The decision on substantiality is a jury question for the judge and in very many cases the judge will be able to make up his mind without the aid of any evidence. Nevertheless, in some cases . . . particularly borderline cases . . . expert evidence may assist the Court and in such cases Order 14 [for the case to be struck out] would not be appropriate. (per Hugh Laddie)

In *Produce v. BMG* (1999), a striking out application came before the court with regard to a claim by Produce Records that BMG had infringed their copyright in 'Higher and Higher', a track composed and recorded in the early 1990s by The Farm. Produce alleged that BMG's 1996 release of Los del Rio's 'Macarena', incorporated a substantial part of 'Higher and Higher' in contravention of CDPA 1988 s. 16. The argument put forward by the defendants was a simple one. It was admitted that Produce had copyright in 'Higher and Higher' and that part of it had been copied into 'Macarena'; the crucial question was whether this was substantial or not. Counsel for BMG contended that this was a matter for the judge alone to decide, and that expert evidence was therefore not admissible. The only conclusion that the judge could come to was that no copying of a substantial part of 'Higher and Higher' had been made. Unsurprisingly, the plaintiffs sought to rely upon experts' reports, and, in particular, on the evidence of musicologist, Guy Protheroe, which argued a substantial part of 'Higher and Higher' was copied. The sample in question was a vocal passage, around seven seconds long, sung by a backing singer, Paula Davis, which was repeated throughout 'Macarena'. In his ruling, Mr Justice Parker held that there was at least a triable issue there and therefore refused the claim to strike out the action. Had he not done so it is arguable that a precedent could have been set that no permission need be sought for similar future use of samples.

The case of JAMMS was discussed by Simon Frith in the first edition of this text (Frith 1993: 4–6). It is, however, useful to recall the relevant issues here as the case perhaps provides one of the clearest examples of the potential for copyright law to censor new work created by the process of sound sampling. JAMMS, alternatively known as the KLF (Kopyright Liberation Front) produced an album entitled *1987: What the Fuck is Going On?*. The album as a whole contained an eclectic sequence of sampled work, ranging from a Petula Clark song to a recording of the TV programme *Top of the Pops*. One track in particular proved problematic, 'The Queen and I' borrowed liberally from the Abba recording, 'Dancing Queen'. No permission was sought to use these excerpts and JAMMS duly heard from the MCPS, as administrators of Abba's UK rights in their recordings, in a letter sent in August 1987. This notified them that Abba was not willing to grant JAMMS a licence for the use of their track and ordered them to:

1. cease all manufacture and distribution;
2. take all possible steps to recover copies of the album which were then to be delivered to MCPS or destroyed under the supervision of MCPS;
3. deliver up the master tape, mothers, stampers and any other parts commensurate with manufacture of the record. (cited in Robinson, undated: 8)

Attempts to persuade the owners of 'Dancing Queen' of the merits of 'The Queen and I' were fruitless (Greenfield and Osborn 1998: 66–7). All masters were surrendered, and the LP was rereleased in 'sample free' format later in the year, resplendent with long periods of silence (and sleeve note instructions as to how to recreate the original LP). The original LP itself became a collectors' item, with urban legend having it that Jim Cauty and Bill Drummond of JAMMS bought the last five copies from a record shop, advertised these in *Face* magazine at £1,000 each, and sold three of them. The importance of this case (which did not reach court and therefore has no value as legal precedent) is that it shows clearly, nevertheless, how new musical works, however creative in their use of samples, can be kept from the public by the exercise of copyright law.

The crucial point here is that a new work, new even if it used a copyright work as its fulcrum, was prevented from being released. This is how copyright exerts censorial control over music. Given the existence of intellectual property rights, future uses of musical works can be fettered on the grounds that someone owns the originals and can therefore control their reuse. It is certainly arguable that this aspect of copyright deters creativity, notwithstanding the traditional view that copyright promotes creative endeavour by acting as an incentive (Greenfield and Osborn 2002: 71).

Outside of the strict copyright arena, it is important to note that the vehicle by which most copyright transactions are made is that of the contract. The second part of this chapter considers how copyright impacts upon music contracts and, in addition, how the contract itself can place restrictions upon musical output.

Copyright and Contractual issues

A crucial factor at the heart of both recording and publishing contracts, indeed in almost all entertainment contracts, is the question of exclusive performance. The music industry seeks exclusive control over artists and their output, at least for as long as they are successful. Success is monitored through a series of option periods that allow the company to discard the artist once economic returns point to diminishing commercial profits. When artists are contracted to write and/or to perform, what is actually being bought is the exclusive right to copyright works, whether compositions or the performances embodied in sound recordings. It is the artist's ability to produce viable copyright works that is at stake in both music publishing and recording contracts.

Ownership of these rights may arise in different ways but their exploitation is determined in contractual terms. The essence of a music publishing contract, for example, is the transfer of copyright from the songwriter to the publisher via an *assignment*. The publisher is buying exclusive rights to exploit the output of the songwriter for a defined period, although the use of options often leaves the final determination of the defined period in the publisher's hands. In other words, although disputes between artists and publishers or record companies are expressed in contractual language, they are, nonetheless, essentially disputes over rights ownership and the control of copyright. The contracts involved are contracts to buy and use copyright, and whilst disputes here are often couched as questions of enforceability or 'restraint of trade', it is copyright that is effectively at the heart of the matter. It is only the third type of this particular class of music business agreement, the management contract, that is not directly concerned with copyright issues, though as management fees are earned largely through the exploitation of copyright there is an indirect link here too.

The doctrine of restraint of trade has been used successfully by artists such as Holly Johnson and The Stone Roses to free themselves from contracts they had signed at an early point in their career. Usually the key to these kinds of legal dispute is the artists' disquiet at the financial package involved, though the argument sometimes concerns the musical direction the artist, but not their record company, wants to pursue (see, generally, Greenfield and Osborn 1998). Publishing and recording contracts may explicitly deal with copyright in a number of ways. As noted above, such contracts are the vehicles via which copyrights in a song are transferred from the original author (or owner) to the publisher. There may be a number of clauses in these contracts dealing with both the quality and the quantity of the work that is to be supplied.

Contracts involve a series of obligations placed upon both parties. One of the crucial aspects, as already mentioned, is the duration of the contract (Initial Period and Option Periods) and the commitment predicated upon these periods (the minimum commitment that must be delivered during each contractual period). Outside of this, and in terms of copyright-based provisions, there will usually also be stipulations about rerecording, and the technical or commercial suitability of what the artist produces, stipulations that along with other clauses about publication go to the heart of the control artists have over their finished work. Of course, as we have argued elsewhere, the artist's bargaining strength, or leverage, will be crucial in determining the extent, or even existence, of such restrictions (see Greenfield and Osborn 2002). That said, all contracts are formulated on the same basic templates:

> Contractual theory is based upon the exchange of obligations, and it is the obligations placed upon artists within these contracts that can operate to restrict artistic freedom. The company will also have a number of positive obligations with respect to the treatment of the artist and exploitation of the product. Music contracts will often be in quasi-standard form, with the same basic constituents, although the details may differ in each case. (Greenfield and Osborn 2002: 72)

For example, the artist will usually agree to indemnify the record company or publisher against any potential third-party actions that might be brought. This is to cover the situation where an artist's lyrics, for example, are defamatory of a third party, or fall foul of the criminal law in terms of their explicit content. In the latter case particular issues might centre around a situation where, for example, the lyrical content is potentially in breach of the Obscene Publications Act 1957, or perhaps might be deemed to incite racial hatred. The former issue was raised in respect of the NWA album *efil4zaggin* although the work was not deemed to be obscene (see, generally, Cloonan 1996; Greenfield and Osborn; 1998, Chapter 3); and the issue of inciting racial hatred might be raised by the activities of far right groups (such as Skrewdriver). Similarly a warranty as to the non-blasphemous nature of the material delivered also persists in some recording contacts although this clause is falling into disuse (Gregg 2002).

Additionally, and more relevant to our concerns here, the artist's warranties usually cover too the situation where the copyright work of a third party is deemed to have been subsumed within the delivered work without clearance. The onus is on the artist to clear such uses and to indemnify the company against any potential legal liability. The obvious effect is to force the group either to remove any work that has not been cleared (such as samples) or to negotiate – and pay for – the clearances themselves.

Perhaps most contentious, certainly in terms of artistic freedom, is the clause in the majority of contracts detailing what type and standard of material will be acceptable as the commitment detailed under the contract. This is the issue of technical, or commercial, suitability. The following is fairly typical, insofar as any clause within a music contract can be said to be typical:

> Each master recording made by you shall be subject to our reasonable approval as being commercially and technically satisfactory for the manufacture of records and tapes therefrom and you shall at our request repeat any performance until master recordings acceptable to us as aforesaid are obtained. Instrumental recordings and recordings other than in a recording studio will not be acceptable unless we have previously agreed to the contrary.

This clause potentially allows a record company or publisher to reject a work on the grounds that it is not 'suitable'. Unless what is suitable is specified explicitly, this can give companies considerable freedom to determine what an artist can do, with the knock on effect of limiting artistic development when or if the contracted artist is taken to be deviating from the blueprint that the company originally laid down for them:

> If the artist is in a strong position, legal advisors can try to adapt such clauses so that they become less of a hindrance. But the ultra-competitive ethos of the record industry, where many agreements are underpinned by a 'take it or leave it' philosophy, means that few artists have strong leverage. Similarly, the contract might empower the record company to choose a producer for the work, the songs that will appear as singles, the artwork to be used, and other features. All of these are potentially severe censorial restrictions and should be resisted, at least as far as individual leverage allows, by the artist who wants to maintain some degree of artistic control. (Greenfield and Osborn 2002: 73)

This was one of the crucial issues at the heart of the George Michael contract litigation (*Panayiotou v. Sony Music Entertainment* (1994);

Greenfield and Osborn 2000). Michael's desire to change image and market, to become more serious and political, was met with less than an enthusiastic response from his publisher and record company who measured his material in terms of potential sales rather than pithy social comment. The issue here comes back to the leverage of the artists. An artist in a strong position when contracts are negotiated (with publisher or record company desperate to sign them) may be able to remove the clauses about 'commercial suitability' and keep control of their own work, but examples of this are few and far between. Morrissey exerted a high degree of artistic control under the terms of his Rough Trade contract while in The Smiths (this was the norm for Rough Trade contracts) which he was able to preserve when signing to EMI, given that every major label was competing for his signature. But the mantra of 'take it or leave it' on the part of the music industry potentially puts them in a very strong bargaining position, and the point about this to make here is that while the ideology of copyright law might be to protect the rights of the artists, the reality of the music business is that such rights are, in effect, exercised by their publishers and record companies.

Conclusion

'Product' is well-known music industry slang for both the physical material that is sold, and, more contentiously, for the people, the musicians, who supply this material. What has been detailed above are some of the ways in which 'product' in both senses is legally regulated by the contractual and intellectual property restraints that are applied in the name of copyright to the dissemination of musical material. Of course, the law's task of dealing with these issues in an age of swift technological change is a difficult one, and perhaps the time has come to reconsider whether copyright is the most apposite vehicle for dealing with the ownership and control of musical (and other artistic) material:

> The law is notoriously slow to respond to technological advance and often by the time that it does act events have been superseded or overtaken. Such problems have been exacerbated in the recent past as the pace of change has become more pronounced creating a number of problems regarding exploitation of rights within the context of changing cultural, geographical, philosophical and electronic boundaries. At the heart of this debate lies the role and function of copyright and perhaps even the issue of whether it can survive the digital challenge. (Greenfield and Osborn 1997: 80)

At the same time, and while the current copyright regime still exists, it is important for creative artists to be cognisant of the ways in which they can best protect themselves. As we have argued above, artists in a strong bargaining position can exert significant influence over their contractual terms and thus the use of their copyrights. It is usually the case, however, that artists at the beginning of their careers are not in a strong position. One key way in which musical artists can protect themselves, then, is by seeking independent legal advice on the contracts they are offered before they sign them. Indeed it has been argued that independent advice is so crucial that if it has not been sought before the contract is signed it may potentially render the contract unenforceable (*Clifford Davis v. WEA* 1975).

The call for proper specialist independent legal advice for all musicians is easier to propose as a theoretical ideal than a practical possibility. In the world of popular music the desire to sign any offered contract immediately almost always outweighs any thought of reading the small print. However, as the case law shows, the courts are able to help artists who sign bad deals in legal ignorance (Greenfield and Osborn 1998, 2000). What case law also suggests is that under the copyright system artists have to consider themselves in commercial (rather than artistic) terms from the outset of their careers. This seems at odds with the ethos of musical production. If commercial issues become music makers' prime consideration, won't their art suffer, just as pre-nuptial agreements doom marriages to failure by commodifying an emotional act? And it might also appear contradictory. Wasn't copyright law developed precisely because artistic creation is not a straightforward commercial activity? But cases such as *Hadley v Kemp* (1999) and *Joyce v Morrissey* (1999), concerning the creative practices of Spandau Ballet and The Smiths respectively, suggest that such a business-orientated approach would have prevented much legal expenditure later, either by enshrining any details of agreements between the group in writing (in the *Hadley* case) or by stipulating the relative worth of each member of the group (as in *Joyce*). In both these cases arguments about who had contributed what to the making of Spandau Ballet's and The Smiths' hits, and how the groups' earnings should therefore be distributed to the groups' members, were decided not by an investigation of the messy collective process in which pop music is actually made, but by an examination of what rights were embedded in what contracts. And it is important to appreciate, finally, that for all the law's safeguards, the party in the stronger bargaining position is always more easily able to exact the contractual terms they wish, and that this party is almost always the corporation rather than the individual. This is as true of contracts involving copyright as of any other commercial deals.

References

Bently, L. and Sherman, B. (1992), 'Cultures of copying: digital sampling and copyright law', *Entertainment Law Review* 5: 158–63.

Bernstein, R. (1994), 'US Supreme Court rules on parody and fair use', *Entertainment Law Review* 3: 95–7.

Bronson, F. (1985), *The Billboard Book of Number One Hits*, New York: Billboard Publications.

Campbell v. Acuff-Rose Music, Inc (1994), 114 S. Ct. 1164.

Carey, M. and Wall, D. (2001), 'MP3: more beat to the byte, *International Review of Law, Computers and Technology* 15 (1): 35–55.

Clifford Davis v. WEA [1975], 1 All ER 237.

Cloonan, M. (1996), *Banned! Censorship of Popular Music in Britain 1967–1992*, Arena: Aldershot

Cloonan, M. and Garofalo, R. (eds) (2002), *Policing Pop*, Temple University Press: Philadelphia.

Francis Day & Hunter v. Bron [1963], Ch 587.

Frith, S. (1993), 'Music and morality', in *Music and Copyright*, Edinburgh: Edinburgh University Press.

Goodwin, A. (1990), 'Sample and hold. Pop music in the digital age of reproduction', in S. Frith and A. Goodwin (eds), *On Record. Rock, Pop and the Written Word*, Routledge: London, 258–73.

Greenfield, S. and Osborn, G. (1997), 'Good technology? Music and the challenge of technology towards the *fin de siècle*', *Information and Communications Technology Law* 6 (1): 77–86.

Greenfield, S. and Osborn, G. (1998), *Contract and Control in the Entertainment Industry*, Aldershot: Dartmouth.

Greenfield, S. and Osborn, G. (2000), 'Spirits in the material world. Musicians, lawyers, and the scope and legal enforceability of music contracts', in E. M. Barendt and A. Firth (eds), *The Yearbook of Copyright and Media Law 1999*, Oxford: Oxford University Press, 149–61.

Greenfield, S. and Osborn, G. (2002), 'Remote control. Legal censorship of the creative process', in M. Cloonan and R. Garofalo (eds), *Policing Pop*, Philadelpha: Temple University Press, 65–78.

Gregg, L. (2002), 'Freedom of expression and music contracts: is there a place for blasphemy any more?', *Entertainment Law* 3: 53–71.

Hadley v. Kemp [1999], EMLR 589.

Hawkes v. Paramount [1934], 1 Ch 593.

Hettinger, P. (1989), 'Justifying intellectual property', *Philosophy and Public Affairs* 18: 31–52.

Hyperion Records Ltd v. Warner Music (UK) Ltd (1991), High Court transcript, 17 May.

Joyce v. Morrissey [1999], EMLR 233.

Ludlow Music v. Robbie Williams [2001], R 271.

Panayiotou v. Sony Music Entertainment [1994], EMR 229.

Produce Records Ltd v. BMG Entertainment International UK and Ireland Ltd (1999), High Court transcript, 19 January.

Robinson, P. (undated), *Justified and Ancient History. The Unfolding Story of the KLF*, East Grinstead: self published.

Tackaberry, D. (1990), 'The digital sound sampler: weapon of the technological pirate or palette of the modern artist?', *Entertainment Law Review* 3: 87–95.

CHAPTER 6

Copyright and the Composer

Roger Wallis

Introduction

The composer is at the bottom end of the music industry 'food chain' and has thus traditionally been in a vulnerable position. The desire to hear one's creation performed has often encouraged composers to sign away their intellectual property rights (IPRs). That this desire has also frequently resulted in poor or even non-existent contractual relationships has further made it hard for many creators to monitor or control what happens to their work in the course of its exploitation. There is a multitude of sad tales of composers seeing very little of the cash their works generate (Wallis and Malm 1984: 163–215), particularly in developing countries where few institutions exist to protect their interests.

Individual holders of IPRs cannot easily enforce their statutory claims to exclusive usage and remuneration. Since the middle of the nineteenth century, composers (and occasionally publishers who represent them) have responded by creating collective bodies, so-called 'collecting societies' which monitor music activity in a given territory, and collect and distribute fees accordingly. As described in Chapter 4, the first European composers' collection agency was SACEM in France, founded by thirteen composers and lyricists in 1851. Its stated aim was 'to defend the common rights of all composers and lyricists, with or without the co-operation of their publishers, in relation to the owners of public establishments where their literary and musical works are performed'.

In his historical overview of the development of copyright protection, Petri observes that:

> The construction was a stroke of genius. The newly won protection of performing rights could not possibly have been monitored by the individual composers. Only an organisation inclusive enough to cover most of the repertoire in question could have done it . . . And it also provided the users of the music with the only possible uncomplicated means of being granted access to the music right they wanted. The

organisation could not possibly have been built up by anyone but the authors themselves – had the publishers joined forces to acquire rights from the composers and sell them on to the users of music, they would have found themselves in a monopoly situation that would have been unacceptable even then. Thus it was logical for the composers to take the lead. (Petri 2002: 105–6)

The rise of the global media corporation combined with new digital production and distribution technologies has seriously undermined these early principles (Wallis et al. 1999). This chapter will focus on relationships between the composer, national composers' organisations and collecting societies, and the international music industry.

The music industry value chain and the creation of composers' rights

Figure 1 illustrates the traditional music industry value chain, as well as the points where IPRs are generated, and where various intermediaries (collection societies) are created to collect and distribute revenues arising from these rights.

A composer creates a work and can either register it with 100 per cent ownership with a collection society ('manuscript registration') or sign an agreement with a music publisher who then retains a share of the revenues in return for assistance in promoting the work. Until the 1960s publishers had two main roles: they printed and distributed sheet music, and they actively sought to persuade artists and record companies to perform and record the works they represented. With reference to the former activity, a typical revenue-sharing agreement for print music allowed the publisher to retain 50 per cent of incomes. Over recent decades publishers' investment in printing and distributing sheet music has become less significant, as market demand has diminished. This could change in the digital world: the Internet provides opportunities to distribute sheet music as electronic files on a one-to-one basis.

Getting a song recorded traditionally involved the publisher contacting a record company's artist and repertoire (A & R) department. Once the A & R staff had decided on a combination of composition and artist, the recording process would be instigated. Record companies would then manufacture, market and distribute the work. They would promote the record on radio and in concert, initiating public performances to generate further revenues (from the exploitation of *performance rights*) for composers and publishers via agreements between collecting societies and broadcasters and venues (between 5 per cent and 8 per cent of box office receipts would be the normal rate of return from the last). Examples of the

Figure 1: Traditional MI value chain

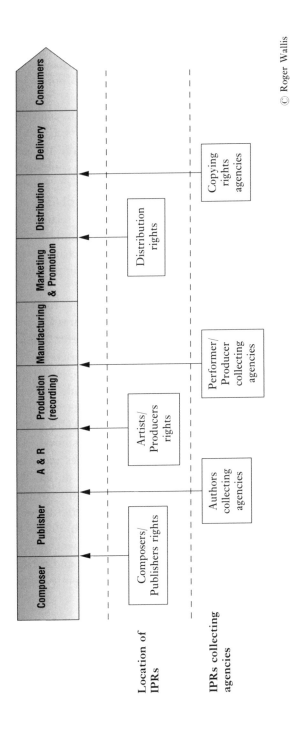

© Roger Wallis

The traditional music industry value chain, linking composers, artists, producers and distributors, in parallel with a series of intermediaries (collecting agencies) which collect and distribute revenues based on intellectual property rights.

collecting societies which collect and distribute performance rights revenues are the Performing Right Society (PRS) in the UK, The Swedish Performing Rights Society (STIM) in Sweden, Irish Music Rights Organisation (IMRO) in Ireland, American Society of Composers and Publishers (ASCAP) and Broadcast Music Incorporated (BMI) in the USA.

Record companies, too, pay copyright revenues to composers/publishers for the use of their works on physical discs (LPs, CDs and so on) via the exploitation of *mechanical rights*. This refers to the mechanical process of reproducing an original composition. Returns to composers/publishers here are in the region of 8 per cent to 9 per cent of the wholesale price of the recording. Such incomes are collected and distributed by mechanical rights collecting societies. These are often closely related to performing rights societies in the same territories. The MCPS in the UK is part of the MCPS-PRS Alliance. NCB, which collects mechanical rights in the Nordic and Baltic area, is owned by the performing rights societies in Sweden, Finland, Denmark, Norway and Iceland.

Over the course of the twentieth century the recording industry discovered both new sources of income and new areas in which revenue could be lost. On the one hand, 'neighbouring rights' allow performers and producers (record companies) as well as composers and publishers to claim fees when recordings are performed in public (generally via broadcasters). And there are by now numerous intangible sources of revenue from recordings, sources arising from the exploitation of rights rather than from sales of physical products (Malm and Wallis 1992). There are collecting societies distributing revenues from sources as diverse as photocopying, cable retransmission, blank tape levies and synchronisation rights. On the other hand, consumer electronics devices have made it increasingly easy for consumers to copy music and share it via physical cassettes, CDs and digital files – the battles to restrict these practices are fought in the name of copyright protection (Frith 1992). These developments are all discussed elsewhere in this book. I will concentrate in this chapter on how they have affected the composers and those representatives and collecting agencies on which their economic welfare depends.

The rigidity of the music industry value chain

From a composer's point of view what is most striking about the music industry is the continuity of its ways of money-making, however much the creative and technological processes of music-making, change. During the first few years of the twenty-first century, much rhetoric has emerged from the record industry regarding the difficulties they are suffering as a result of file sharing and other 'misuse' of digital networks (Kretschmer and Wallis 2000). Publishing revenues, though, seem to have remained lucrative, probably because of the large number of older copyrights that continuously generate publishing and composer income. It is certainly arguable that the large music publishers have become in effect investment houses: rights and catalogues are purchased on the assumption that they will, without any further investment, generate income for decades to come since they exist for up to seventy years after a composer's death. EMI's publishing arm, for instance, accounted for 21 per cent of the EMI group's revenues during the period April–June 2002, but no less than 60 per cent of its operating profits (*Music & Copyright*, 27 November 2002). As the leading US trade journal, *Billboard*, commented in March 2002:

> In contrast . . . [to record companies] . . . music-publishing assets have been fetching high prices of late. Publishing assets are seen as a relatively safe haven within music and media because of the stable revenue streams they generate. Making music publishing assets even more attractive is the cheap availability of financing. (*Billboard* 2002)

Billboard concluded that the current value of EMI publishing was as high as the combined stock market evaluation of the whole of the EMI conglomerate (including record company, manufacturing and distribution interests).

The contrast *Billboard* is pointing to here – between the 'crisis' of the record industry in the face of the digital revolution and the 'stability' of music publishing revenues – can be interpreted another way, as reflecting the *resistance* of the copyright regime to change. What is surprising is how little the structure of the music industry value chain has been altered by technological change. The only institutionalised example, albeit short-lived, of how short the value chain between composer and consumer could now be was provided in the late 1990s by the digital distribution company, mp3.com. Creators who controlled all the rights to their own productions (music in the form of digital files) could post such offerings on the mp3.com site. Figure 2 illustrates the consequence.

Revenue generation in the mp3.com system came from banner advertisements sold by the digital distributor. Fifty per cent of this revenue was shared amongst those offering music for downloading, distributed according to the actual number of downloads. To attract a critical mass of users, though, mp3.com also made other copyrighted materials available to consumers for free. The record industry sued the company and it ended up being purchased by one of the Big 5 record corporations,

Figure 2: The dis-intermediated vision

Simple value chain

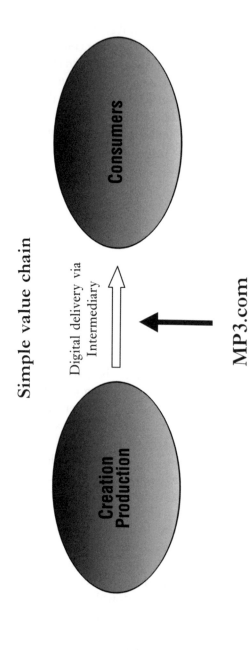

Creation Production

Digital delivery via Intermediary

Consumers

MP3.com

The ultimate short value chain between creator and consumer as illustrated by mp3.com (acting as an intermediary collection and distribution body).

Universal Music Group. Since then the easy-access, intermediary role of mp3.com has lost its significance, not least because of the charges introduced to those wanting to post their own creations. Mymp3.com Europe was closed down by Universal in the autumn of 2003 – the company claimed it was not breaking even. Alternatives are appearing, notably altnet.com (www.altnet.com) which allows individuals to post their own copyrighted materials for a standard fee. Consumers who download pay a charge which is returned direct to the copyright owner.

Thus, whatever the theoretical opportunities for shortening the value chain between creator and consumer made possible by digital technology, in practice change is remarkably sluggish. The underlying structure of existing contracts between creators/performers and their media representatives, which is on the whole unaffected by changes in the music industry environment, is undoubtedly one of the factors hindering any adjustment to the value chain. Publishing contracts, for instance, are particularly vague concerning any obligations of the publisher to demonstrate more than their 'best efforts' to achieve success in the market-place, and it is hard for a composer to extract himself/herself from them. The interlocking relationships between entities in the value chain and the various collecting agencies also serve to decrease the dynamics of the business, as I will now describe.

The Control of Copyrighted Musical Works

Vertical integration, producing larger and larger music and media corporations, has been a key feature of the past two decades. (Wallis 1990, Hirsch 1992): A major entertainment conglomerate such as AOL-Time Warner included in 2003 the world's largest Internet Service Provider, a major record company, a major music publisher, broadcasting and cable interests, printed publications and so on. For the individual composer the traditional 'personal' nature of the relationship between creator and exploiter has inevitably changed. The traditional publisher–composer relationship assumes close ties between creator and representative, with the publisher being entirely independent of the recording industry. As publishers have grown in size and corporate complexity, the relationship between creator and publisher has inevitably shifted from the personal to the impersonal. For example, the largest publisher in Sweden controls almost 600,000 works. It is clearly impossible for such an organisation to inject personal effort into promoting all but a small percentage of these works. This allows for a situation where three different types of activity can be described.

1. The *active promotion* of particular works.
2. *Neutral participation*. Publishers do little but retain of a share of copyright income when works do happen to be exploited, for example broadcast on the radio or covered on a recording.
3. *Negative control*, or the *de facto* blocking of access to copyrighted works so as to establish higher market rates for their exploitation. In their objection to the EMI–Time Warner merger, the Disney Corporation complained to the European Commission (EC) that the combined publishing outfit would dominate ownership of music required for use in films and commercials, and would therefore be able to manipulate market prices by withholding materials and not accepting current fee levels.

In the Internet world, the control of music use raises different questions. How can publishers even follow what is happening to their work once a recording has found its way into digital networks? (Hugenholz 1996, Hulsink and Tang 1997). The issues here are further complicated by tensions between different rights–holders, with publishers controlling music copyrights and record companies controlling the rights to specific recordings. One effect of (and reason for) vertical integration is the attempted alignment of interests between rights–owners (publishers) and rights–users (record companies). In the distribution of IPR revenues, that which is a cost in one division of a global media company (the record company) becomes a source of revenue for another division (the publisher). What is not clear is how such synergy benefits either composer or consumer. Increased corporate profits in this model are achieved by using combined publisher/record company power *over* actors outside this synergy relationship, which means, in essence, either forcing consumers to pay more or creators to receive less.

This is the context in which questions are raised about the intermediaries between creators and consumers. Is there still a need for both record companies and publishers? Do they really add the value that is reflected in their share of revenues? What nowadays should be the role of the collecting societies in the collection and distribution of revenue from users of music? Are they still essential?

Most music authors, including lyricists and arrangers, do still rely on the efficient functioning of music copyright societies to regulate the flow of IPR revenues. Historically, as we have noted, such societies were founded by authors and composers. Publishers may be members of their boards but their influence varies from society to society. In the Nordic area, for instance, composers' associations are part-owners of their national collecting societies, though this is not found in any other music territory.

Figure 3: The collecting society as an intermediary

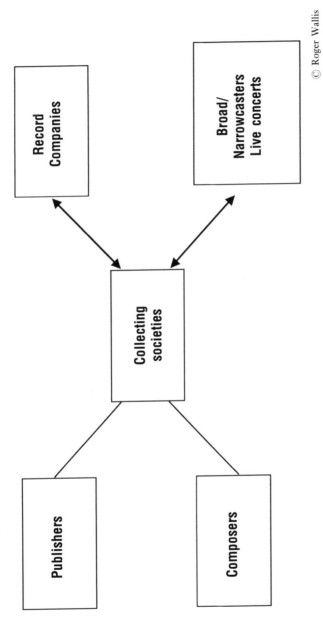

Composers' collection societies function in theory as independent intermediaries between owners of copyrights (composers/ publishers) and those that exploit them (e.g. record companies and broadcasters). Their role is to balance the interests of owners/ users, to collect revenue and distribute fairly according to actual usage.

Copyright organisations obviously need to be efficient and fair, and in recent years there have been growing demands for increased transparency in their operations. The EU competition authorities have been particularly critical of some aspects of collecting society operations (Temple Lang 1997), and an extensive study of PRS by the UK Monopolies and Mergers Commission (MMC) in 1996 made specific demands for a better alignment between moneys collected from different sources and moneys paid out to those whose works were actually performed. In general, copyright societies need to be capable of handling four categories of data:

1. a register of members whose rights they represent;
2. details of registered works (titles, authors, publishers and the agreed split of revenues between them);
3. details of users with whom agreements are signed;
4. details of music use by such users.

The amount of data involved in the societies' work, in short, is huge! The Swedish copyright society STIM, for instance, has no fewer than 45,000 registered members and a register of almost 5.5 million works (2004 data). Radio alone, even in a small country like Sweden, can account for several million performances of musical works per year. All these data here to be analysed as efficiently and cheaply as possible, with the moneys being distributed to rights-holders in a manner that is deemed as correct as possible by rights holders, users, and other observers. Collecting societies, that is to say, as intermediaries, have to satisfy demands from three major sources:

1. from copyright owners (who want efficiency and success in hunting down music users);
2. from music users (who do not, as a rule, enjoy paying copyright dues);
3. from official watchdogs, monitoring their behaviour as *de facto* monopolies.

Most copyright societies in Europe are *de facto* monopolies. This is generally accepted by exploiters of music as a practical advantage since it allows them to sign 'blanket licences' giving them access to virtually all repertoire. National *performing rights* societies are all members of the International Confederation of Societies of Authors and Composers (CISAC), based in Paris. CISAC members agree to abide by a series of international rules. One of these stipulates that the share which should be paid to an author when revenues are collected in another territory should not be less than 50 per cent (after deductions of taxes and administrative costs). If US$100 is collected by ASCAP in the USA

Figure 4: IPR intermediaries under pressure

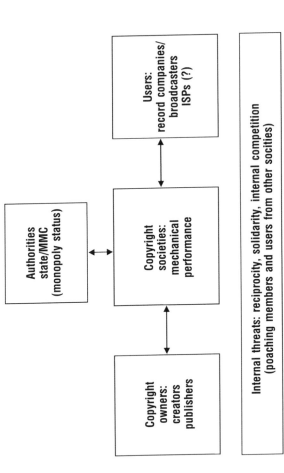

© Roger Wallis

Copyright societies under pressure from different interest groups: national/international competition authorities, users and copyright owners. Established principles of solidarity (same administration fees for all) and reciprocity (same treatment in all territories by all societies) are also coming under pressure. Demands that such societies compete with each other could lead to the poaching of members.

for a song written by a composer registered with the PRS, then a minimum of US$50 should be received by the UK composer. (The other US$50 would normally be paid to a US 'sub-publisher', the publisher who had acquired the right to promote the song in the USA.) Successful composers can negotiate higher percentages with their publishers by signing so-called 'at source' agreements. These stipulate the percentage of moneys collected "at source' in different territories which the composer has the right to receive.

Mechanical rights payments, for the reproduction of a work on a carrier such as a CD, DVD or VHS cassette, are not covered by CISAC rules and usually involve a higher degree of control by publishers (the UK's Mechanical Copyright Protection Society, MCPS, for example, is owned by the Music Publishers Association). Until the 1970s, payments composers received from the sales of physical carriers of their works abroad were usually governed by 'receipts contracts'. Composers received a percentage of the moneys received by their original publisher in the home territory (usually 50 per cent) but such moneys were transferred via a chain of different sub-publishers, each of whom took a slice (as well as sometimes an administrative fee). The result could be a net receipt for the composer of as little as 10 per cent of their original entitlement. An important legal decision in the early 1970s regarding Elton John and his publisher, Dick James Music, questioned whether this practice was 'reasonable', and found that in that particular case, it was not. The gradual replacement of 'receipts' publishing contracts with 'at source' contracts was clearly a result of this judgement.

In the world of digital distribution, as we have already observed, the distinction between performance and mechanical rights is blurred. Downloading a song from the Internet could, on analogy with other uses of music, be regarded as involving both performance and mechanical rights but no-one has yet come up with an agreed way of splitting *digital rights* income. The extensive revenues collected in Scandinavia in 2000–02 for downloading mobile phone ring tones were split 70:30 between mechanical and performance rights holders but the global structure of music revenue streams from digital rights management has yet to be settled: is music delivery on a digital channel to be regarded primarily as an equivalent to record distribution (the consumer downloading a virtual object)? Or is such delivery rather a form of public performance like a radio broadcast (the receiver simply making a copy for personal use, as if time-shifting)? The answers to these questions will determine the relative roles of performing and mechanical rights societies in digital income distribution, and the relative power of composers, publishers and record companies. (Or more likely, the relative power of these interest groups will determine how digital rights revenues come to be assigned.)

Composers and their publishers can also claim revenues from the exploitation of *synchronisation rights*. These arise when audio and visual elements are linked together, for example when pictures are superimposed over a melody. Such rights originally emerged in the shift from silent to talking movies. In some cases such rights are administered by collecting societies but as a rule publishers prefer to administer synch rights themselves. Large sums of money can be involved when, say, advertisers negotiate the price for the inclusion of a popular song in a television commercial, and, if only for reasons of business secrecy, publishers see it as in their interests to handle both the collection and distribution of such fees on their own.

Finally in this list of composer rights, in some countries there exist *moral rights* which allow rights-owners to refuse uses of their works that are deemed to be in conflict with their integrity. Such rights usually arise in contexts involving religion, politics or pornography. Moral rights can also function as economic rights if they are used, for example, as a reason for raising the price when someone wishes to use a piece of music in a particular commercial context.

Different rights apply, of course, to the same work and to the same act of exploitation. Music written for a film will involve a synchronisation right (when the film is edited and a final version is produced), a performing right (when the film is shown in a cinema), and a mechanical right (if the film is mass-marketed in VHS or DVD format or its soundtrack sold on CD).

Threats to the copyright system

As economic monopolies, collecting societies have traditionally presented themselves as guardians of the cultural system, as essential facilitators for the creation and dissemination of intellectual (musical) property. Since monopolies are open to abuse of power, various safeguards have been introduced to prevent this. In Sweden, for example, from the early 1940s the state appointed the chairman of the board of STIM and two of its governors. In May 2003 this system was changed: the board now elects the chairman and two external directors. This reflected a general recent tendency for competition authorities to exercise the prime monitoring function over national collecting societies. But the most significant challenge to collection societies in the last two decades has come from the commercial rather than the state sector, as the largest record companies and publishers have demanded increased efficiency and, in some circumstances, preferential treatment. These moves threaten the principles of *reciprocity* and *solidarity* which hold the international collecting society system together. Traditionally composers in country A could be sure that their rights were looked after without prejudice by the collecting societies in country B, and vice versa, while within any particular country, rights administration costs were more or less equitably shared by all rights–owners, big and small (Wallis et al. 1999). In general this is still the rule but exceptions are appearing as exemplified by the case of large concerts where superstars such as U2 perform their own creations (as described below).

In discussing this I will focus on three of the most important of recent issues in the international copyright fee distribution system: Central European Licensing, the CASINO or Cannes Agreements of 1995 and 2002, and 'cultural deductions'.

Central European Licensing (CEL, later renamed Central Licensing Agreements or CLA), was introduced in the late 1980s. Under this system an international record company pays all its European mechanical rights dues to one collecting society, irrespective of where in Europe the recordings were manufactured. In return the collecting society (the Dutch mechanical rights collecting society was the first to accept such a deal) gives the record company a discount on the agreed percentage of the retail price of the recording. The savings in administrative costs, in other words, are passed on to the company rather than to the copyright holders. This may seem mutually beneficial – the cost of mechanical rights falls for the record company while the return to the composers stays the same – but it clearly leads to a weakening of the reciprocity principle, as other collecting agencies face a decline in their income (and ability to absorb their own administrative costs) (Montgomery 1994).

The problem was clear when EMI Publishing attempted to set up an independent 'collecting society' to handle all the incomes from the mechanical rights to several songs published by the group Simply Red. This scheme was short-lived but the seriousness of the threat (and the market power of EMI Publishing) is illustrated by the fact that the costs of discontinuing EMI's would-be new collection agency were partly covered by the established collecting society in the relevant territory. The group U2 also sought to the challenge the principle of solidarity (in this case in the administration of performing rights) by demanding a better deal for the distribution of rights income from its own live concerts. They argued that since they were playing their own works, the costs of handling the distribution process were minimal. Societies should therefore charge them a lower rate than groups who performed work from a variety of sources in their concerts. Following U2's campaign, several European societies have agreed to implement both lower administrative rates and speedier payments for certain so-called Mega Concerts.

The *CASINO* or *Cannes Agreement* of 1995 was the result of demands from the major publishers for a general decrease over time of the commission rates charged by the mechanical collection organisations for handling revenues from Central Licensing Agreements. The threat to collection societies here was that the publishers, as divisions of major record labels, would where possible bypass them altogether, moving the rights fees that flowed from record company to composer/publisher internally, as it were. But to fulfil the terms of the Cannes Agreement, some societies were forced to charge higher commission rates for the distribution of payments from copyrighted materials on smaller record labels (outside the CLA system) to compensate for the increasing amount flowing to the majors. In the case of the Nordic Copyright Bureau, for example, which collects mechanical copyrights for the five Nordic countries, it was deemed necessary to charge 12.5 per cent on revenues from small labels as opposed to the roughly 6 per cent on revenues due to rights-holders on CLA schemes. The major publishers were, in essence, demanding lower commission rates for the distribution of mechanical rights revenue arising from CLA records, in other words, from records released by the recording divisions of their own corporations. Once again, the principle of solidarity was weakened.

That Cannes Agreement ran out in July 2001. The major publishers indicated a desire to renegotiate the terms, and included a demand this time for greater representation on the boards of the mechanical collecting societies. A new Cannes Agreement between the five major publishing companies and the European mechanical copyright societies was signed in late 2002. The societies negotiated a slight increase in CLA commission rates but in return had to guarantee, amongst other things, not to change any distribution rules which might have the effect of decreasing the publishers' share when mechanical rights revenues are passed onto composers.

The Cannes Agreements are good examples of how the vertical integration of the music industry has increased the power of the major corporate players even within the collecting societies, supposedly set up to protect the interest of individual composers. The tension between corporate and other kinds of public interest is equally apparent in the debate about *cultural deductions*. International agreements between collecting societies allow them to deduct up to 10 per cent of their national income and use it for "cultural purposes". Such deductions have been increasingly (and loudly) opposed by some British and American composers and publishers on the grounds that this is, in fact, a way of "stealing" "their" money. Continental European societies argue that the deductions are used in a way that strengthens respect for copyright and supports musical culture, thus benefiting everyone, irrespective of nationality. There is no doubt, though, that this argument will not go away.

From outside the music industry, it appears that collecting societies play a pivotal role in its operations, controlling tariffs and regulating the flows of money between exploiters (record companies, broadcasters and so on) and rights owners (authors, publishers). As my discussion of current pressures on copyright societies shows, though, this is a gross simplification. The reason for this, as I have also suggested, can be found in the effects of vertical integration, with the large entertainment corporations now controlling publishing, recording and, in some cases, even broadcasting. As Petri notes:

> Publishing contracts tend to be for very long periods of time. The activities of the Big 5 also include channels of distribution and dissemination. Thus one and the same corporation may represent all the parties concerned in negotiations regarding the value of music rights. 'Catalogues of Rights' are bought and sold without consultation with the author. Now that there are agreements running throughout the entire seventy year period of protection of the work, we are not far from a situation where 'eternal' copyright applies but – just as the critics of the idea originally feared – with the rights in the hands of interests with at least an oligopoly if not a monopoly position. (Petri 2002: 147–8)

Figure 5 illustrates how the collecting societies have been weakened. Major publishers who are members of these societies inevitably have dual loyalties, to the collecting society and to their corporate bosses. Such publishers, via their corporate links to major record companies and broadcasters, enjoy preferential deals not available to individual creators or smaller independent companies. More recently, broadcasters and even some advertising agencies have started their own 'publishing houses': composers who are offered commissions to write music for television programmes or commercials have to assign their publishing rights as part of the deal, thus cutting their fee by up to 50 per cent. As a rule, these 'pretend' or 'phantom' publishers, as they are known, are administered by one of the major multinational publishers, which probably explains why collecting society regimes have not challenged their validity. The BBC publishing arm, for instance, is administered by BMG Publishing, itself owned by BMG Music. Sweden's national commercial television network, TV4, has a publishing arm that is administered by Sony Publishing.

Figure 5: Vertical integration → instability

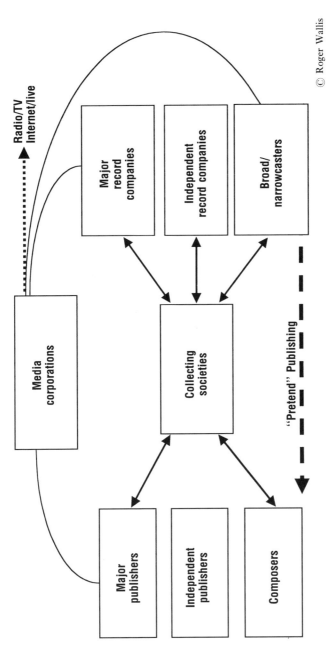

Vertical integration can result in a small number of major corporations representing all the rights holders involved in negotiations. It also allows 'publishing companies' to be set up with the sole purpose of clawing back a share of the fees paid to societies (and so composers) for the exploitation of rights.

The British PRS did attempt to introduce a rule to curb such practices in the film industry in the early 1990s. Rule number 2 (f) ii. read as follows:

> In the case of any work specially written for a film, the performing right in which work was first controlled by the Society on or after the 4th day of July 1990, the share of the publisher shall not exceed one-half of the share allocable under the normal basis of division, unless in the agreement between the publisher and the writer(s) of the work, the publisher has undertaken to use all reasonable endeavours to exploit the work for the benefit of the writer(s) by means additional to the inclusion of the work in the soundtrack or film for which it was commissioned and the public performance or broadcasting of the film in question or its inclusion in a cable programme service.

In the event this rule has been fairly toothless. All the 'pretend' publisher needs to do is to include in the contract with the composer an undertaking to 'use all reasonable endeavours' to achieve secondary exploitation, that is, exploitation over and above that which goes naturally with the original commission. If the publisher does nothing further to exploit or promote the work, the composer has to take legal action against it – enforcement is outside the realm of the society and its distribution rules. British composers reacted strongly to this development but have enjoyed little success in their efforts to oppose it. In a speech to the 1999 Congress of the International Confederation of Musical Authors, Mark Fishlock of the British Academy of Composers and Songwriters maintained that:

> We've made virtually no progress on this issue over the last 20 years: what began as a shady practice is fast becoming the industry norm. One of the main reasons is the problem of getting beyond contractual considerations. The argument composers are forever hearing is: 'if you don't like it, don't sign the contract'. This is all very well, but the composer's bargaining position has never been weaker. So the reality is, if you don't accept their [the music industry's] terms, you don't get the job. (Fishlock 1999)

Conclusion

At the end of the twentieth century the 'new economy' was the buzzword among academics, journalists, consultants and IT suppliers. Dot.com companies then collapsed, sales of physical products like mobile phones and DVD players took off, and file sharing applications are now being steadily brought into the world of the major players. Can one still expect any significant changes in the music industry value chain?

Much will depend on the activities of the agencies which collect and distribute "intangible" revenues to artists, publishers, composers and producers. They have extensive databases of artists, composers and works. They could, in theory, offer new platforms through which creators could find a shortcut to users, both business users and individual consumers. The Spanish collecting society, for example, has invested heavily in an Internet site known as Portalatino (www.portalatino.com), which offers composers the opportunity to create their own home pages and make recordings available to consumers who visit the site, without the involvement of intermediaries such as record companies or publishers. The society was taken to court by the major publishers who claimed that this was a misuse of members' funds, since they too are members of collecting societies. Another interesting initiative is the Phonofile digital base in Norway, which allows commercial users to browse and purchase from over 25,000 digitised recordings, mostly from independent Norwegian record companies (www.phonfile.no). Such initiatives might not be appreciated by sectors of the existing music industry value chain, but they do indicate one way in which the route between creators and listeners can be made much shorter in the digital environment.

The degree of concentration of power in the contemporary music and entertainment industry is unprecedented. Regulators have a crucial role in restraining corporations which are now seeking complete control of IPRs – and the people who create them – on a global level. But so do consumers. Fortunately, the interaction of people and technology in the media field always seems to result in applications that have not been foreseen either by their inventors or the financial forces that seek to exploit (or block) their use.

References

Billboard (2002), 'Consolidation seen on the fast track', 22 March: 10.

Fishlock, M. (1999), 'The relationships between authors and publishers', speech presented at the 1999 Congress of the International Confederation of Authors of Musical Works (CIAM), Helsinki, Finland.

Frith, S. (1992), 'The industrialisation of popular music', in J. Lull (ed.), *Popular Music and Communication*, Beverly Hills: Sage, 53–77.

Hirsch, P. M. (1992), 'Globalization of mass-media ownership: implications and effects', *Communication Research* 19: 677–81.

Hugenholtz, P. B. (ed.) (1996), *The Future of Copyright in a Digital Environment*, The Hague: Kluwer.

Hulsink, W. and Tang, P. (1997), *The Winds of Change: Digital Technologies, Trading Information and Managing Intellectual Property Rights*, Rotterdam: Rotterdam School of Management, Management Report No. 44.

Kretschmer, M. and Wallis, R. (2000), 'Business models and regulation in the electronic distribution of music', in B. Stanford-Smith (ed.), *E-Business: Key Issues, Applications and Technologies*, Amsterdam: IOS Press, 197–204.

Malm, K. and Wallis, R. (1992), *Media Policy and Music Activity*, London: Routledge.

Monopolies and Mergers Commission (1996), *Performing Rights*, London: HMSO, Cm 3147.

Montgomery, R. (1994), 'Central licensing of mechanical rights in Europe: the journey towards a single copyright', *European Intellectual Property Review* 16 (2): 45–65.

Petri, G. (2002), *The Composer's Right*, Stockholm: Atlantis.

Temple Lang, J. (1997), *Media, Multimedia and European Community Antitrust Law*, working paper of the European Commission Competition Directorate (DGIV).

Wallis, R. (1990), *Internationalisation, Localisation and Integration: The Changing Structure of the Music Industry*, working paper of the Department of Mass Communication, Gothenburg University.

Wallis, R., Klimis, G. M. and Kretschmer, M. (1999), 'Globalisation, technology and creativity: current trends in the music industry', final summary report from the ESRC study at City University Business School, London. City University website publication: www.city.ac.uk/multimedia

Wallis, R., Baden-Fuller, C., Kretschmer, M. and Klimis, G. M. (2000) 'Contested Collective Administration of Intellectual Property Rights in Music: the challenge to the principles of reciprocity and solidarity', *European Journal of Communication* 14 (1): 5–35.

Wallis, R. and Malm, K. (1984), *Big Sounds from Small Peoples: The Music Industry in Small Countries*, London: Constable.

CHAPTER 7

Musicians

Jason Toynbee

Introduction

More than a set of laws, copyright is a key institution for musicians, one which structures the way they work and get rewarded. Most importantly, it divides them up into types, assigning a different value to each one. The paradigmatic case in Western culture is that of the composer, librettist or songwriter. People in these roles are granted copyright in the product of their labour, something which is then given the special title of the 'work'. Further down the pecking order comes the performer who plays music written by someone else. Here the musician has no copyright, since – in terms of the law at least – she produces no work.[1] Traditional music represents a different case again. If you play music passed down and adapted from one generation to the next, the material is said to be in the 'public domain' and therefore freely accessible to anyone, including those outside the community where it originates. Musicians in this situation are likely to have the label 'folk' applied to them, the significant point about folk being that it consists of many people besides yourself, most of them anonymous and dead. As a result, the argument goes, attribution of the kind of individual authorship enshrined by copyright is neither possible nor desirable (traditional music is discussed in detail in Chapter 9).

It seems, then, that copyright rests on a set of norms. We can set them out as follows:

1. Writing and performance constitute distinct functions.
2. Writing is a special kind of activity which merits a special kind of legally protected relationship to the product of one's labour – copyright.
3. In cases where a named writer cannot be identified or where writing and performance cannot be distinguished (as in traditional music) no copyright applies.
4. Inasmuch as they carry out the instructions of composers or perform music of a folk tradition, performers do not receive full copyright protection.

Over the course of the chapter I will argue that these norms, and the laws which enshrine them, are flawed. Not only does copyright arbitrarily privilege one form of musical production (Western, compositional) at the expense of another (non-Western, traditional), but it sets up on dubious grounds a system of value in which performance is inferior to composition. As well as being unfair, these distinctions fail to take account of an increasingly important characteristic of music in the twentieth century and after; the renewed convergence of the functions of writing and performance through techniques like improvisation, repetition-variation and sampling. Musicians who want to adopt these methods are strongly disadvantaged by the structure of rights. Lastly, copyright does not provide an equitable system of reward. Above all, it has favoured big corporations over the supposed beneficiaries of the system, music makers. Copyright also accentuates inequality between music makers, especially between stars and small-time music makers. In what follows I will investigate these issues, examining what's wrong with copyright from the musician's point of view. And in the conclusion I'll ask how copyright might be reformed, both for the benefit of music makers, but also for the social good more generally.

Perhaps it's worth considering first *why* copyright has failed musicians. Despite being presented as a way of protecting creators, arguably it is more a device for coping with the special conditions of music markets. Music, like all symbolic forms, presents a problem for the capitalist mode of production (Garnham 1990: 160). Once originals are made – the expensive part of the process – it is difficult to prevent competitors from exploiting them through the use of relatively cheap copying technologies like printing, tape or the Internet. Copyright addresses this problem by instituting a form of property in music. With ownership of the work established, so-called free riders can be kept out, or charges made to those who want to copy. Simply put, copyright law turns music from a public into a private good. As such it has been central to music industry strategies of profit-making.

Copyright is rarely, however, discussed in terms of a device for enabling commerce in music. Most often it is presented as a way of protecting composers. Now it is perfectly true that traditional copyright law grants the creator rights in the first instance. But the fact remains that industry control over the means of exploiting music leads to a situation where most writers and composers are forced to sell on their copyright. No-one can make it without a publishing deal, something which always involves the assignment of rights. Arguably, then, it is the power of capital that counts when it comes to copyright, and the right of the creator serves as a pretext for corporate control of music, a way of legitimating the whole system of intellectual property (Boyle 1996; May 2000).

Copyright, the work and division of labour

If copyright *covers* up corporate power over musicians it also *conjures* up a certain kind of musicianship, as I suggested at the beginning. Anne Barron (2002) argues that the central problem in copyright law has been how to make clear-cut property out of intangible art. In responding to this problem, she suggests, the enumeration of broad principles about the nature of creativity has generally been avoided, because these principles would be difficult to apply in law. Instead, a different approach has been adopted, one centred on the concept of the work. The great advantage of the work is that it can be described in quite concrete and specific terms.

In the case of music, several causes coincided in the early nineteenth century to determine the work's *written* shape: the ascendancy of total composition (and thus the end of improvisation in classical music), the advent of the rotary steam printing press and typography for music notation, the growth of a mass, middle-class market for pianos and, thus, of a market for sheet music. As well as these cultural and economic factors, there was a juridical issue. The two-dimensional, visual form of the musical work meant that it could become the object of a rational legal process. 'Pirate' publishers might now be challenged through the comparison of texts, original against alleged copy. Reducing music in copyright law to basic elements, most importantly melody and (in the case of a song, opera or other such genre) words, made this process even more straightforward. And, critically, it ensured a regime of enforced originality. From now on all kinds of citation or similarity between existing pieces of music would be highly suspect.

In an important sense the institution of the work also enabled the emergence of a music industry based on a strict division of musical labour. On one side were composers, librettists, Tin Pan Alley songwriters and arrangers, not to mention all the ancillary roles involved in publishing. On the other, the performance side, was another set of roles; orchestral players, pit musicians, vocalists, song and dance acts as well as entrepreneurs and administrators. Indeed it was the growth of a mass market for musical performance in vaudeville, music hall and so on, which drove the next big development in copyright in Britain and the US, the introduction of performing rights at the beginning of the twentieth century.[2] Now publishers could claim remuneration in respect of the performance of works on stage. By the 1920s these rights were being claimed in respect of the broadcasting of music. Copyright was also extended to cover the 'mechanical reproduction' of works on recordings and, after the advent of the sound film, the 'synchronisation' of music on soundtracks.

In effect, then, the arrival of mass media reinforced the copyright system and the labour process based on it. The pattern was broadly similar in all advanced capitalist countries. Publishers supplied music on the basis of copyright protection to the media and live entertainment industries where most musicians worked as performers. A much smaller group, the composers and song writers, was contracted to the publishers.

Phonographic orality v. copyright

However, even as this work-performance model was being embedded, a parallel system of music making began to develop alongside it. What happened was that new forms of popular music, most importantly jazz and blues, carried forward into the age of mass media certain characteristics of the traditional, 'folk' mode of production. Indeed, these characteristics increasingly took on a mediated shape. I want to call this new method of making music, *phonographic orality*.[3] Its earliest manifestation was the way musicians in jazz and blues learned their craft and their repertoire through listening to records, as well as (sometimes instead of) reading music or being formally trained. But new material was created in a distinctively phonographic way too. Blues songs were effectively variations on an embedded form, whose structure (the twelve-bar, I/IV/V chord sequence) was repeated over thousands of record releases. As several writers have argued, it was the circulation of records across African-American communities that facilitated the crystallisation of new blues sonorities and styles (Eisenberg 1987; Jones 1995). In the same period, from the 1920s onwards, improvised jazz found its fullest expression on recordings. These fixed the fleeting moment of creativity, allowing it to be contemplated and heard again and again (Small 1987).

As sound technology developed, so too did phonographic orality with the result that it quickly became the dominant way of making popular music. The successive musical revolutions of rock'n'roll, soul, punk, disco, hip hop and electronic dance music were all products of the phonographic mode of production. Critically, however, copyright law does not match such a form of musical creativity. For one thing, the law specifies that the work be created independently, without imitation of other works. But this can hardly be the case in, say, twelve-bar blues, where every new blues repeats (while varying) the basic format. As for an improvised jazz solo this *will* tend to be independent from other solos, yet it cannot be the subject of copyright, because only the notated, invariant components of the song are protected.

Another aspect of the disjuncture between phonographic orality and copyright has to do with the latter's premise that composition and performance are different functions. But in an important sense the two are intertwined in most forms of popular music making. Improvisation provides one example: a jazz or rock solo consists in composition *through* performance. Another example is the way songs are 'written' by trying out ideas, or jamming, often in the studio. In neither case is there a first stage of score production, followed by a second of pure performance. In both cases recording constitutes the moment of fixation or completion of the work, and it therefore becomes the 'primary text' (Moore 2001; but see also Gracyk 1996).[4]

Interestingly, when new rights were enacted to protect the recording in the first half of the twentieth century there was no recognition of this.[5] Granted as a response to demands from an emergent recording industry, phonographic rights were invested in the record company or agent who commissioned the recording. In other words they simply enshrined a new commodity form, the 'sound image' of the master recording, and there was no question of recognising the role of the creator. The contrast here is with traditional copyright which, because it is originally vested in the composer, at least gestures towards the value of creative acts. With recording rights there is no acknowledgement of authorship, no understanding that in much popular music the musical work *is* the recording.

Put bluntly, then, copyright law doesn't mesh with the practice of popular music. What are the effects of this on musicians in the contemporary period? At a general level, the biggest problem is a deep confusion about the attribution and ownership of creativity, a confusion which has got worse since the advent of digital sampling. Digital sampling is now the most ubiquitous phonographic technique. It involves the reuse of existing recorded materials, and so runs against the grain of the rights regime – the central thesis of copyright being, of course, that works must be original. Despite this difficulty, an ad hoc system for the clearing of samples emerged in the late 1980s which has enabled a trade in the supply of samples from rights-owners to users. Sample clearing is certainly testament to the pragmatic nature of capitalism. Yet it has hardly cleared up the host of problems which musicians face on an everyday basis. For one thing obtaining clearance can be extremely expensive, and disputes about what might be appropriate use of samples are legion. But more than this, controversy continues over the key issue of the attribution of authorship – is a piece based on samples the work of the sampler or the one who is sampled? In short, sampling points up key problems of working as a musician in a system of production based on phonographic orality, yet regulated by copyright. One recent court case has demonstrated these problems all too well. It's therefore worth discussing at some length.[6]

Pass the mic (and steal the riff)

In 1978 the jazz flautist and composer James Newton registered a work called 'Choir', a solo piece for flute, with the US Copyright Office. Rights in the composition were assigned to a publishing company, Janew Music, owned by Newton. 'Choir' was then recorded by the musician and issued on his 1982 album *Axum* for the ECM label. ECM held the rights in the recording. In 1992 the Beastie Boys obtained a licence from the label to use a six-second sample from this recording. They did not consult Newton, nor did ECM inform him about the agreement (Korn and Berchenko 2001). The sample was inserted as the introduction to the track, 'Pass the Mic'. It also provided a continuous loop behind the beats and rapping featured on that song. Originally issued on the Beasties' hugely successful come-back album *Check Your Head* (Beastie Boys 1992), 'Pass the Mic' was rush released as a single with supporting video. It became a big hit.

Seven years passed and the Beastie Boys' career flourished. Then, one day in January 2000, James Newton was giving a jazz analysis class at the University of California, Irvine when a student mentioned that he had seen the flautist's name on the liner of a Beastie Boys' CD. A week later the student brought in *Check Your Head*. Newton played it in class, and was horrified to hear the six-second sample from 'Choir' being repeated over and over again on 'Pass the Mic'. He sought legal advice immediately, and a year later began an action against the Beastie Boys on the grounds of breach of copyright (Korn and Berchenko 2001). In May 2002 the Central District Court of California found against Newton, dismissing the complaint on all counts.

In the order issued at the end of the proceedings District Judge, Nora M. Manella, makes three basic points (*Newton v. Diamond et al.* 2002). First, Manella directs attention to the distinction between the musical composition and the sound recording. She makes it clear that because the Beastie Boys obtained a licence from ECM for rights in the recording, only use of the composition is at issue. The question then becomes what in the composition is protected. As Manella defines it: '[a] musical composition consists of rhythm, harmony and melody, and it is from these elements that originality is to be determined . . . A musical composition protects an artist's music in written form' (*Newton v.*

Diamond et al. 2002: 8). Such a formulation, of course, encapsulates that reduction of music in copyright law we noted earlier. Not only are just three parameters isolated (of these melody has always been most salient in law), but the work becomes identical with its score.

In court Newton's expert witness, Christopher Dobrian, responds to this line of argument by proposing that it is the 'special playing technique described in the score' which establishes the uniqueness of 'Choir'. He is referring here to a technique Newton calls 'multiphonics'. It involves singing along with the flute-sound. Manella is not persuaded by the testimony however, and points to the acknowledgement by another of Newton's experts that 'vocalization performance techniques' have a long history and can be traced back to Africa (9). In other words, notwithstanding the instruction shown in his score, Newton does no more here than play the role of a folk musician. As such he cannot be protected by copyright. But there's worse to come: Manella points to another concession by Dobrian, namely the latter's acknowledgement that 'neither the timbral effect nor the portamento [further aspects of Newton's multiphonic technique] is notated in the score' (11). As for the over-blowing and breath control invoked by the Newton team, these are performance devices pure and simple (12). Bearing all this in mind, Manella concludes, only the three-note sequence played in the sample, and not its particular sonority, can be at issue (13).

The second point of the judgement concerns whether this sequence of notes is then protected under copyright law. Judge Manella's main thrust here is that only 'those components of the work that are original and non-trivial 'are protected' (14). She cites the case of *Gaste v. Kaiserman* where the court had observed that 'common themes frequently appear in various compositions, *especially in popular music*' (14, my emphasis). Manella concludes from this that the sequence in question (C – F flat – C) cannot be protected because of its ubiquity. A couple of pages in the judgement are then given to establishing a minimum threshold of originality through a review of the case law: on their own, three notes are insufficient (15–16). What's more, the three-note sequence in the sample is not original and lacks distinction. Manella quotes the defendants' expert Lawrence Ferrara who suggests that the same sequence 'has been used over and over again by major composers in 20th Century music, particularly the '60s and '70s just prior to [plaintiff's] usage'. Druckman and Ligeti are mentioned in this connection (17). It seems, then, that by avant-garde, as much as by pop, standards the sequence from 'Choir' is derivative.

Finally, Manella turns to the question of whether the sample is *de minimis*, in other words whether the appropriation by the Beastie Boys is so small and trivial that it would fail to be recognised by the average audience. According to case law, the focus here is not on the repetition of the sequence, and hence its significance in 'Pass the Mic'. Rather what matters is its importance for 'Choir' (21). In quantitative terms this is very low, being a mere three-note sequence, or 2 per cent of the whole. Still, case law suggests that qualitative factors may also count. In considering them Manella once again cites Newton's expert witness Dobrian. Dobrian had said that the two works 'are substantially dissimilar in concept and feel' (23). So, Manella concludes, there can hardly be breach of copyright on the grounds of significant similarity. And even if the six-second sample might be recognised as coming from 'Choir' then it is the *sound* of the sample which is recognisable, and sound – being covered by the ECM licence – is not an issue (24).

Newton v. Diamond et al. is a crucial judgement in that it involves one of the fullest interpretations yet of the way copyright law impinges on creative practice in contemporary popular music. It also reverses a trend in legal disputes which has seen the ascendancy of rights-owners over samplers. By rigorously isolating and removing all those elements which belong to the realm of performed sound, Judge Manella reduces 'Choir', the composition, to the status of musical skeleton. Arguably, to do so just reflects the nature of copyright law in the USA. Yet this is clearly absurd. For, like so much jazz, 'Choir' is a composition-in-performance, with James Newton's score inevitably being a mere shadow of the realised work. In its focus on notation, copyright law fails to do the very thing it promises, namely to protect creators and their creativity.

But suppose there was a way of protecting Newton. Suppose, for example, that he held the rights in his 1982 *recording* of 'Choir'. Immediately one class of problem defined by Manella disappears, that is to say the performance aspects of the sample are now covered. Or are they? Newton's own witnesses argued that the original elements in 'Choir' are actually techniques which derive from a long, African-American tradition of music making. How, then, can Newton claim them as his own? In a letter to a friend subsequently published in an online jazz newsletter, Newton addresses this issue, arguing that Judge Manella:

> consistently used European paradigms to judge my music. An aria from Purcell's 'Dido and Aeneas' and Cole Porter's 'Night and Day' were examples of what is protectable. 'Choir' is about four black women singing in a church in rural Arkansas. The work is a modern approach to a spiritual. (Newton 2002)

Implicit here, I think, is an alternative way of thinking about author-ship, one where the composer-improviser becomes, in effect, the most recent link in a historical chain of African-American music making. Cultural critics like Henry Louis Gates (1990) and Paul Gilroy (1993) have developed this idea. They suggest that the culture of the people of African slave descent is grounded in a process of dialogue and exchange which results in a constant recoding and reworking of the tradition. The movement of the people across continent and ocean then accentuates the process. I want to suggest there are actually strong arguments for extending this model of musical creativity further, beyond African diasporic cultures to *all* forms of music making – like, for example, the New York, Jewish hip hop of the Beastie Boys.

As the sociology of culture has shown, art works, including music, are the product of a complex web of social relations (Becker 1982, Wolff 1993, Bourdieu 1996). Even in classical music where acts of creation appear to be solitary, composers invariably depend on discussions with colleagues and friends, advice from performers, relationships with impresarios, feedback from critics, audiences and so on. Just as importantly, composers use forms, themes and aesthetic assumptions inherited from earlier practice in the field. Thus, even in this heartland of aesthetic individualism, authorship is social and compositions are more like moments in a continuing cycle of production than unique and original creations.

Clearly, copyright law doesn't see things this way. Quite the reverse, it unequivocally attributes authorship, and, ideally at least, places the individual work on a pedestal high above the historical continuum of music making. Perhaps, then, the way forward in reforming copyright might be to recognise the social nature of both authorship and the work. Instead of the European art model of production with its hierarchy of labour, its fetishised 'work' and institutionalisation of individual genius, a model derived from the cultural practice of people of the African diaspora might be more appropriate. This would recognise versioning, repetition and quotation. Above all, it would reduce the grand figure of the author (which, anyway, provides an ideological cover for corporate control of rights) to the status of co-worker and collaborator. I'll have to leave the problem of how these broad principles might be applied in law till the end of the chapter. Other factors need to be fed in now, most of all the question of money; of how copyright rewards – and fails to reward – music makers.

Copyright, musicians and reward

By definition, copyright grants composers a special economic status. Strangely, though, this may not be in their best interest. The reason is that copyright and the royalty system that goes with it effectively transfer risks from publishers to creators (Towse 2001). As I pointed out earlier, creating the work is the expensive part in the production of music. To use economic jargon, fixed costs are high. Think about writing your first album's worth of songs. Quite apart from writing, demo-ing and rewriting you will already have spent a considerable amount of time acquiring the knowledge, skills and equipment needed to undertake the task. Of course you may have negotiated an advance on royalties from your publisher. But this will usually be small compared with the huge amount of time and effort you have already expended. What's more, given the uncertainty of musical markets, the chances are that your songs will *not* be successful, and that you will therefore earn little or nothing in the way of royalties. As for any advance, this represents a debt and can be subtracted from earnings you might – if you're lucky – receive in the future.

So, the copyright system effectively makes the writer carry the costs of failure in a market where failure is endemic and fixed costs are high. The reason the system persists is because writers are hungry for success and prepared to work for very little, or to subsidise their music making from other employment, sometimes for years on end. Actually, for the small number who develop successful careers or have a few big hits the system works quite well. The terms and conditions of publishing contracts are much better than in, say, the early 1960s when Lennon and McCartney were beginning their song-writing careers. As a result copyright ensures that successful writers, as well as publishers, receive significant income from the exploitation of rights.

If star writers and composers earn large amounts from rights, and people on the bottom rung get little or nothing, what of the typical writer-musician if we can talk about such a person? Actually, the position is difficult to assess because the collecting societies do not publish informa-tion about how much money goes to particular individuals – all we have are annual pay-outs and numbers of recipients. So, if we look at UK music copyright revenue for 2000 (these figures do not include overseas earnings) 2,700 composers and song writers earned £328m (National Music Council 2002: 11). That is an average of £121,481 per person. Clearly, however, this figure is misleading – it's hiked up by the star system, the fact that only a few extremely successful composers and writers earn most of the money. Significantly, a survey of musicians' employment commissioned by the Musicians' Union in Britain suggests that this is indeed the case. Among musicians across the categories of jazz, folk, classical and rock/pop less than 5 per cent of earnings came from broadcasting, recording, writing and royalties (York and Laing 2000: 8). It seems that, for most music makers, copyright is an irrelevance.

Of course it could be argued that this situation is perfectly fair. Copyright rewards success, and only a few writers and composers are successful because the market for music is of the winner-takes-all type, in which consumers want a small number of big hits and big stars (Adler 1985). But there are at least two problems with this. First, notwithstanding the market, collection and distribution of copyright revenue have tended to be unfair. In the case of public performance rights, relatively indiscriminate 'blanket' licensing of broadcasters and venues has been used for collection. This is quite an efficient method because it enables prices for the use of musical works to be agreed on the basis of large scale and therefore easily assessed factors like turnover (in the case of venue) or overall amount of music used (in the case of broadcasting). In this way the costs of administration are kept down. When it comes to distribution, however, the goal of minimising administration costs can lead to rough justice. With all the money received going into a pool, collecting societies like the UK's Performing Right Society use fairly crude sampling methods to find out which songs are being played. These methods inevitably privilege hits, which turn up disproportionately in the survey returns filled in by broadcasters and venues.[7] So, when it comes to paying out, the writers and publishers of hits are disproportionately rewarded too.

The second way in which the copyright system skews the economics of music making is through its intensification of the winner-takes-all tendency in music markets. The key issue here is that beyond the consumer's desire for stars, the music industry has a structural interest in producing them. Stars represent stability in an otherwise volatile market, and they slow down innovation and reduce diversity. Despite the relatively large payments which stars attract, the likelihood that their products – songs, symphonies, CDs – will sell in large quantities can actually lead to a reduction in costs. There is less need to invest in risky unknown talent. What's more, stars are monopoly suppliers of their own stardom, so all the advantages of a monopoly market accrue to the publishers and record companies which contract them. And of course big companies can usually outbid small ones for the services of a star. How does copyright impact on the star system? The most important factor here is term, the period during which copyright applies, and before the work reverts to the public domain. A long term encourages the music industry to promote stars and 'classic' songs and recordings, because they can continue to extract economic value from them with very little extra investment. Extension of term, as in the recent shift in copyright from fifty to seventy years after the death of the author (now adopted in all the advanced capitalist countries), only increases the tendency of the music industries to 'sit on' their existing stars and back catalogue at the expense of developing new talent (Smiers 2002).

All the criticisms that have been made so far of copyright as a way of rewarding writers and composers can also be applied to a recent development – the extension of rights to cover musical performance. Since 1996 in the UK recording artists have been granted statutory, non-waivable rights in respect of performance. When a recording to which an artist has contributed is reproduced or broadcast then she is entitled to payment. Fifty per cent of the net phonographic rights income goes to the artist. The idea behind the European Union directive which generated this UK law (and similar measures elsewhere in the EU) 'was to prevent performers, who generally have a weak bargaining position vis-à-vis record companies, from being forced to agree to a buy-out of their rights' (Towse 2000: 13). However, Ruth Towse makes an interesting argument about the new right, namely that recording musicians may be no better off as a result. This is because the cost of monitoring their individual contributions track by track will be high, and so will be likely to absorb much of the revenue collected. More, record companies may recover the money they are forced to pay out under the scheme by reducing conventional royalties to newly contracted artists, or by paying smaller fees to session musicians. In other words, the record companies' power in the labour market may trump any grant of rights to musicians by the state.

Conclusion: reforming rights

This chapter has painted a fairly bleak picture. In terms both of the practice of music making and form of reward it has been suggested that musicians are badly served by copyright. So the question arises of how the system might be reformed.

One strong defence of copyright is that there can be no market in music without it, because there will be no incentive for music makers to create if their work can be copied without restriction. This is the free-rider argument, which I mentioned at the start of the chapter. But we might ask how *much* protection is needed to provide an incentive. The current term of seventy years after the death of the author effectively turns copyrighted works into property of the order of land. 'Rent' can be charged for its use, yet there is little or no cost in making it available. As a result rights-owners like record companies and publishers make good profits but it is difficult to see how a significantly greater incentive to music makers is created. In fact, the reverse happens: as we have seen, enhancing the value of back catalogue may lead to a reduction in music industry investment in new talent. Reform One would be, then, to decrease the term of copyright, perhaps to no more than ten years after the moment of creation. Such a measure would immediately make more works available in the public domain, help push down the price of music and reduce the dominance of the big rights monopolists in the market place.

Actually, this approach – the *weakening* of copyright – could be adopted in other areas. One of the biggest problems identified in this chapter concerns sampling or, more generally, the creative reuse of music. It was suggested that when thinking about copyright and reuse an African diasporic model of culture, where versioning is the norm, might be more appropriate than the European ideal of original creation. Reform Two would enable the versioning aesthetic to flourish through the compulsory licensing of musical materials for reuse. The principle of compulsory licensing is already well established, for example in relation to the 'mechanical' reproduction of music. Record companies do not need to ask publishers' permission to record copyrighted works, or negotiate deals for this use. Instead the state has intervened to provide a fixed royalty rate, and a compulsory license. In the UK the royalty paid by record companies to copyright owners is set at 8.5 per cent of the retail price per record shipped. A compulsory licence for sampling could not be so clear-cut, of course, because the size of samples varies. There would need to be a sliding scale of charges, perhaps based on sample time, or maybe the percentage of the original piece being used. Crucially, though, rates would have to be set well below the current rates for 'clearing' samples. These effectively censor the use of found materials by small-time musicians. Interestingly, James Newton's lawyer Alan Korn has advocated compulsory sample licensing – and on an anti-copyright web site to boot (Korn 2002).

Term reduction and compulsory licensing for samples are realistic goals for copyright reform in that they involve variations on the way things are now. But musicians might actually go further, or in different directions, under the existing law – by employing licenses which grant a *part* of their copyright to users of their music. The Terms and Conditions offered by the group, Musicians Against Copyright of Samples provides one example on its web site. The aim here:

is to unify artists and musicians seeking a method to grant any person, or persons, the right to replicate portions of audio from 'granted material'. The usage of replicated portions of audio must conform to the following conditions: (1) in which the audio replication shall not conflict with the copyright of said material, and (2) shall be used solely for the use of musical composition. (MACOS 2004)

Condition 1 simply reiterates the existing position under the law. You cannot grant material which is already under copyright, as might be the case when your work incorporates a sample of another person's piece of music. Condition 2 represents an attempt to limit the scope of use. Employing samples in musical composition is fine, but other use is restricted, for example, repackaging an entire song.[8]

The campaigning group Creative Commons (2003) provide much fuller documentation for their eleven licences. Each one varies in scope across a 'spectrum of rights'. So, with the Attribution license '[y]ou let others copy . . . but only if they give you credit',[9] while the No Derivative Works licence allows people to 'copy, distribute, display, and perform only verbatim copies of your work, not derivative works based upon it'. The Creative Commons licences certainly offer flexibility, but by the same token this can involve a considerable degree of restriction. For example, No Derivative Works explicitly prevents sampling.

It seems, then, that there is a range of strategies which musicians might adopt faced with the problematic copyright regime: campaigning for legal reform, using 'copyleft' licences of one sort or another, or simply hoping that the copyright clouds will drift away in the heaven of Getting A Deal. Whichever strategy is chosen, though, it's worth recalling a point made at the start of the chapter. Ultimately, production of music for profit under private ownership underpins the institution of copyright and drives its continued expansion. Musicians have never been the real beneficiaries. Any attempt to reform the system of rights or, more boldly, to eliminate intellectual property in music altogether, needs to include recognition of this. And that in turn suggests that advocating change in the copyright regime means making common cause with opposition to rampant capitalism everywhere, from Glaxo to Warner-AOL.

Notes

1. Actually, as we will see later, in Europe musicians do now have certain rights in their performance on recordings.
2. These changes had already been made in France and other European countries. Publishers in the USA and Britain were relatively late to lobby for performing rights because they continued to see public performance primarily as a means of promoting sheet music sales (Ehrlich 1989).
3. See Toynbee (2001) for a fuller discussion.
4. By the same token when sheet music is published for songs produced in this way it is necessarily derivative; more, the notation constitutes an inadequate, and often inaccurate, reduction of the record-text.

5. The home of these so-called 'neighbouring rights' is Europe; in the USA rights in the recording came later and were never extended to cover broadcasting of recordings, although rather perversely a right in the recording in respect of *web*-casting has recently been instituted.
6. This is an American case, but the issues raised are of a sufficiently general nature to make it a useful case study in copyright and musicianship everywhere.
7. National (but not local) broadcasters do have to submit 'census' returns in which all works played are itemised. See PRS (2004).
8. This raises interesting questions about the scale of reuse. Might not 'framing' a whole track by putting your name to it actually constitute composition? And what about the bootleg genre in which as few as two recordings are combined?
9. Actually, in most countries these days (but not the USA) the so-called 'moral right' of authors to be attributed is enshrined in copyright law.

References

Adler, M. (1985), 'Stardom and talent', *American Economic Review* 75 (1): 208–12.

Barron, A. (2002), 'Copyright law and the claims of art', *Intellectual Property Quarterly* 4: 368–401.

Beastie Boys (1992), *Check Your Head*, Capitol [compact disc], CDEST2171.

Becker, H. (1982), *Art Worlds*, Berkeley: University of California Press.

Bourdieu, P. (1996), *The Rules of Art: Genesis and Structure of the Literary Field*, Cambridge: Polity Press.

Boyle, J. (1996), *Shamans, Software, and Spleens: Law and the Construction of the Information Society*, Cambridge: Harvard University Press.

Creative Commons (2003), 'Licenses explained', < http://creativecommons.org/learn/licenses/ > [accessed 21 January 2004].

Ehrlich, C. (1989), *Harmonious Alliance: A History of the Performing Right Society*, Oxford: Oxford University Press.

Eisenburg, E. (1987), *The Recording Angel: Music, Records and Culture from Aristotle to Zappa*, London: Picador.

Garnham, N. (1990), 'Public policy and the cultural industries', in *Capitalism and Communication: Global Culture and the Economics of Communication*, London: Sage, 154–68.

Gates, H. (1990), *The Signifying Monkey: A Theory of African-American Literary Criticism*, New York: Oxford University Press.

Gilroy, P. (1993), *The Black Atlantic: Modernity and Double Consciousness*, London: Verso.

Gracyk, T. (1996), *Rhythm and Noise: An Aesthetics of Rock*, London: I. B. Tauris.

Jones, L. (1995), *Blues People*, Edinburgh: Payback Press. [orig. publ. 1963]

Korn, A. (2002), 'Re: [rumori] newston vs. beasties – alan korn's reply' [sic], *Detritus.net*, < http://www.detritus.net/contact/rumori/200211/0115.html > [accessed 13 June 2003].

Korn, A. and Berchenko, J. (2001), *First Amended Complaint* (USDC CDC, Case no. CV 00–04909–NM).

MACOS (2004), Musicians Against Copyrighting of Samples, < http://www.icomm.ca/macos/ > [accessed 21 January 2004].

May, C. (2000), *A Global Political Economy of Intellectual Property Rights: The New Enclosures?*, London: Routledge.

Moore, A. (2001), *Rock: The Primary Text: Developing a Musicology of Rock*, Aldershot: Ashgate.

National Music Council (2002), *Counting the Notes: The Economic Contribution of the UK Music Business*, < http://www.musiced.org.uk/features/ counting_the_notes.pdf > [accessed 28 November 2003].

Newton, J. (1999), *Axum* [compact disc], ECM 8350192. [orig. publ. 1982]

Newton, J. (2002), 'From James Newton', *All About Jazz*, 28 August, < http:// www.allaboutjazz.com/news/pf/20020823/1682/james_Newton_loses_to_ beastie_boys > [accessed 12 June 2003].

Newton v. Diamond et al (2002), United States District Court, Central District of Calfornia, Case no. CV 00–04909 NM.

PRS (2004), 'Distribution principles', Performing Right Society, < http://www.prs.co.uk/broadcasters/ > [accessed 21 January 2004].

Small, C. (1987), *Music of the Common Tongue: Survival and Celebration in Afro-American Music*, London: Calder.

Smiers, J. (2002), 'The abolition of copyrights: better for artists, third world countries and the public domain', in Towse, R. (ed.) *Copyright in the Cultural Industries*, Cheltenham: Edward Elgar, 119–39.

Towse, R. (2000), 'Copyright and the cultural industries: incentives and earnings', paper for presentation to the Korea Infomedia Lawyers Association, Seoul, 30 October, < http://www.kafil.or.kr/seminar/171.PDF > [accessed 24 June 2003].

Towse, R. (2001), *Creativity, Incentive and Reward*, Cheltenham: Edward Elgar.

Toynbee, J. (2001), 'Creating problems: social authorship, copyright and the production of culture', *Pavis Papers* 3, Milton Keynes: Pavis Centre for Social and Cultural Research, Open University.

Wolff, J. (1993), *The Social Production of Art* (2nd edn), Houndmills: Macmillan.

York, N. and Laing, D. (2000), *Nice Work – If You Can Get It! A Survey of Musicians' Employment 1978–1998*, London: Musicians Union.

CHAPTER 8

Technology, Creative Practice and Copyright

Paul Théberge

Introduction

Over the course of the past half-century, the technologies of sound recording and reproduction have become central to our understanding of popular music as creative practice, commodity, and cultural form. For musicians, in particular, the relatively recent adoption of electronic and digital technologies in music production has resulted in new ways of composing music, new concepts of musical sound, and new forms of social interaction and collaboration. Indeed, what it means to be a 'musician' has, in many ways, also changed: musicians have become 'technologists' – and with this term I refer not only to contemporary composers and performers, but also producers, engineers, synthesiser programmers, turntablists, sample artists, mixers and remixers – individuals whose knowledge and skill in the uses of the recording studio, and the various technologies associated with it, have become as important as their knowledge of music, style, or vocal and instrumental performance. For technologists, a musical sound is not an ephemeral event but a reproducible entity and, as such, can be considered as both a fundamental building block of music, to be modified, altered and combined in myriad ways, and an object of economic exchange, whose ultimate value is highly contested.

The regimes associated with intellectual property in music, however, have lagged far behind these developments. And, where revision in copyright laws have sought to address the new realities of musical practice that stem, in part, from technological innovations in music making, they have been adopted and applied in such an uneven fashion that confusion, inequality, and the stifling of creativity have been the result. In this chapter, I will examine some of the shifts in musical practice that have accompanied, and in some instances driven, technological innovations in the production of popular music, primarily during the past forty years. I will argue that the cumulative effect of these shifts has redefined the nature of music, and what it means to be a musician, in fundamental ways and that nothing short of an equally fundamental rethinking of copyright law in relation to music will be required if we are to progress beyond the patchwork of legal instruments that presently enable and constrain music making at the beginning of the twenty-first century.

The Burden of History

The origins of music copyright law are rooted in a particular, restrictive notion of the musical work (defined as a combination of melody and harmony) and its fixation in graphic form (the musical score). Thus, from the outset, copyright law valorised composition (and by extension, the composer) over performance as a form of musical practice. Initially, this 'strategy of forms' (Mosher 1989) was perhaps understandable, given that performance, ephemeral in nature and lacking a means of fixation and reproduction, did not lend itself to the evolving economic system based on fixed commodities and exclusive property rights. But it was not inevitable: it was the interests of composers and publishers that prevailed in the formation of early copyright law and, as a result, many forms of music not based in notation – including various types of folk music, jazz, and indigenous people's music – have not been well served by copyright. It is not that these musics are lacking in a sense of ownership as is often assumed: in the music and dance of various indigenous peoples, for example, forms of individual and collective ownership can be seen to operate (see Harrison 2002).[1] But the protocols associated with such ownership are often incompatible with the particular notions of fixation, assignable rights, and other premises upon which the exploitation of property rights in the world of music publishing are based.

Far from being a simple point of departure, the formation of copyright law around a particular technology (the notated score) has had a significant influence on the formulation of subsequent laws and continues to have important repercussions to the present day. With the introduction of mechanical reproduction (both in the form of player pianos and sound recording) at the beginning of the twentieth century, the reproduction of musical performances became possible. Not surprisingly, it was the musical performer who became the artist (and star) of the recording medium and the first generations of performers, from Enrico Caruso to Bing Crosby, were able to secure lucrative contracts and royalty arrangements from their record companies.

From the standpoint of copyright law, however, the performer remained remarkably absent: copyright in the recording was vested in the producer, or the owner of the original 'plate', usually taken to mean the record company itself. The shift in emphasis here is significant: whereas the composer and lyricist are considered the 'creators' of the musical work, and thus entitled to copyright protection, it is by virtue of a simple contractual agreement – an agreement that specifies who organises and pays for the recording session – that the record company becomes owner of the sound recording and the rights associated with that ownership. In this way, performers continues to be denied the status of 'artist' or 'creator' of their recorded sounds – an unjustifiable inequality when one considers, for example, the role of the performer in improvised forms of music such as jazz.[2]

It was not until the Rome Convention of 1961 that performers were recognised within international copyright law but, even then, the application of the Convention was far from universal: many countries, most significantly the United States, were not signatories to the agreement. In Canada, it was not until the relatively recent adoption of Bill C-32, in 1997, that producer and performer rights were introduced but, again, these so-called 'neighbouring rights' did not enjoy equal status with the rights accorded to composers, lyricists and publishers. Indeed, in the months leading up to the introduction of Bill C-32, the Society of Composers, Authors, and Music Publishers of Canada (SOCAN) felt compelled to pay lip service to the idea of extending copyright protection to performers while, at the same time, insisting that it had no intention of sharing any of its income from broadcasters and other copyright users with the new neighbouring rights collectives; new monies would have to be found. Thus, the extension of copyright protection can be seen to create hierarchies within rights regimes and to put musicians in competition with one another rather than to foster cooperation.

A New Mode of Production

With the introduction in the 1960s of multitrack recording technology and the recording practices associated with it, popular musicians began to explore the possibilities offered by the recording medium, to regard sound recording not simply as a means of reproducing music but as an integral part of musical creation. In the decades that followed, several trends emerged that had significant implications for copyright law.

Firstly, the use of the multitrack studio fostered new forms of creative collaboration between musicians, producers and engineers. In some cases, producers became closely connected to the artists with whom they worked: for example, George Martin, in his various roles as producer, arranger and occasional performer on recording projects for The Beatles, came to be regarded by many as 'the fifth Beatle', and his contribution to the sound of their recordings has been widely recognised. And it was precisely the stature of producers like Martin that allowed him, and others, to argue for significant royalty concessions from record companies during this period. As more producers have broken away from record companies and pursued independent recording projects, they have also been able to avail themselves of some of the benefits of copyright protection by claiming ownership of recordings.

Perhaps even more dramatic was the transformation of the sound engineer from a mere technician into a full-fledged member of the creative enterprise within the studio. Edward R. Kealy (1979) has argued that during the 1960s the role of the engineer gradually changed from the level of craft union worker to that of 'artist' by virtue of increasingly significant contributions to the sound of pop music. Some engineers were eventually able to break their conventional status of wage labourers by arguing with producers and record companies for 'points' on record sales and, by the early 1990s, some remix engineers could negotiate lucrative, long-term contracts with record companies based on their ability to deliver marketable hits, but the status of the engineer-as-artist has yet to be fully realised in copyright legislation. Even in countries where 'neighbouring rights' have been established, engineers are seldom among those who enjoy the financial benefits of these rights, despite the importance of their contribution to the sound of any recording and their ability to rearrange digitally recorded material in a seemingly infinite variety of ways.

Secondly, as suggested above, the changes in the nature of the collaboration between musicians, producers and engineers (and more recently, synthesiser and computer programmers) have, in many ways, called into question the conventional claims to authorship within popular music. With the increasing reliance on studio techniques, automated drum machines, digital sequencers and other devices, producers and engineers have taken on a larger role in the production of popular music, especially the various genres associated with dance music. Will Straw has argued that, beginning with disco during the 1970s, record companies have had difficulty in promoting dance music because of the industry's conventional reliance on artists (especially vocalists) as the focal point of both the star system and as the apparent authorial source of the music (Straw 1999: 204–6). With disco music, performers were often little more than a front, an alibi for a system of production that was more reliant on producers and engineers as the functional source of musical sounds. At the same time, however, musicians in other genres of pop, especially rock, became interested in the techniques of recording and built sophisticated home studios where they could experiment with recording and mixing, thus asserting greater levels of control over the sound of both their music and the music of others for whom they acted as producers. The point here is that, in the recording studio, the roles of musician, arranger, producer, engineer and programmer have become increasingly fluid, with any given individual sometimes filling more than one role. As a result, traditional assumptions surrounding musical authorship simply do not hold.

Finally, as the recording studio became the primary site in which the creation of popular music takes place, it displaced the musical score as a means of musical composition. In the case of jazz, where the elements of composition are often little more than the outlines of a melodic and harmonic structure that is to be fully realised in performance, the status of the musical score had already been called into question; in rock and pop music the notated score has also become increasingly irrelevant, an artificial mode of fixing certain elements of a song after the fact. Indeed, by the late 1960s, musicians no longer came to the studio to record a pre-existing song; the song was constructed *in* the studio, not only out of the possibilities offered by words, melody, harmony and rhythm, but also out of the sonic possibilities offered by the studio itself. Technical practices within the studio are oriented towards the production and manipulation of musical sounds and, like the rock guitarist's obsession with the quality of amplifier distortion, it is the *sound* of music that is the focal point of the technologist's aesthetic concerns and the musical feature that consumers most readily recognise.

Thus, to a large degree, the conventional division enshrined in copyright law – the division between the underlying musical work and the sound recording, each bearing its own claim to copyright protection – becomes meaningless: for all intents and purposes, the recording *is* the work, and it is this fact that is attested to by the prevalence of sampling from the 1980s onward (the significance of sampling will be discussed in greater detail below). Even where a score predates the recorded work, there is some evidence to suggest that the courts are beginning to recognise that music, as it is performed and recorded, can sometimes be more 'original' in character and substance than the score from which it is derived. In a judgement handed down in 2002 (*Newton v. Diamond*), a California district court ruled that the Beastie Boys, who had obtained clearance to use a sample from a recording by jazz flautist James W. Newton in their song 'Pass the Mic', were *not* required also to obtain a licence from Newton for the corresponding portion of his underlying composition (Newton had sold his rights in the recording to ECM Records, from whom the Beastie Boys had purchased the sample licence, but retained his rights to the composition). As already discussed by Jason Toynbee in the last chapter, the court in this case reasoned that the portion of the score that had been included in the sample was not sufficiently original, in itself, to support a claim of copyright; indeed, concerning the sample, it was the *sound* of Newton's recorded performance that was the more important feature of the music. It is perhaps ironic that the composer and the performer, in this instance, were the same individual but the case does highlight the constructed character of the hierarchy between score and sound recording, and the contradictions embedded in the copyrights assigned to each.

The complete reversal of the primacy of the score in the score/ recording hierarchy, however, has never been fully reflected in the economic regimes of copyright: as noted above, performance royalties accorded to songwriters and publishers continue to be among the most lucrative of all musical rights. Record companies own music publishing houses, not because publishing, as such, is an essential part of their operations (they make relatively little from the actual sale of printed music), but because the securing and exploitation of copyright has become recognised as an important stream of revenue, one that is essential to the profitability of the overall enterprise.

Sounds as Objects

Given the increasing importance placed on the production of a unique 'sound' in popular music recording practices, it should not be surprising that individual, isolated sounds have become the next ground upon which the extension of musical rights, and their protection, have been sought. The initiative for this development came from two distinct sources: the first from the ranks of entrepreneurial sound designers who created sound programs for digital synthesisers and samplers; the second from musicians, record companies and music publishers who sought to protect their works from (or at least profit from the use of their works by) another breed of technologists, sampling artists.

During the early 1980s, the programming of digital synthesisers became a highly complex process. Only the most technically knowledgeable musicians were able to create effective sounds for the instruments and some among them, recognising that there was a growing market for desirable sound programs, began to devote their energies to supplying those sounds. For these specialised technologists, the need for some form of copyright protection for their work became evident very early on: unscrupulous retailers were often too ready to give away entire banks of sounds if it might help sell a big-ticket item like a synthesiser, many musicians freely traded sounds among themselves, and pirates sometimes copied sound programs and then sold them under their own name.

Ironically, in 1989, when the Copyright Office of the Library of Congress finally began accepting sound 'patches' as individually copy-rightable entities, the twin requirements of fixation and proof of originality demanded that programmers submit their sounds in the form of synthe-siser parameter settings: like a musical score, copyright protection would extend to the parameter settings (as written or digitally stored), but not to the sounds themselves (McCaffrey 1989: 24). The problem with this particular manifestation of the 'strategy of forms' is that while synthesiser parameters often cannot be generalised – they are either unique to the synthesis models used in a given instrument or, in the case of common elements such as envelope settings, varied in their implementation – it is nevertheless possible to create very similar sounding programs through different means. To the ear, the resulting sounds might suggest that some form of copyright infringement has taken place but an analysis of the parameters would not necessarily support such an assertion.[3]

Because the cost of creating sound libraries for digital samplers can be quite high (in addition to looping and programming, the samples themselves are usually recorded in professional studio facilities), sample developers have also sought the protection of copyright to prevent the illicit copying of their work. Sample developers treat their products – often referred to as 'soundware' – much as software developers treat theirs in the world of computing: users purchase a 'licence' that allows them to use the sampled sounds in a musical composition, royalty-free (although, interestingly, some developers request that users credit the source of the samples on CD liner notes much as one would credit the contributions of session musicians); however, *ownership* of the sounds remains with the original developer/producer. In this way, sample developers hope to control the illicit copying of their work, on the one hand, and the use of their sounds in isolated form in other media, for example, in the way that the creators of computer games might use isolated sounds as sound effects, on the other.[4]

Sample programs were originally distributed on floppy discs and, later, as part of large CD-ROM collections, each containing hundreds and even thousands of sounds; more recently, sample developers have turned to the Internet as a means of distribution and have created pricing schemes where even individual sounds can be purchased, in some cases with different pricing structures for limited and commercial uses. But like the record industry's more general problem of controlling the digital distribution of songs, the increasing popularity of downloading and sharing sounds on the Internet has challenged the sample developers' ability to control the distribution of their work. The problem is compounded by the fact that synthesiser programmers and sample developers seldom have the financial resources to pursue legal proceedings against violators of their copyright.

While there have yet to be any major, precedent-setting cases that have set the legal terms or limits of synthesiser or sample program ownership and use, the significance of these developments lies more in the general manner in which sound developers have staked a claim to the aesthetic and economic value of their work in the first place. In this sense, entrepreneurs working on the fringes of the music industry have helped to reinforce the notion that individual sounds can be considered as aesthetic objects and, as such, assigned commercial value.

To assert the value of the isolated sound object in this way is important because it is precisely the assumption of such value that underlies much of the intimidation and litigation surrounding the use of samples in hip-hop, dance remixes, and other forms of popular music during the past two decades. Indeed, until relatively recently, the actual musical significance of a sample – of a vocal sound or a break beat – when found *within* the context of the original sound recording or, conversely, *within* the new musical creation, has tended to go unexamined. Once the act of copying from the original has been established, the value of the object is assumed, and a case for infringement seemingly guaranteed.

Proceeding on this assumption, the recording and publishing industries have, since the 1980s, litigated against artists who sample from their copyrighted works. While most sampling cases were (and continue to be) settled out of court, usually for undisclosed sums of money, rapper Biz Markie decided to fight a suit brought against him in 1991 by Gilbert O'Sullivan for sampling from the latter's song, 'Alone Again (Naturally)'. Ultimately, Markie lost what became a precedent setting case: in his ruling, Judge Duffy defined unlicensed sampling as 'stealing', plain and simple, and thus sent a chill throughout the sampling community (*Grand v. Warner* 1991). What made the case important for the industry was not the specific details nor the merit of the claim of infringement against Markie so much as the simplicity of the ruling: by not allowing for any possibility of a counter claim of fair use, the ruling upheld the idea that the isolated sound object had value and that virtually any act of sampling undertaken without first obtaining necessary permissions and clearances was essentially an illegal activity.

The widespread fear of litigation that ensued from Judge Duffy's ruling permitted the industry to exact copyright clearance payments in advance from would-be samplers. Since 1991, the oppressive character of the legal climate and the financial burden of advance clearances have placed considerable constraint on sampling artists and inhibited their ability to create new works: when one considers that many recording projects sample from more than one work, the prospects of paying for each sample in advance can make such projects financially unviable from the start (in addition, depending on the material being sampled, clearances may have to be sought from both the owners of the recording *and* the underlying musical composition, thus potentially doubling the cost of clearances). Because the practice of clearing samples in advance is unregulated (there isn't even an agreed standard for clearances), it has afforded the industry a way of reaping excessive profits from its copyrighted material: unlike compulsory licensing schemes that set the cost of licences at fixed amounts (such as the compulsory licences associated with making cover versions of a song), the industry can set the price of sampling arbitrarily, at whatever level the market will bear. Typically, sample licences cost anywhere from US$1,000 to US$5,000 per sample but sampling from some popular recordings can cost several times that amount and/or involve signing away a percentage of the future profits in the new work.

Such practices place an undue emphasis on isolated fragments of sound as objects of exchange and virtually ignore the significance of the creative uses to which they are put. The degree to which the status quo has come to be taken for granted can be discerned by the number of large record companies that have established departments dedicated to the clearance of copyright licences and the rise of specialised, third-party firms that perform such services for smaller record labels and music publishers. A recent US court decision, however, *Bridgeport v. Dimension*, rendered in 2002, has called into question some of the assumptions upon which the profitability of this status quo is based, and as I will describe below, it places a very different kind of emphasis on the relationship between the value placed on isolated sound objects and that given to the transformation of those objects by creative technologists.

Sampling as an Art Form

Sampling as a creative practice is at odds with copyright in that it is fundamentally based on the idea of 'unfixing' recorded sounds: that is, the aesthetic 'value' of the recorded object lies less in the form of its original fixation than in its *reuse* in a new musical context. Even before the rise of digital sampling technology, the practices associated with hip-hop and dance music DJs – practices such as 'scratching' and mixing LPs in real time – had challenged the idea that recorded songs were essentially 'finished' works, fixed in some immutable way, or that turntables were simply reproductive devices. By isolating break beats and other bits of recorded sound and music, DJs (now often referred to as 'turntablists') could extend and intensify the effect of rhythmic passages within songs and combine them with other music to create a new form of live, improvised music. Turntablism thus posits a new equation between performance and reproduction – an equation that, more than anything, changes the nature and value of the recorded object.

Sample artists have extended the techniques of the DJ, combining them with a powerful new technology: digital sampling. Sampling allows virtually any sound that can be recorded to be looped, altered in pitch, and subjected to a wide variety of other manipulations before being sequenced together with other sounds or tracks in a multitrack composition. While samplers can be used in conjunction with digital keyboards in performance contexts, their more typical use among hip-hop and dance music producers has been in the recording studio where they have become a central component in the remixing of popular songs for the dance floor and for the creation of entirely new works.

It is in this latter activity that samplers have been implicated in cases of alleged copyright infringement. In part, because studio uses of sampling appear to be more detached and calculated in character (like the work of studio engineers and producers more generally) they have tended to invite traditionalist critiques that pit conventional instrumental performance skills and romantic notions of originality against technology as an artificial and falsifying influence on music production (such arguments are not unfamiliar, and have long been a feature of more general critiques of technology in music making, see Frith 1986). Within such arguments, even the appropriative nature of turntablism is made somewhat more acceptable by the very fact that it is a performance-based art.[5] But what is perhaps most important is that this ideological separation of sampling techniques in the studio from more traditional forms of music making has given sampling artists a tenuous purchase on notions of authorship, creativity and authenticity (Sloop and Herman 1998: 301–2).

Partly as a result of this, sampling projects are typically understood to be derivative: that is, their value can only be assessed in relation to some other, more 'original' source. In court cases, this usually takes the form of arguments based on the idea that the very success of the sample-based work of art is ultimately dependent upon its use of some particular bit of appropriated material (no matter how minimal). Indeed, insofar as the charge of infringement usually also involves a claim that the market for the original has been somehow negatively impacted by the very existence of the infringing work, it suggests that the relationship of the latter to the original is not simply derivative but *parasitic* in character.

One sees such a relationship in operation even within the legally sanctioned areas that generally come under the rubric of 'fair use' (in the USA) or 'fair dealing' (as it is known in some countries, although there are fine distinctions to be made between the two concepts). The most famous case of sampling to avail itself of the fair use clause in fending off charges of infringement involved the group 2 Live Crew and its parody of Roy Orbison's song, 'Oh Pretty Woman' (*Campbell v. Acuff-Rose* 1994). While the case has achieved the status of a 'landmark' (see the discussion in Chapters 4 and 11), by setting a certain precedent in legal case law regarding sampling, it has perhaps closed down more avenues for technologists than it has opened. Indeed, even while allowing for fair use doctrine to be employed as a defence in the 2 Live Crew case, the court was careful not to suggest that all uses of sampling could similarly avail themselves of this part of the copyright statutes: only in cases where sampling made direct reference to an original for the purposes of satire or parody could this defence be allowed. While it could be argued that artists often sample specific works with the expectation that listeners will be able to identify the origin of at least some of the samples, thus arriving at a layered sense of meaning, they seldom do so with the explicit intention of parodying the originals and thus their actions are still subject to legal action.

What is perhaps most important to understand in this context, however, is that sampling is part of a larger musical practice, compositional technique and aesthetic and, as such, its specific musical effects are not always dependent upon the identification of the original source of the samples employed. Indeed, the aesthetics of sampling are more about original *uses* of sound material – their manipulation, transformation, and combination with other sounds – than with simple copying (and in this sense, it could be argued that the act of sampling does not always, nor necessarily, make one work 'derivative' of another, in musical or legal terms). Michael Chanan, drawing on the work of Roland Barthes, has argued that we need to think of sampling as a new form of *musica practica*, one that has arisen out of the various possibilities offered by new technologies; including not only sampling but sound recording, mixing and reproduction more generally (Chanan 1995: 162–3). Furthermore, he argues, this new form of practice, by its very nature, calls into question the fixity and singularity of the musical work, as well as notions of authorship, ownership, and the like.

While it might appear that this new form of practice is the negation of an older *musica practica*, one based in more conventional forms of composition and performance (Chanan 1995: 162–3), it is perhaps more important to understand where both differences *and* continuities exist between these forms of practice, and where notions of musical skill, originality and ownership need to be redefined in order to accommodate it. While the climate of threat and intimidation surrounding sampling that has prevailed over the past two decades has not been conducive to a rethinking of fundamental principles, a recent copyright case does suggest that the courts are perhaps now willing to be more subtle in their application of the law and, in so doing, may lay the basis for a shift in the balance of power between simple ownership and creative use.

During the spring of 2001, in what must be regarded as an all-out assault on sampling as an art-form, Bridgeport Music, Inc., filed a complaint against approximately 800 defendants, claiming close to 500 cases of infringement. Bridgeport holds the copyright to a number of musical compositions by George Clinton and other artists of the 1970s, a repertoire that has been particularly important to many rap technologists (see Demers 2003) and, in this sense, their legal action could have a major impact on hip-hop culture as a whole (it does not appear that Clinton has any direct interest in the claims pursued by Bridgeport). The courts refused to hear such a massive action and severed the complaint into some 476 separate cases. One of those cases, *Bridgeport v. Dimension Films* (2002), which involved a sample taken from a George Clinton song, 'Get Off Your Ass and Jam', and used initially by the group N.W.A. in their recording of '100 Miles and Runnin'', and subsequently in the film *I Got the Hook Up*, is of particular interest here because of the logic employed by the judge in denying Bridgeport's claim of infringement.

In his decision, Judge Thomas A. Higgins applied the principle of *de minimis non curat lex* ('the law cares not for trifles') in arguing that the material sampled from the copyrighted work was insufficient to support the claim of infringement. More important than the principle itself was the justification (or perhaps even the motivation) behind its use:

> The Court's role in making a *de minimis* analysis is a tricky one. It must balance the interests protected by the copyright laws against the stifling effect that overly rigid enforcement of these laws may have on the artistic development of new works. (*Bridgeport v. Dimension* 2002: 16)

In taking such a position, Judge Higgins was clearly going against the dominant trend in cases of sampling where simple ownership has most often taken precedence over creative use. His position is also significant concerning to the wider field of copyright legislation as well: while the ideal of encouraging the creation of new works is one of the founding principles of copyright, it has taken a back seat in recent years to industry-dominated appeals for the extension, in both the scope and duration, of copyright protections.

In his analysis, part of the justification of the decision rendered by Judge Higgins was based on the fact that the sample in question had been transformed to the point that it would be barely recognised, even by an individual familiar with the music of George Clinton (*Bridgeport v. Dimension Films* 2002: 20). If this were the only reason for applying the *de minimis* analysis, however, then relatively little would stand to be gained from his decision: as in the case of parody, the requirement of altering a sample beyond the point of recognition would simply place a new kind of restriction on the kinds of samples that can, or cannot be used in a recording – it would draw a new line in the shifting sands of 'fair use'. Indeed, such a regime would serve only to reinforce current practices among some technologists who, out of fear of litigation, disguise their appropriations or otherwise bury their samples deeply within musical textures in the hope that they will not be noticed in the first place (see Schloss 2004).

The ruling rendered by Judge Higgins is significant, however, for two reasons. Firstly, the ruling recognises, in principle, that sampling is an art form based in the copying and transformation of pre-existing sound material and, perhaps most important, that the transformative aspect of sampling technique may, in certain circumstances, outweigh claims to ownership and control over the source material. As noted above, the particular case considered by Higgins may suggest that such transforma-tions must be quite significant, even extreme, if they are to act as a challenge to ownership; but in his analysis Judge Higgins makes clear that it is not so much the degree of transformation as the musical context in which the sample is placed that is perhaps the more decisive factor.

It is this second area of analysis that is perhaps the most remarkable aspect of Higgins' ruling: in support of his use of the *de minimis* principle, Higgins offers an analysis of the sampled material, in the context of both the original song and the one in which it has been placed, that is both quantitative and qualitative. The analysis extends beyond the simple assessment of the duration of the sampled material and even its location and relative prominence within the two works. It includes a consideration of the overall thematic context of each song (as suggested, for example, in the lyrical content) and even the particular mood or tone evoked by the use of the sample (that is, the particular musical effect of the sampled material in terms of how it creates feelings of tension, apprehension, or other emotions in each of the works).

It should be noted here that neither the idea of 'transformation' nor the use of both quantitative and qualitative comparisons are particularly unusual in cases of copyright infringement. However, in the past, most courts dealing with music and sampling have either been ill-prepared or unwilling to apply such considerations in a methodical or consistent manner, thus allowing the interests of copyright owners to dominate the proceedings. Perhaps the most interesting thing about Judge Higgins' decision in this regard is the subtlety, depth, clarity and methodical character of his analysis. While it is too early to know whether this ruling will be eventually regarded as a precedent-setting case, it does offer an exceptionally well-formulated model for balancing the conflicting interests of ownership and creative use in cases of copyright infringement and, for this alone, technologists in the future may have reason to be grateful.

Conclusion

Many technologists, including recording engineers, sound designers and programmers, turntablists, sample artists and remixers, occupy an ambiguous position within the record industry. They play essential roles in the creation of many forms of contemporary music yet they continue to be marginalised, in terms of public recognition and the dominant structures of remuneration within the industry, and are even overtly intimidated whenever the appropriation of copyrighted material is at issue. In the last case, the industry has been unusually duplicitous, encouraging sampling when it has the potential for creating new hits but, at the same time, inhibiting its use through litigation or by insisting on the payment of excessively large, advance clearances.

In this regard, sampling will perhaps only become fully accepted (as opposed to simply tolerated) if it is understood as part of a larger, relatively new mode of production or, put in Chanan's terms, a new form of *musica practica*. At the heart of this new set of practices, whether they be the sound manipulations and mixing techniques of the recording engineer, or the looping and layering practices of sampling artists, is the transformative power of new technologies when put to creative use by technologists. And certainly, not only technologists but also conventional performers and composers have benefited from the realignment of their practices with the transformative and productive potential of the new technologies. In this sense, while some practices associated with new technology may appear to be the negation of older forms of musical practice (and the negation of copyright as well), they in fact do not entirely negate or replace older forms of practice so much as *displace* them, forcing a redefinition of our notions of creativity and originality (and thus also requiring of copyright law a redefinition of the balance between ownership and creative use).

The evolution of this new form of *musica practica* has continued unabated in recent years and with the increased availability of transformative production technologies, such as those associated with basic audio editing software for PCs, is now in the process of becoming a widespread amateur phenomenon (in Barthes' original formulation, amateur music making is at the heart of the idea of *musica practica*). Indeed, the distinction between 'professional' and 'amateur' is often undermined by the use of technology and a recognition of this tendency can be found in a recent release by Public Enemy: during the production of *Revolverlution* (2002), the group invited fans to remix some of the Enemy's earlier tracks and some of these remixes were eventually released, along with the group's own work, on the album. In this way, Public Enemy highlights the fact that what separates professional from fan in popular culture is largely an economic relation and, by allowing the authors of the remixes to retain the copyright in their work, they demonstrate a willingness to address their fans as equals.

A more widespread phenomenon can be found in the rise of so-called 'mash-ups', also known as 'bootlegs' or 'bastard pop' recordings. An outgrowth of DJ culture, these recordings typically layer two songs (not brief samples but entire vocal or instrumental tracks) by disparate artists from diverse musical genres; the resulting juxtapositions are pastiche-like in character, humorous and often satirical in intent. While some have appeared on commercial releases, they are more often played in dance clubs, are widely distributed on the Internet, and have garnered a considerable amount of mainstream press in recent years (see for example, Phillips 2002, Rojas 2002, and Ryan 2003). There is an artlessness to mash-ups – they tend to be technically unpolished and appear to require little by way of conventional skill to create – but this characteristic belies the musical knowledge that is at the root of the combinatorial strategies that are required to make, and interpret, the works.

Even more than sampling did twenty years ago, however, mash-ups challenge the very basis of copyright law by further blurring the boundary between simple copying and transformation. Perhaps not surprisingly, the record industry has already employed legal intimidation, in the form of cease and desist orders, in an attempt to prevent club DJs and radio stations from playing the music. In the basic layering of tracks, however, it could be argued that mash-ups do transform the original recordings in a fundamental way: through their radical juxtapositions, they recontextualise the originals, forcing a reevaluation of their meaning both individually and in combination with one another. But copyright law may ultimately be a crude instrument with which to restrain or control the spread of this particular manifestation of *musica practica*, much less understand it; and as noted by Judge Higgins, little is to be gained by an 'overly rigid enforcement of these laws'.

Rather than allow it to be used in an attempt to stifle yet another creative form of musical practice, the industry, legislators and the courts need to reexamine copyright law and its commitment to outmoded notions of originality, creativity and ownership, and to balance the economic interests that these ideas support with a recognition of the technologists' capacity to transform musical sounds and their right to make creative use of recorded material in the production of new works.

Notes

1. Copyright law with respect to indigenous people and the use of their music raises special problems of both a legal and ethical nature. For a discussion of some of these issues as they relate to the appropriation of World Music by Western musicians see Feld (1994), Taylor (2001), Théberge (2003), and Chapter 9 in this book.

2. In a number of cases in the United States, performers have had to turn to the common law notion of publicity rights rather than copyright in order to protect their recorded sounds from unauthorised use by others. Publicity rights grant individuals the exclusive right to use their name, image, sound, and so on, for the purposes of merchandising, advertising, product endorsements and the like. In copyright law, performers do not 'own' their recorded sounds (copyright resides with producer of the recording), so they have turned to these common law 'publicity rights' to control who can use their sounds and for what purpose. One of the most famous cases involving music is Bette Midler's suit against the Ford Motor Co. and its advertising agency (*Midler v. Ford Motor Co.* 849 F.2d 460 [9th Cir.] 1988) in which she was awarded US $400,000. in compensation for their use of a 'sound alike' performance of one of her songs. In ruling against Ford, the court argued that the deliberate imitation of Midler's voice was equivalent to appropriating her identity for its advertising campaign. An even more spectacular case involved singer Tom Waits and Frito-Lay, Inc. (*Waits v. Frito-Lay, Inc.*,

978 F.2d 1093 [9th Cir.].1992): as Waits had been an outspoken opponent of celebrity endorsements the courts awarded him some US$2.5m in compensation and punitive damages.

3. The relationship between digital information, fixation and sound is an extremely varied and contradictory one. Recently, the combination of MIDI sequencers and digital audio recording software has made it possible to extract 'the groove' – the unique sense of timing and rhythmic phrasing contained in an instrumental performance – without reference to the sounds that produced it. The groove can then be applied to other sounds such that they have virtually the same feel as the original recording but are distinctly different in timbre. The question as to whether technical practices of this kind can be considered a violation of copyright have scarcely been raised, in part, because of the difficulty in proving that an act of infringement has indeed taken place.

4. For an example of the type of agreement associated with sound samples see the various sample distribution web sites such as < soundsonline.com >.

5. Some music schools, such as the Berklee School of Music, in Boston, have even begun to debate whether turntable techniques should be taught as part of the regular curriculum in instrumental performance. For a discussion of the relationship between DJ practice and performance and its extension into studio composition via sampling; see Fikentscher (2003).

References

Bridgeport Music, Inc. v. Dimension Films LLC (2002), 230 F. Supp. 2d 830 (M.D. Tenn.).

Campbell v. Acuff-Rose Music, Inc. (1994), 510 U.S. 569, 114 S.Ct. 1164.

Chanan, M. (1995), *Repeated Takes: A Short History of Recording and its Effects on Music*, London: Verso.

Demers, J. (2003), 'Sampling the 1970s in hip-hop', *Popular Music* 22 (1): 41–56.

Feld, S. (1994), 'From schizophonia to schismogenesis: on the discourses and commodification practices of "World Music" and "World Beat"', in C. Keil and S. Feld (eds), *Music Grooves*, Chicago: University of Chicago Press, 257–89.

Fikentscher, K. (2003), ' "There's not a problem I can't fix, 'cause I can do it in the mix": on the performative technology of 12–inch vinyl', in R. Lysloff and L. Gay (eds), *Music and Technoculture*, Middletown: Wesleyan University Press, 290–315.

Frith, S. (1986), 'Art *vs* technology. The strange case of popular music', *Media, Culture and Society* 8(3): 263–80.

Grand Upright Music Ltd v. Warner Brothers Records, Inc. (1991), 780 F. Supp. 182 (S.D.N.Y.).

Harrison, K. (2002), 'The Kwagiulth dancers: addressing intellectual property issues at Victoria's first People's Festival', *The World of Music* 44 (1): 137–51.

Kealy, E. R. (1979), 'From craft to art: the case of sound mixers and popular music', *Sociology of Work and Occupations* 6 (1): 3–29.

McCaffrey, T. (1989), 'Copyright okayed for synth patches', *Keyboard* 15 (12): 24–5.

Mosher, J. (1989), '20th century music: the impoverishment in copyright law of a strategy of forms', *Intellectual Property Journal*, 5 August: 51–70.

Newton v. Diamond (2002), 204 F. Supp. 2d 1244, 1256 (C.D. Cal.).

Phillips, D. (2002), 'Smells like teen booty', *The Guardian*, 27 February.

Public Enemy (2002), *Revolverlution*, Koch Records, CD 8388.

Rojas, P. (2002), 'Bootleg culture', *Salon.com*, http://www.salon.com/tech/feature/2002/08/01/bootlegs/ [accessed 23 March 2003].

Ryan, M. (2003), 'Mashups pair up unlikely musicians', *Chicago Tribune*, 31 August: 8.

Schloss, J. G. (2004), *Making Beats: The Art of Sample-Based Hip-Hop*, Middletown: Wesleyan University Press.

Sloop, J. and Herman, A. (1998), 'Negativland, outlaw judgements and the politics of cyberspace', in T. Swiss (ed.), *Mapping the Beat. Popular Music and Contemporary Theory*, Malden and Oxford: Blackwell Publishers, 291–311.

Straw, Will (1999), 'Authorship', in B. Horner and T. Swiss (eds), *Key Terms in Popular Music and Culture*, Malden: Blackwell, 199–208.

Taylor, T. D. (2001), *Strange Sounds: Music, Technology and Culture*, New York: Routledge.

Théberge, P. (2003), ' "Ethnic sounds": the economy and discourse of World Music sampling', in R. Lysloff and L. Gay (eds), *Music and Technoculture*, Middletown: Wesleyan University Press, 93–108.

CHAPTER 9

Traditional Music Ownership in a Commodified World

Anthony Seeger

Introduction

It lasts the whole night. Song after song fills the air and dancers, encouraged by experience-altering chemicals, move their bodies in coordination with the beats, their feelings, and the traditions of the genre. Ecstatic transformations inflame the minds and bodies of the participants. The dawn finds them drained, recalling the night with pleasure and anticipating other such nights.

A rave party? Amazonian Indian ceremony? From the outside the two events may appear to be similar. Sounds, movement, drugs, and profound personal experience characterise them both. But looking at the meanings attributed to the sounds by the participants can make them seem totally different. Rave occurs in a capitalist country in which music is secular and commodified and the entire performance is associated with marginality, youth, and subculture. The Amazon Indians consider the music and the mind-altering substances to be sacred. Community elders at the centre (not the margins) of the social order use them. One group thinks it is having a party; the other group thinks it is communicating with sacred beings. One is dancing to popular music; the other is dancing to the sounds of the gods themselves. Applying the word "music" to certain structured sounds in such different societies lumps together things that have vastly different meanings to the participants. And therein lies a fundamental problem with copyright and traditional music.

An essential difference between rave parties and worship lies in the attitudes the participants have toward the music. Popular music is by definition a commodity – it is produced for sale to as many people as can be convinced to consume it. But music is not everywhere a commodity, even though international legislation treats it as such. Some communities would exclude their music from such a definition because its objectives are so different – although any music can become a commodity. From such fundamentally different ideas about the essence of music and creativity come many of the inequities created by copyright legislation and much of the anger of artists and communities around the world about the use, and misuse, of their cultural traditions in commodified products.

This chapter begins with a brief discussion of Euro-American copyright legislation and how it fails to address a great deal of what can be termed "traditional" music. It goes on to describe the distinctive ideas about music ownership found in a single Amazonian Indian society that make it difficult to apply copyright legislation to their music. It then shows how the popular music industry has repeatedly exploited the creativity of traditional artists, and discusses some of the options being considered to improve the current conflict-ridden situation.

Euro-American Copyright Legislation

In its simplest form, music copyright is a limited-term monopoly granted to the creators (and to some extent the performers) of musical "works". For a fixed period of time (now the lifetime of the creator plus seventy years in the USA) other people are prohibited from making money from those works without the permission of, and usually some form of payment to, the copyright holder. When the fixed term expires, the work passes into what is called the "public domain". This is a kind of well of ideas that may be used by anyone, without permission or payment, to create more new things. For example, 'White Christmas' is a composed song, but after its copyright term expires anyone will be able to perform it or use the musical ideas in it without paying fees. The public domain includes anything old enough to have gone out of copyright, as well as some kinds of works that were never in copyright – oral traditions without an identifiable author, and in some legislation all "folklore".

Copyright legislation does not cover all kinds of knowledge or all kinds of music, only identifiably new creations. Traditional and folk music are generally excluded from coverage either because they do not have a "composer" or they are too old. They are available for people to use to make new works, which they can then copyright. Intellectual property legislation assumes that all works should be treated as commodities. Little attention has been given to other possibilities, because the objective of the legislation is to provide those who produce commodities with a recompense for investment, and to encourage them to produce more. But by failing to recognise and protect other types of works, the legislation fails to address part of what music is, how people feel about it, and the various motivations behind its performance, publication, and dissemination.

Every society in the world apparently performs structures of sounds similar to what we in English call "music". But not every society shares the same ideas about the origin, control, and rights over those sounds. The intellectual property laws that are being used as the basis for international legislation arose in Europe during a particular moment of its history. The laws were developed at a time when very specific ideas about the nature of the individual, the essence of the creative act, and the protection of industry were taking shape.[1] Even within Europe, countries had quite different legislation covering intellectual property – or no laws at all. But the regulations that were then formulated soon spread from Europe to the rest of the world as an aspect of colonialism. Today, the General Agreement on Tariffs and Trade (GATT) that governs trade also includes rigorous standards for the creation of a standardised intellectual property code covering not only copyright, but also trademark, trade secret and other types of intellectual property.

Many industrialising countries had only fairly limited copyright legislation before signing the GATT treaty, and most of them are updating their national legislation in an effort to comply with the basic principles articulated in the GATT agreements. Yet even when a government decides to adhere to the international intellectual property legislation, there are often communities within their nation whose ideas are at variance with the national legislation. Some of them are minority communities within the country that are referred to as the "Fourth World" – communities isolated within nation states by accident or conquest, whose ideas may not be reflected in national legislation at all. Examples abound: the American Indian (descendants of pre-Colombian populations) societies in North and South America, the many linguistically and culturally distinctive local communities within nations in Africa and the Pacific region, and the aboriginal peoples in Australia are only a few of them. While they are found within nation states, their ideas and attitudes often conflict directly with the national legal codes. Many of these communities have ideas of music and its ownership and control that are at variance with the national and international legislation that is emerging.

Most of the attention to music copyright has focused on popular music, where fortunes are being lost (at least according to the record companies), and won (at least by law firms), and a large part of the music–consuming public is being accused of piracy by the recording industry. Much less attention has been paid to traditional music, largely ignored by law courts and largely invisible in the press because its practitioners lack financial backing and have little legal standing. Yet intellectual property legislation is of great importance to the artists and communities whose lives are affected by the superimposition of an "international" (that is, European and North American) intellectual property code that overrides their local concepts of music ownership, creativity, and ethics. What are the implications of copyright legislation for communities whose cultural heritage is not considered by them to be a commodity, and who are unable to protect their arts from exploitation?

Early European copyright legislation developed where literate people were creating new works for publication. The purpose of most copyrights was to give a short-term monopoly to the publisher of a literary (and, later, musical) text, and then to allow the work to be freely accessible to anyone who later chose to use it. The legislation was not originally designed to protect authors so much as publishers (see Woodmansee and Jaszi 1994). Since the rural and the poor were generally thought to be backward and ignorant, and the indigenous peoples of Africa, Asia and the Americas possibly less than human, little thought was given to their control over their knowledge. Under the terms established by the literate elite, knowledge that did not have a single, named, author could not be copyrighted. Folklore – including folk music and many forms of traditional knowledge – is specifically excluded from the copyright acts of many countries.

Yet in the twentieth and early twenty-first centuries, traditional knowledge has become very profitable for those able to adapt it and turn it into a commodity. The knowledge of plants and their qualities acquired over centuries by members of tribal societies in ecologically rich zones has proved extremely useful to pharmaceutical companies. As tourism has grown to become one of the world's largest industries, the appreciation of traditional arts has grown, as have the fortunes that can be made from imitating traditional styles. Yet even as opportunities for benefiting from a degree of commodification of their arts appear, members of societies whose arts are considered "traditional" find their works are not protected in the same way as those of urban musicians.

This exclusion of traditional knowledge and folklore from copyright legislation resembles colonial relationships established by military might in an earlier era. Subject communities provide raw materials to other communities who then "improve it" (through manufacture or arrangement) and make money by selling the "improved material" as a commodity. This happens when a pharmaceutical company develops a drug from a shaman's knowledge, or when a composer takes a folk tune, arranges it, and puts his name on it as the creator – something some popularisers of calypso and a number of contemporary musicians have been accused of doing (this is discussed below). This unequal relationship is partly created by intellectual property legislation passed by those countries who are benefiting from the relationship: the countries who have most strongly supported the current European-American based legislation also have the most to gain from its implementation.

This has its counterpart in popular music. The popularity of "world music" over the past fifteen years has led to a remarkable increase in the commodification of what were once fairly obscure local traditions. When the party that makes the most money from something also writes the rules for it, the potential for exploitation is considerable.

When Non-Humans Create

Ethnomusicological descriptions from many parts of the world reveal that music is often considered to be revealed rather than composed by a human agency. Musical creativity is often attributed to powerful beings, and said to be superhuman. Many musical genres are associated with religious matters, and performed for serious purposes, rather than for entertainment alone. In Australia, for example, many aboriginal communities and clans have their own songs, particular to their members and not necessarily meant to be shared (Payne 1984; Toner 2001). In parts of the Pacific, such as Vanuatu, knowledge of many kinds is particular to specific individuals or social groups, and its use prohibited to others (Amman 2001). But rather than piling one example upon another, I will describe music among the Suyá Indians in greater detail.[2]

The Suyá are a small (300 members), horticultural society who live in Mato Grosso, Brazil, where they hunt, fish, plant subsistence gardens, and spend a good deal of their time in ritual activities that include singing. Music is an important part of Suyá life. It is intimately intertwined with their understanding of the universe, their concepts of space and time, their relations with other indigenous societies, and their sense of self and community identity (Seeger 1987). When I first began fieldwork among them, in 1970, there was no 'entertainment' music at all.[3] There were no lullabies, no songs of protest, no love songs, and no social dance parties. All music was associated with ceremonial life in some form or another. This does not mean that all music was serious. Suyá ceremonies are also fun and their objective is make people euphoric. Elderly men and women had the ritual obligation to sing songs the younger members of the society considered obscene, funny, or scandalous. They also played the role of clowns, and appeared to parody the earnest young performers. South American Indians, whose music is nearly always sacred, are some of the greatest experimenters with chemical mind-altering drugs and introduced the world to tobacco, coca, Banesteriopsis Caapi, and chocolate. Music is neither all serious nor always performed sober, but certainly has very different meanings and uses from those in capitalist societies today, where music is by and large a commodity.

According to the Suyá, all music comes from less-than-human sources, not from the Suyá mind. They do not claim to be 'composers' or 'creators' of any music. Music comes from three other sources. Old songs, which have been sung for generations, are attributed to events described in mythology, where songs were learned from spirits, animals, or monsters. Another group of songs originated with other peoples not considered fully social by the Suyá. At least six other indigenous societies and two European ones have contributed to their repertory. A third group of songs comes from the natural world, learned by living people who understand the language and introduce new songs they have learned from nature to the rest of the community, which then sings them.

Contrary to the stereotype of "traditional" communities doing the same thing year after year, the Suyá constantly introduce new songs into their repertory. They say it is tiresome to sing the same song over and over again. Certain Suyá men and women, after they recover from an illness or dramatic personal experience, are recognised as having a special ability to hear the songs of the spirits of the trees, the fish, the bees, certain mammals, and human "ghosts". The songs of the spirits of the natural species should not be confused with the sounds the rest of us can hear. Bee songs do not sound like the humming around a bee hive. The Suyá say that people who understand the bees hear beautiful melodies and poetic texts. Before a ceremony, the men and women who have this ability take a walk in the forest, paddle along the rivers, or go to sleep in their hammocks, learning the songs of the species whose language they understand.

Each specialist can usually only understand the songs of a certain species or group of species. Sometimes his or her spirit, which enables him or her to learn songs, moves from one species to another. For example, one old man's spirit once lived with armadillos, and he had taught people armadillo songs for many years. Late in his life his spirit moved to women's vaginas, and he taught his peers songs he learned from vaginas (which taught him some pretty bawdy songs). Another man's spirit was with the trees, but fled to the arrow cane after he had been hit by a bullet in an angry altercation. He then began to sing songs of the arrow cane – some of them filled with fear. In these cases we have a clear relationship between an individual's experience and the songs he performs. But according to the Suyá, the songs themselves all come from spirits, not from the psyche of the individual, or directly from his experiences. The songs do not "belong" to either man.

The Suyá do talk about control over their songs. They describe individual songs by the name of the person who sang it publicly for the first time (as in "Peti's Shout Song") rather than by the natural being who composed it or the person who introduced it to the village. Group songs are recalled by the name of the group that first sang them. These individuals or groups are called the "masters" of the song (I have also translated this as "owner-controller"). A "master" of a song must give permission for it be sung, and may complain that the singer isn't singing it seriously. But permission is always granted. And if a social group is "master" of a song, their control never expires.

How do we fit Suyá ideas into copyright legislation? What is the lifetime of an armadillo species that teaches a man a song? And how does the spirit of the armadillo assert its rights, since it neither speaks nor can afford to hire a lawyer? More cogently, since songs are revealed by supernaturals, what is the lifetime of a spirit or a god? What is the lifetime of a kinship group that has a collective right to a song? None of these would be equivalent to the lifetime of the transmitter of the song plus seventy years. The Suyá don't even recognise the role of the "transmitter" as a creative one. Suyá calculations are totally different because their concepts of music and its origins are totally different. The concepts of mastery or control illustrate how wide the differences can be between international legislation and local attitudes.

The Suyá case, although it has some specific features, is not unusual among the native peoples of North and South America. In many indigenous societies individuals seek spirits and learn songs from them. The songs then become personal property of some kind, which may be given to others or kept as a source of power. This is one of the reasons that certain North American Indian communities forbid all recording of their sacred music. The only way they can protect control over their sounds is to prohibit anyone from making recordings, transcriptions, or other uses. Protecting community or artist rights to traditional music can be very difficult, however. First, if it is ever published, it will eventually enter the public domain and be available to everyone, regardless of which group they belong to, to create new things from. Second, it is hard for non-literate people without legal representation to protect even what the legislation does allow them. Sometimes the difficulty is caused by the laws; at other times the difficulty is created by the power of commercial interests.

When Traditional Music Becomes Popular

A few communities do not want their music used by anyone for any purpose. Other artists and communities object when someone takes their music and makes money out of it, while they do not. They do not object to a researcher or tourist recording or photographing a public performance for their personal use. The problem arises when that document is used to make a profit, and above all when the commodified product neither credits the original producers nor gives them a share of the profits. In fact, many artists around the world think everyone is getting rich on their music but them, and distrust is widespread.

Moneymaking uses of music, for groups like the Suyá, are a fairly recent phenomenon. Even commercial recordings of such communities were once obscure documents of interest to only a few hundred people who were specialists in the field. The sudden popularity of World Music caught many scholars, small record companies, and traditional artists unprepared. Ethnomusicologists who had thought they were producing recordings for small, non-profit companies suddenly discovered the same recordings were being used for popular music recordings promoted by multinational conglomerates. Reports of this kind of problem have been appearing only recently, but a consistent picture is emerging from those reports (Feld 1996; Zemp 1996; Guy 2002; Rees 2003).

Once an obscure ethnographic recording is released, even with very limited circulation, it becomes available to musicians, filmmakers, and advertisers who may see in it opportunities for furthering their own artistic and commercial goals. The compositions may be listed as "traditional" and thus in the public domain, available for arrangement. The sounds them-selves (master rights) are often copyrighted by the record company, and then sub-licensed by it without consulting the original artists. Technically sophisticated sampling allows studio artists to mix a wide variety of sounds into a contemporary groove, and a little 'authentic' music can deepen a scene's background in a film, or help sell everything from SUVs to perfume. In his excellent examination of the use of the music of several groups referred to as 'pygmies' in central Africa, Steven Feld writes:

> The primary circulation of several thousand, small-scale, low-budget, and largely non-profit ethnomusicological records is now directly linked to a secondary circula-tion of several million dollars worth of contemporary record sales, copyrights, royalty and ownership claims, many of them held by the largest music entertainment conglomerates in the world. Hardly any of this money circulation returns to or benefits the originators of the cultural and intellectual property in question. It is this basic inequity, coupled with the reproduction of such negative caricature, that creates the current ethnomusicological reality: discourses on world music are inseparable from discourses on indigeneity and domination. (Feld 1996: 27)

One of the examples described by Feld is the use of ethnographic recordings from West Africa in the CD *Deep Forest*, released in 1992.

Deep Forest was a great success. It sold over two million copies in the succeeding years, and selections were also apparently used in a number of commercials for large companies, including Sony, Porsche and Coca-Cola. The recording notes for the album indicated that an unspecified portion of the profits would be donated to The Pygmy Fund in California. The director of that fund, however, would not respond to Feld's request for information about the amount of royalties donated, and Feld's investigation of the fund's tax returns for several years after the recording revealed little change in the base contributions – which Feld suggests might indicate that the 'pygmies' did not receive much money from the *Deep Forest* recording in spite of its popularity.

Feld's observations are supported by Hugo Zemp's article in the same issue of the *Yearbook for Traditional Music*. Zemp also notes that 'more and more, ethnomusicological research and commercial exploitation are getting intertwined" (Zemp 1996: 36). A researcher at the Centre National de Recherch Scientifique (CNRS) in Paris, who has published many ethnographic recordings and films, Zemp has had extensive experience serving as an unwilling intermediary between local communities and commercial industry. He has tried to be scrupulous in his dealings with local communities, and also with respect to his obligation as a scholar to make some of his materials available to other scholars. In his article he describes eight different experiences with the music industry, the most dramatic and complex of which concerned how a Polynesian lullaby ended up on the song 'Sweet Lullaby' on the album *Deep Forest* – the same CD discussed by Feld. It turned out that 'Sweet Lullaby' did not use a West African sample (as the packaging suggested) at all. The lullaby was, in fact, taken from a recording that Zemp had made in Polynesia among the 'Are'Are, whose use he had not approved. Furthermore, the liner notes gave him credit for something he did not do and misspelled his name in the process: 'Deep Forest has received the support of UNESCO and of two musicologists Hugo Zempe [sic] and Shima Aron [sic] who collected the original documents." Their names are actually spelled Hugo Zemp and Simha Arom, and the 'Are'Are melody sampled on 'Sweet Lullaby' was originally published on a UNESCO recording. Zemp was unable to discover how permission had been obtained to use the lullaby – everyone denied having granted it.

Hugo Zemp wrote a letter to the musicians who created the track asking for an explanation:

> You have been disrespectful first to the musical heritage of the Solomon Islands, using without permission a piece of music and concealing the source of your arrangement on the CD notes (you are mentioning only African sources), and second to the ethnomusicological discipline in usurping my name making believe

> that I have given my support to your purely commercial enterprise . . . it is time to
> put your good words into action and pay back part of your profits to the real owners
> of this music, to a cultural/scientific association of the Solomon Islands that really
> cares for the preservation of artistic heritage . . . as soon as I have your answer, I
> will communicate to you, with the agreement of cultural leaders of the Solomon
> Islands the name of one of several associations to which you could pay back part of
> your profits taken from 'Sweet Lullaby'. (Zemp 1996: 48)

The artists would not comment except to advise him to contact Sony Music, which did not respond. His article reports that his last contact was a letter from the musicians who 'maintained that my position was erroneous and what they had done had been appropriate' (Zemp 1996: 54). If renowned ethnomusicologists cannot get an answer from a record company, what does it take? That becomes clearer in the next example.

A recent article by ethnomusicologist Nancy Guy highlights a similar problem, but with a different outcome. She discusses the use of a sample of two musicians of Taiwan's Amis tribe in the song 'Return to Innocence', released in 1993 by Michael Cretu, who works under the name Enigma (Guy 2002). Like the 'Are 'Are, the Taiwanese musicians were originally recorded by a scholar and their work issued on a small record label. As in the 'Are 'Are case again, their song was extensively sampled on a popular song. Over two minutes of the four-minute-fifteen-second Enigma track feature the voices of Kuo Ying-nan and his wife, Kuo Sin-chu.

> Cretu, however, gave no indication of the source of his materials. The CD liner
> does not give the names of the aboriginal singers, it does not indicate where the
> music originated, nor does it name the recorded source from which the sample was
> taken. Printed boldly on the last page of notes are the words 'All songs written by
> Curly M. C." (also known as Michael Cretu). At the bottom of this page, in small
> print, is a list of sampled sources. Absent from this list, however, is any reference to
> the materials heard in 'Return to Innocence'. (Guy 2002:197)

Cretu had his manager contact the company that published the original recording, and pay them a licensing fee so he could use the music. Unfortunately, the musicians had not been consulted about the original use of the music on the Taiwanese recording, and were again not consulted on its licensing for Cretu's use.

What differentiates this case from the previous two is that the Taiwanese record company agreed to prosecute the artist and his record company in the United States. There were several reasons to do this in the USA. Most of the copies of the recording were sold there and the best way to protect local artists from this kind of abuse is to establish case law in the United States that supports the rights of artists whose recordings are used without their permission. Guy's article describes the general nature of the case, but does not enter into details because she was an expert witness in it, and obligated to keep certain things secret.[4] The eventual outcome was an out-of-court settlement whose details are not public. While the case did not set any legal precedents in the United States, because it was settled out of court, it apparently did benefit the surviving artist. Since both Feld and Zemp were barely accorded a response to their requests for information, the case demonstrates why filing a lawsuit can be more effective (but far more expensive) than expecting voluntary restitution.

There is a common thread in all of these cases. An early, research-based recording was sampled as part of a piece of popular music. Even when benefits were promised to the original artists for their music's use, evidence is not forthcoming to show any were delivered. Scholars have little leverage with the multinational record companies, who have large legal departments and considerable funds to battle lawsuits. The hard truth is that those who can afford lawyers may exercise rights and negotiate. Those who cannot, or whose resources are seen to be insufficient to pursue a long legal case, will be ignored.

The proliferation of highly publicised cases, like those described above, has engendered a great deal of uncertainty among scholars as well as among local musicians. Scholars suddenly become responsible for the use of their collections decades after they have recorded them. The cases reveal that people with the best of intentions can find themselves powerless to reverse exploitative uses of the materials they have acquired on the understanding that they were not to be used for commercial purposes. Artists are also concerned that people are recording their music only to exploit them. Is it any wonder that local communities today view with suspicion the arrival of a researcher carrying a tape recorder or videocamera? The Taiwanese musicians agreed to sing for Guy, but only after she turned off her tape recorder. Artists in many countries are becoming increasingly aware of the (often inflated and imagined) value of their art. And they are quite concerned about misuse of it.

The public is often deceived as well. Reading the liner notes the public assumes that local artists have been consulted and that the attributions are correct. Part of the consuming public is aware of exploitation and supports efforts to reduce child labour and promote better working conditions in sweat shops, coffee plantations, and other places whose exploitative practices have been denounced. Improving local conditions has become part of marketing special products – but the use of un-protected music by popular artists suggests that the exploitation of traditional arts and artists remains a problem in popular music today.

Conclusion

What should be done to rectify this? There are two possibilities, which are not mutually exclusive:

1. Changes in copyright legislation that provide some protection for traditional knowledge would help. Both UNESCO (United Nations Educational, Scientific, and Cultural Organization) and WIPO (World Intellectual Property Organization) have been working on ways to address these issues. It is difficult to achieve agreement on the subject because nations have an interest in different outcomes.

2. Legislation is being developed that specifically protects indigenous knowledge, which would have its own legal rights (Janke 1997 and Mills 1996). Brazil is one among a number of countries that is granting to indigenous groups perpetual rights to their knowledge. This would protect the Suyá when they sing their own music; they might get into trouble for singing the songs of the six other indigenous groups. Such laws tend to fix and restrict knowledge circulation, which concerns many critics.

The extension of the time limit for the control of knowledge rights has an impact on another area of copyright law – the creativity implied by a constantly renovated public domain. If materials keep entering it, the ideas can be re-used. If companies, or indigenous groups, keep rights to things in perpetuity, the public domain shrinks. The public domain is often likened to the common land to which all members of English villages once had rights – all residents were free to use what they held in common. Just as the English commons were fenced and privatised, so large corporations (and some defenders of indigenous rights) are increasingly shrinking the public domain and trying to keep their property (the right to Mickey Mouse is a famous one) from entering it (McCann 2003; Lessig 2001).

There are good arguments on both sides of the debate over the recognition of communities like the Suyá. Michael Brown (1998) gives a very clear evaluation of some of them, and suggests that an accommodation might be reached that would be morally acceptable and practical. But we are far from reaching it.

It is important to make allowances for works that are not meant to be commodities in the first place. There need to be mechanisms to keep secret songs secret, and without danger of entering the public domain. It is also important to recognise the rights of all artists to benefit from their arts if they so desire. The Suyá, who are happy to be paid for their songs and can work things out with the natural world if they choose, should have the same rights as rock stars to their artistic output.

The world is in a very difficult period of transition, when more and more ideas are becoming thought of as commodifiable "intellectual property" in a global economy. Aspirations and reality do not meet for anyone. There are immense inequalities and there is considerable injustice. The time has certainly come to find a solution, but there is no certainty as to which direction things will go in. Addressing the current inequalities in the recognition of "traditional knowledge" will take a combination of improved legislation, changed ethics on the part of composers and musicians who take inspiration from traditional works, and high enough penalties to discourage others from being equally unethical. Legislation will require a delicate balancing of community and individual rights with the rights of access to a public domain. Above all it will require recognition of the perspective that not all that is music is necessarily appropriate to becoming a commodity. The differences between a rave party and an Amazonian ceremony must be recognised: music is not the same thing everywhere.

Notes

1. During the past decade a number of extremely interesting books that focus on this culture-bound history of what is now considered a universal right have appeared, among them Woodmansee and Jaszi (1994) and Boyle (1996).
2. I have been writing about the Suyá for nearly thirty years. Particularly relevant for this article is Seeger (1987).
3. Since the 1970s, however, technological innovations and other changes have also changed the way they produce and attend to music. Some of these are addressed in Seeger (2003).
4. This is an interesting problem in research – those who know the most are often prohibited from communicating it in such a way that it can become the source of wider analysis and reflection. In addition to expert witnesses, ethnomusicologists who have been initiated into certain religious performance groups also find that their knowledge prevents them from communicating what they know.

Reference

Amman, R. (2001), 'Using ethnomusicology to assist in the maintenance of *Kastom*, with special reference to New Caledonia and Vanuatu', in H. R. Lawrence (ed.), *Traditionalism and Modernity in the Music and Dance of Oceania, Essays in Honor of Barbara Smith*, Sydney: University of Sydney, 151–63.

Boyle, J. 1996, *Shamans, Software, and Spleens: Law and the Construction of the Information Society*, Cambridge: Harvard University Press.

Feld, S. 1996, 'Pygmy POP. A Genealogy of Schizophonic Mimesis', *Yearbook for Traditional Music* 28: 1–35.

Guy, N. (2002), 'Trafficking in Taiwan aboriginal voices', in S. R. Jaarsma (ed.), *Handle with Care: Ownership and Control of Ethnographic Materials*, Pittsburgh: University of Pittsburgh Press, 197–236.

Janke, T. (1997), *Our Culture, Our Future: Proposals for the Recognition and Protection of Indigenous Cultural and Intellectual Property*, Canberra: Australian Institute of Aboriginal and Torres Strait Islander Studies.

Lessig, L. (2001), *The Future of Ideas: The Fate of the Commons in a Connected World*, New York: Random House.

McCann, A. (2003), 'Beyond the commons: the expansion of the Irish Music Rights Organization, the elimination of uncertainty, and the politics of enclosure', PhD dissertation, University of Limerick, Ireland. Version on the Internet: http://www.beyondthecommons.com/shop.html

Mills, S. (1996), 'Indigenous music and the law: an analysis of national and international legislation', *Yearbook for Traditional Music* 28: 57–86.

Payne, H. (1984), 'Residency and ritual rights', J. C. Kassler and J. Stubington (eds) *Problems and Solutions: Occasional Essays in Musicology presented to Alice M. Moyle*, Sydney: Hale & Iremonger, 265–78.

Rees H. (2003), 'The age of consent: traditional music, intellectual property, and changing attitudes in the People's Republic of China', *British Journal of Ethnomusicology* 12: 137–71.

Seeger, A. (1987), *Why Suyá Sing. A Musical Anthropology of an Amazonian People*, Cambridge: Cambridge University Press.

Seeger, A. (2003), 'Globalization from a local perspective in Brazil: the Suyá Indians and Música Sertaneja', in S. Loza (ed.), *Musical Cultures of Latin America, Global Effects, Past and Present. Selected Reports in Ethnomusicology Volume 11*, Los Angeles: Ethnomusicology Publications, 121–8.

Toner, P. (2001), 'When the echoes have gone: a Yolngu musical anthropology', PhD dissertation, Department of Anthropology, Australian National University, Canberra, Australia.

Woodmansee, M. and Jaszi, P. (eds) (1994), *The Construction of Authorship: Textual Appropriation in Law and Literature*, Durham and London: Duke University Press.

Zemp, H. (1996), 'The/An ethnomusicologist and the record business', *Yearbook for Traditional Music* 28: 36–56.

CHAPTER 10

Music and the Media

Simon Frith

Introduction

No work on music copyright is complete without the story of the French composers in the café. It has occurred at least twice already in this book and I want to use it too. A reminder, then, of this famous event (in Dave Laing's words, taken from Chapter 4):

> In 1849, several composers were drinking in a Paris café when they recognised their tunes in the repertoire of the café orchestra. Enraged at receiving no payment for this use, they refused to pay their bill and brought a court case against the proprietor. The ruling in the composers' favour confirmed the existence of a 'performing right' for music authors and established the legal principle that they should be paid whenever their compositions were performed in public.[1]

This story, usually presented (as here) as a key moment in composers' fight for their rights, interests me for different reasons. To begin with it makes the point dramatically that the development of music copyright is tied up with two key aspects of modernity: the ubiquity of music in everyday life and the related importance of music to the history of commercial entertainment. And before expanding on these points I also want to note the people missing from the standard version of the Paris café story. What of the other coffee drinkers? Were they there for the music or would they rather have been drinking to different sounds or without any background noise at all? And what about the orchestra itself? Who decided its repertoire? Why were they playing these tunes? As a response to audience demand? Under instruction from the café proprietor? The economics of this situation may not be as straightforward as the composers' version suggests. It was, after all, common enough for publishers later in the nineteenth century to pay bands (or, at least, their leaders) to perform their latest numbers.

In other words, what we have here in capsule form is an early indication of what was to be the most significant aspect of the twentieth-century technological revolution in the popular music trade: songs and melodies (musical 'works') became an essential component of all forms of mediated entertainment, from the cinema to the mobile phone. In this chapter I want to examine copyright law as an effect of the extraordinary development of mass entertainment media and also to show how it helped to shape them.

These days cafés are not the only public places in which strolling composers are likely to hear their music. Indeed, a traditional Parisian café may be one of the few public places in the city where there isn't background music. These days, one might say, certainly in cities, music is everywhere and always. There are occasional attempts to halt the spread of sound but though the public use of music has to be licensed (this is the defining feature of a copyright regime) its increasing presence in our lives is, it seems, unstoppable.[2] Consider what we now take for granted:

1. A great variety of public occasions and places *for* music – concert halls, dance halls, clubs, discos, bars, etc.
2. A great variety of public occasions and places for entertainment to which music makes an essential contribution – cinemas and theatres, video arcades, theme parks and fairgrounds, fashion shows, ice rinks, etc.
3. A great variety of public occasions and places for leisure activities to which music has seemingly become a necessary accompaniment–shopping, eating and drinking, sporting events, etc.
4. A great variety of public occasions and places when and where it is assumed that music can offset tedium – the tedium of waiting in airports and bus and rail stations, in bank queues, in doctors' and hospital waiting rooms, in lifts and on the telephone; the tedium of routine work in factories, garages, and offices; the tedium of routine work-outs in keep fit classes and sports clubs and swimming pools.[3]

There are still public occasions and places where music is regarded as unseemly (libraries, churches, some museums and galleries, educational settings such as schools and universities, law courts and Parliament), but more of our activities seem to have a musical background these days than not. This reflects, too, the way in which technology has transformed the private and domestic use of music. This is no longer fixed, formal or collective, the family gathered round the piano or gramophone or radio in the living room (which is how I remember my childhood in the early 1950s); but mobile, informal and individual. Music on portable radios and tape, CD and MP3 players accompanies domestic activities from the moment we wake up (to a clock radio) to the moment we fall asleep (to a chill-out CD). And our music goes with us out of the house too – in the car, on the aptly-named Walkman.

This may seem to be taking us away from copyright but detail is important here. The fact is that since those French composers met at that Parisian café 150 years ago, there has been a phenomenal growth in the amount of time most people in the Western world spend listening to music, a phenomenal growth in the proportion of our lives which has musical accompaniment.[4] The questions raised 150 years ago remain the same. What kind of control should composers have over the use of their music by other entrepreneurs? What kind of economic return should they expect from such use? But the problems of exercising such control and the amount of money potentially at stake have grown phenomenally too. The Parisian composers recognised the tunes being played in the café because in those days musical worlds were relatively locally defined: the audience for whom popular composers wrote was the same sort of audience for whom the café orchestra played; the musical tools and resources the composers used were used by the orchestra too. There was a shared musical culture that made it relatively easy to trace a work from composition to use.

Today such a link is quite tenuous. There is hardly any limit to the kind of music we get to hear in everyday life: it's not just that music is everywhere but that *all* music is everywhere. Works composed for specific secular or religious occasions (marches or masses) in specific places (Thailand or Texas) can turn up as if at random on TV commercials and restaurant tape loops. There's no longer any apparent connection between the occasion for making music and the occasion of listening to it. This is, of course, to increase greatly composers' opportunities to make money from their work. But it is also to make the logistics of getting the money to them for the use of their music – in distant places, at random times, for no particular reason – extremely difficult. Still, these are the problems that copyright regimes are meant to solve, and in this chapter I want to draw attention to two issues in particular: on the one hand, copyright's place in the organisation of the entertainment media; on the other hand, the media's effects on the economics of music. I will then raise some questions about the meaning of the term 'public domain' now that to be in a public place is to be listening to music whether we want to or not.

Music Copyright and the Media

The history of music is a history of entertainment, just as the history of entertainment is a history of music: theatre, dance and opera, court revels, pleasure gardens, circuses, fairs and parades, music halls, vaudeville and burlesque, bandstands and pier-ends. Public gatherings have always involved music, whether markets, harvest festivals, sports contests, political demonstrations or even hangings. Crowds are a source of income – they need entertainment which musical performers can instantly provide. And music is both an emotionally effective way of creating a community (as with military bands and church choirs) and a socially effective way of attracting an audience by making an occasion more enjoyable.

I make these points for two reasons: first, as a reminder that the twentieth-century media did not so much change the role of music in society as provide new opportunities for its commercialisation; and, second, in order to emphasise that, in the end, the economic importance of music depends on its social importance. I'll return to this point at the end of the chapter. Immediately, I want to sketch out how the media offered new opportunities (and problems) to music rights-owners. (I should perhaps stress from the outset that 'the media' describes a number of different institutions, institutions that compete, on the one hand, for people's attention, time and money, and, on the other hand, for musical 'content'. To talk about the interests of the media is to talk about the different, often conflicting interests of different media.)

It is obvious enough that the last 100 years have seen an ever-increasing number of ways in which music can be carried: by records, discs, tapes, and digital files; across airwaves, through cables, via electrical microphones and amplifiers. Each new technological means of storing and distributing sounds and images means a new use of music which a rights-holder can license as a new source of income. And each new technological device, each new medium of communication, has also meant new opportunities for *other* people to use music as a way of pursuing their commercial ends. Records and recording were, from the start, the basis of the commercial radio industry; music has always been essential to the audience appeal of the commercial production of films and television programmes. On the other hand, there are also clear continuities in the use of music in nineteenth- and twentieth-century entertainment. The earliest recordings featured established live performers and familiar works, whether from the music hall or the opera. 'Silent' films were in fact accompanied by 'live' musicians, whether orchestras in the larger, prestige city centre cinemas or pianists in the smaller local film houses or, later, cinema organs everywhere. The earliest radio programmes featured established musicians, whether on record, in the studio, or in outside broadcasts from concert halls and dance floors.

What emerged from all this activity were the new rights discussed elsewhere in this book – the mechanical rights regulating the recording of songs, the neighbouring rights of the companies producing those records, the synch rights controlling the use of music to accompany moving images – and the new rights-owners, the record companies and their collecting agencies. Copyright laws had to be amended to establish such rights; payment regimes put in place to set fees and licence terms. But this is not just a story of rights expansion, with music rights-holders licensing more and more musical uses, receiving higher and higher returns from their work. The new media also had a profound effect on what might be called the ecology of the music business, on the distribution of power, the role of creativity, and the understanding of the music market. To use Roger Wallis' term from Chapter 6, composers found themselves part of a new kind of 'value chain'.

The first point to make from this perspective is that as the entertainment media established themselves commercially so they sought to use their market clout to establish a clearer control over the music that they needed. Two strategies were possible here: on the one hand, to buy up existing musical rights; on the other hand, to originate music rights themselves. Once talking pictures were established at the beginning of the 1930s, for example, Hollywood studios both started taking over established music publishers and commissioning and recording film scores to which they therefore retained the rights. For the next forty years or so 'film music' in the Hollywood industry primarily meant commissioned scores and studio-owned music (with only musicals working differently). When, from the late 1970s, film scores began to feature pre-existing music again (as the studios used cult tracks or pop hits to target the youth market – as in *Dirty Dancing* and *Top Gun*), a new kind of deal between music publishers, record companies, film studios and music television was established *within* new kinds of global leisure corporation. What's involved in the exploitation of music rights today is not the composition of a song that then just happens (if it is successful) to be licensed for various media outlets but the composition of a song *for* the use of radio, film, television, and so on.[5]

The second point to note here is the role of advertising in the development of the mass media and so in the development of the music business. All new forms of entertainment have given advertisers new ways to reach the public, of course, but the most important is broadcasting, which, in commercial terms, is advertiser driven. Commercial radio and television stations cover their costs and make their profits from the sale of airtime, not from viewer or listener payments; their commercial raison d'être is delivering audiences to advertisers rather than programmes to audiences. And music is the key to this: to attract the right audience means to broadcast the right music. From the advertisers' perspective music is thus important in two ways: the adverts themselves have to use music to hold listeners' attention – hence the rise of the jingle; and radio music has to be in itself a kind of sales pitch, putting listeners in the mood for consumption, as it were.

Put these two approaches together and you get the use of hits and other 'found' tracks in advertisements themselves and, more to the point, a rich new opportunity for composers and publishers and performers and record companies to exploit their rights.[6] But, again, this has not just meant adding something else to the rights basket. It has also given advertisers and advertising agencies a role in the music (and rights) making process itself. If advertisers use a track because they think it might help sell a drink or a building society or a pair of trousers, music publishers and record companies quickly realise that whether or not an ad is successful in its own terms, it certainly increases sales of their song. For many years now major publishers have had divisions whose task is to find tracks for advertising agencies while, more recently, some advertising agencies have effectively become A&R departments (discovering and promoting acts and tracks) and are even, now, setting themselves up as publishers.[7] Add to this the key role of companies like Coca-Cola as sponsors of stars and tours and *image rights* come into the picture too.

By the end of the twentieth century, the media demand for music was a crucial incentive to commercial music production. Providing sounds for radio and television, for films and advertisements, for computer games and mobile phones, for public spaces generally, is nowadays as commercially important as directly pleasing the public.[8] The 'music industry' describes a complex network of rights-owners and licensed users, a continual flow of rights income which seems inexhaustible and sometimes, indeed, quite random.[9] One well-publicised consequence is that songwriters and recorded performers can receive unexpected windfalls as songs written or recorded long ago and for quite other reasons turn up on film soundtracks (Ewan MacColl's 'The First Time Ever I Saw Your Face' on Clint Eastwood's *Play Misty for Me*, for example) or television commercials (Ladysmith Black Mambazo in a Heinz advertisement). But perhaps even more significantly the media use of music has also meant the development of a routinised, corporate system of musical production: much of the music we hear in everyday life is effectively anonymous. It is no coincidence that the name of one particular brand of background sound, muzak, has become a general term for a kind of musical noise for which the underlying principles of copyright (authorship, for example) seem quite irrelevant.

Adding Value

The economic value of the media for music rights-holders is reflected not just in the business statistics but also in the energy with which unlicensed music users (like pirate radio stations) are pursued for 'depriving composers and performers of royalties' and rights ownership disputes are fought out in the courts.[10] How much a particular song earns from one use as against another remains, though, difficult to discover, even for its composer. The best sources of systematic information about at least part of the British rights economy are still the 1996 Monopolies and Mergers Commission investigation of the Performing Right Society and the PRS's own follow-up investigation of the quality of its music use data.[11] PRS divides its revenue stream into various categories, depending on the types of licence involved. The heading *public performance* thus includes *live* (licensees involved in performances, venues, tours, events, and so on); *featured recording* (licensees involved in performances of records in discos and clubs, karaoke nights, and so on); *jukeboxes*; *miscellaneous recorded* (all those people using recorded music in the background – rather than as a feature – in shops and so on); *aircraft*; *cinemas* (in the foyer and the intervals, rather than on the film soundtracks); and *public reception* (licensees using radios and TV in public places like hotel foyers). There is a separate set of entries under *broadcasting* (note that the BBC has a single licence to cover music use on all its radio and TV outlets).

Already by 1997 the income under the 'miscellaneous recorded' (or background music) heading was larger than that from any other public performance category (at £18.5m or 31.8 per cent of the total – live performance brought in £17m or 30 per cent of the total), while broadcasting revenues (c. £64m) exceeded total public performance revenues (c. £57m). Bearing in mind that the PRS is concerned only with song composers' performing rights, and not with mechanical or neighbouring rights in records, this is a good indication of how important the media are in the size and shape of the music economy.

In 1997 the PRS received a little under £1m from airlines for the rights to play PRS members' works as part of inflight entertainment and as piped-in 'taking-off and landing music'. The fee charged to each airline was calculated according to the number of passenger hours involved (the flight time multiplied by the number of passengers). In 1998 British Airways appealed to the Copyright Tribunal for a reduction in its annual fee (which the PRS had raised to £953,000). BA argued that this fee was unreasonable when compared with the fees charged by ASCAP and BMI to airlines using US airports, but in the course of the proceedings BA's counsel made a number of other points about the unfairness of the existing airline fee formula. Most passengers, he argued, weren't actually listening to music during take-off and landing; no passengers were listening when inflight entertainment was not available (during pilot or steward announcements, for example); few passengers listened to inflight services *all* the time they were available. The tribunal reduced the fee to £700,000. It didn't regard US practices as relevant but it did accept that the underlying calculation of music usage needed amending. It rejected the argument that passengers not using inflight entertainment should be excluded from the calculation of passenger hours. Such passengers could use the service if they chose (the charge for juke box licences, by analogy, depends on the size of a venue and how many customers *can* use the juke box, not on how often they do). But the tribunal did agree that the number of passengers should be the basis of fee calculations, not the length of the journey, and it ruled that in future the PRS airline tariff should involve two rates – one for the inflight entertainment, another lower one for the take-off and landing music – a distinction which seemed to be based on the quality of the musical experience involved.[12]

I cite this case at length as a reminder that copyright is a regulated monopoly. Licence fee levels and conditions are not just a matter of market forces; they must also take account of the way music is actually being used; they must consider the public good. This can be seen equally clearly in the history of negotiations between the PRS and the satellite broadcaster, BSkyB. In BSkyB's early days, the PRS sought to base the tariff for music use on a percentage of BSkyB's revenue while BSkyB argued it should be based on its audience share. In this case the tribunal ruled that the PRS was only entitled to a revenue-based tariff when there was 'an adequate nexus between the use of music and the revenues earned' (not the case with BSkyB though it might be for a music cable or satellite channel). In other rulings the tribunal has established a different fee rate for radio stations and companies providing piped music: the former 'add value' to the music they play, the latter don't; the latter therefore pay a higher percentage of their revenues for a PPL licence (Ware et al. 2000: 227–9).

The tribunal's position is that a radio station's revenue – the measure of the value of its audience to advertisers – isn't just an effect of the music played. A radio station's appeal also reflects what it does with and around the music – the disc jockeys, the programming, the news services, and so on. But from the music industry's point of view a radio station might also be said to add value in a different way: it brings a record to the attention of music consumers, it is part of the star making process (think of the value added to an indie release by a play on John Peel's Radio 1 programme, or to a contemporary jazz singer by an appearance on Michael Parkinson's

Radio 2 show). And here we come to the nub of the twentieth-century entanglement of music and media, and its contrary consequences for copyright. Up to now in this chapter I've been writing as if the media just gave music rights-holders new opportunities for licence fee income, but the media also became crucial for the promotion of record sales and the construction of star images, crucial enough indeed, under certain circumstances, to be *paid* for using music.

One could regard this situation as neatly symbiotic – the media paying for music to use, the music industry paying for media exposure – but in practice the economics of the relationship (and the way copyright is deployed) tends to shift over time. Take the case of the juke box in the USA. By the 1930s juke box owners had become as important record buyers as domestic consumers. Half the records manufactured in the USA in 1936 were sold to juke box operators and over the next decade (as domestic sales continued to fall in the face of the depression and then war) they came to dominate the market. One result (particularly as juke boxes serviced Southern migrants to the North, and servicemen far from home) was that they became more important than radio in promoting record sales in some cities, more responsive to the demands of new urban black and white communities, more likely to programme R&B and country music. Juke box operators began to form their own record companies, and existing record companies to do deals to ensure their records were prominently programmed by the bigger juke box chains (Laing 2003). There are obviously parallels here to payola (record company pay-for-play on US radio in the same period), and it is perhaps not surprising that juke box operations, payola and later forms of radio promotion (involving gifts of sex and drugs and goods in kind, rather than simple payment) should be the three areas of the American music business that have been systematically investigated by Congress for Mafia involvement. If copyright payments from juke box operator and radio station to rights-owners was the official business arrangement, payments in the other direction provided an unofficial, often illegal, but just as financially significant, counter-flow.

An alternative strategy is for record companies simply to waive their rights (and to exclude 'promotional' copies of records supplied to radio stations, television producers and club DJs from the royalty contracts signed with musicians). This is in the tradition started by nineteenth-century publishers (who would pay to get their latest numbers played by dance hall or seaside musicians) and living on in the 'product placement' of tracks in films and television programmes. In the 1980s small British labels, particularly those in the dance field, would put out records labelled 'non-PPL', meaning that radio stations didn't need to pay a PPL licence fee to use them. There was a fine economic calculation to be made here: when do the promotional/sales effects of unlicensed radio play cease to outweigh the forfeited rights income? When is it better to try to raise the costs of licences rather than to provide free or cheap music? As I write, the European press is reporting a dispute between MTV Networks Europe and local independent record labels:

> MTV Networks Europe has warned independent labels, which produce 22% of the European music market, that their stars' videos might not be shown unless they sign a deal that halves their payments for the music.[13]

There are a number of interesting aspects to this story. First, the independent labels had originally negotiated, through the video rights collecting society, Video Performance Ltd (VPL), a special rate for the use of their videos on MTV (an agreement that expired in 2002). One justification for the new MTV proposal (which would cut the annual amount paid to indie labels from £1.9m to £840,000) was that independent labels were getting 'double the rate that we were paying other rights holders'. (This was presumably because when MTV Europe was establishing its brand image it needed a guaranteed supply of local indie music.) Second, the independent labels are arguing that 'appearing on TV channels is no longer aiding promotion of artists but instead is contributing to a slump in sales.' They now believe, it seems, that MTV no longer adds much value either to their records (by way of additional sales) or to their videos (by the way they are presented). Rather it is getting cheap programming, the cost of which is carried primarily by the labels themselves.

In the end, MTV backed down in the face of record company resistance to MTV's attempt to bypass VPL altogether and to sign a series of individual agreements. (The motivation here seems to have been MTV's determination to 'obtain a far wider bundle of rights' than just those for TV content so that it could use music in new revenue raising activities like licensed MTV downloads or ringtones. Such rights are not VPL's business.) What is apparent is that in such company by company negotiations, corporate power matters. In this case the would-be music user would be more powerful than the individual company rights-owners. As *Music Week* puts it:

> Whatever its motivation, MTV's latest tactic strikes straight to the heart of the future of rights administration. Many indies fear that they will be in a far weaker bargaining position if they are forced to negotiate fees on their own with a large multinational media company that wields hefty clout in the market place.[14]

In many other cases the balance of power tips the other way: it is the rights-holders, major media corporations, who have power over would-be music and image users, small companies and individuals.

Where is the public domain?

The word most dreaded by popular music scholars is 'permission'. To quote a lyric or piece of music means to get permission to quote a lyric or piece of music, usually from its publisher, sometimes from its author. To clear a permission is time-consuming and expensive and quite often impossible (which has had its own effect on scholarship – on which works are discussed and in what sort of detail). From the academic point of view the copyright system here is inconsistent (some music publishers accept scholarly quotation as fair use, some don't) and irrational (I have been given permission to quote a Gershwin song for nothing; the publishers of two lines of a song by the British reggae group, Aswad, demanded a fee considerably more than my entire advance and likely royalty earnings from the book in which it was to be included). Sometimes what's at issue isn't money but control: writers are asked to provide music publishers with the passage in which the quote occurs; if the publishers don't like what's said about a work they refuse permission for its quotation.[15]

The underlying issue here is obviously fair use, something discussed in different contexts elsewhere in this book, but there is, I think, an equal problem with the music publishers' suggestion that what is at stake is unfair competition. How can an academic book or journal with a sale of hundreds rather than thousands possibly be competing in the mass music market? The concept of value added is relevant here. I originally quoted the Aswad lyrics in a review in the *Sunday Times* which has a readership of millions. No permission was sought; no licence fee claimed – presumably such quotation is regarded by music publishers as a normal part of song promotion. It was only when I wanted to reprint the piece in an academic collection with a tiny print run that a hefty fee was required. What I realised then was that the problem was not Aswad's publishers' particular concern with the effect of academic publication, but that all music rights-owners now operate in a kind of competitive culture of exploitation. There are divisions in every major music publisher and record company tasked with maximising the returns from every right in the basket. Tariffs are set accordingly: so many words, so many notes, so many dollars. Corporate rights-holders have no incentive to consider licence applications on their own merits; to be interested in any outcome except what's on the balance sheet. In my experience many music publishers' rights departments simply aren't resourced to *negotiate* terms.[16]

The point here is that for the entertainment industry as a whole copyright is its most important corporate asset. When David Bowie invited people to invest in Bowie bonds, he wasn't inviting them to share the risk of future record sales but, rather, to get a cut of the steady flow of fee income from the multiple media uses of his back catalogue (one little part of which might indeed come from his academic exegetes). And from the corporate point of view a copyright is not only open to cross-media use (songs on film soundtracks; images on pop videos) but is also a property which needs protecting from uses which might cause its value to diminish (an approach which seems directly contrary to the argument that copyright is a way of ensuring the public availability of art and knowledge).

Academics are marginal to this system. There are far more seriously restrictive consequences for what one might call the smaller players in the copyright game itself: the independent filmmakers and record companies who can't afford the rights fees demanded for the use of protected material; the creative artists who find that they are legally banned from the use of certain samples or images or even phrases and terms – Aqua had to fight a lengthy legal battle with Mattel in defence of its right to use the title and lyrics of 'Barbie Girl'; and the White Stripes were threatened with a similar suit from Warner Bros for the use of material from *Citizen Kane* on 'The Union Forever'.[17] The financial and administrative costs of clearing rights for the use of even the shortest snatches of music on film and television programmes has become so great as to be prohibitive for filmmakers and TV producers who are not part of major corporate structures. If my conversations with fellow academics quickly turn to horror stories about lyric rights, conversations among independent film and TV producers turn equally quickly to the nightmares experienced organising soundtracks.[18]

One particularly disturbing aspect of this situation is that documentary filmmakers have found themselves being charged for showing images or using musical material that was part of the public space being documented. As *The Philadelphia Inquirer* reported in 2003:

> Increasingly, documentary filmmakers must get clearances for songs, product advertising on a billboard, and other copyrighted material that crops up incidentally in their footage, things that once passed under the copyright radar. In one case a few minutes of *The Simpsons* visible on a television in the background in a film about an opera company got the director slapped with a licensing fee of $10,000.[19]

Such cases draw attention to the extent of control entertainment companies now seek to exercise over their intellectual property, but also raise questions as to what is nowadays meant by 'the public domain'. The usual account of public domain in copyright courts is that a tune is in the public domain if there is no-one who can claim to be its originator. But one aspect of modern life, as I suggested at the beginning of this chapter, is that music is everywhere, and occupies public spaces in such a way as to compel us to listen to it whether we want to or not. Such music-as-noise could be said to occupy the public domain because there is no-one who has actually chosen to hear it. Public music (whatever its source or origin) is 'found sound' just as much as a dog bark or a police siren, and occupies just as 'natural' a place on a documentary record. In what way, then, can its original composer or publisher still lay claim to it? The words of David Lange, which I cited in the original edition of this book, seem more apposite than ever. (He was reflecting on the trademark case of *DC Comics, Inc v. Board of Trustees*, in which a group of students was sued for calling their newspaper the *Daily Planet*, but his argument equally applies to music rights.)

> When the proprietor of a mark presumes to intrude into the relationship which the subject of the mark may have contracted with the public in some setting essentially beyond the proprietor's own undertakings – Superman and all his friends and enemies have a place in the estimation of the American public that simply has nothing to do with the parochial interests of DC Comic, Inc – the proprietor goes well beyond any purpose legitimate in the law of trademarks and begins, indeed, to engage in an appropriation of its own. It is tempting, but inadequate, to see this as simply a corollary of the rule that trademarks are lost as they take on generic significance. The lesson in the *Daily Planet* case ought to derive from a more fundamental recognition of separate rights in the public domain. (Lange 1981: 168)

The corollary for music would be that some records ('Whole Lotta Love', say) become so ubiquitous that they too take on a 'generic' significance – should they be credited, paid for, every time they are quoted?[20] Classical composers, certainly, have long drawn on found sounds (such as folk tunes or church bells) in their work – think of Charles Ives' 'documentary' evocations of the early twentieth-century American soundscape. The problem is that found sound is now mediated sound, comes from radio and records, is fixed and owned in new ways by new sorts of rights-conscious corporations. Among other things this means the steady extension of the definition of a 'derivative work'. As Lange points out, once upon a time the Marx Brothers put together an act by drawing on, imitating and quoting a host of long-forgotten music hall and burlesque acts; now a theatre company can be sued for using the 'image' of the Marx Brothers owned by a film studio. The value of that image may have been created by the public in the first place, but the exploitation of its value means removing it from the public domain or, rather, not allowing it free play there.[21] In Lange's words:

> As access to the public domain is choked, or even closed off altogether, the public loses too: loses the rich heritage of its culture, the rich presence of new works derived from that culture, and the rich promises of works to come . . . The

resulting protection guards against the adverse consequences of unfair competition, as it always did, but it does more than that, by far: in effect, it runs against any diminution in the value of any hypothetical interest, and thus it converts each interest into a mutable species of mutant property distastefully reminiscent of *The Alien*. (Lange 1981: 165, 168)

There's an echo here of the overall history of copyright law in the USA, ignored when it was not in the corporate economic interest, relentlessly expanded now that it is. Once upon a time Disney depended on public domain material; on fairy stories and myths. Now it is reported as sending a cease-and-desist letter to a children's party performer who was twisting balloons into the shape of the genie from *Aladdin*![22]

Conclusion

In 2002 Robbie Williams signed a deal with EMI which was, unusually, much discussed in the non-music press. The contract was newsworthy not just for its value but also for its terms. EMI's advance was based partly on Williams' likely record sales, but also seemed to give the company a cut of all his future earnings as a star (or as a brand), a cut from concert receipts, TV deals, DVDs, merchandise, and so on. At the time this deal was seen to reflect record labels' anxiety about sustaining record sales in an age of digital downloading. Recording deals would now, it seemed, be used as promotional devices, less important as a direct source of income than as a way of upping the value of the basket of rights as a whole. People might be able to download a Robbie CD for free, but they would still need to pay for a concert ticket or a T-shirt.

A couple of years on and this investment seems less like a defensive move at a time of crisis than an astute reading of the new rights possibilities when *all* aspects of a musical performer are part of the same digital information system. EMI's contract with Robbie Williams positioned the company brilliantly to exploit DVDs as the newest kind of cross-media platform. There's nothing really new here, though. Twenty-five years ago Madonna and Michael Jackson, Warners and Sony similarly exploited the new cross-media possibilities of video and music television; twenty-five years earlier Dean Martin became the USA's most popular entertainer by exploiting television; and twenty years earlier again Bing Crosby had become the USA's biggest singing star thanks to radio and electrical recording. Ever since the invention of the phonograph, musical success has been tied up with the media use of music and musicians, and copyright regimes have evolved accordingly. Underlying all this, though, is a simple point: the system only works because people –

regardless of copyright – want to make music, listen to music and share musical experiences. These days it seems clear to me that if musical cultures still flourish it is despite copyright not because of it.

Notes

1. See page 71 in this volume.
2. For further discussion of this point see Frith (2003).
3. Music is also now used, it seems, to offset fear – of airplane journeys, job interviews, medical procedures. (I got to choose the music to accompany the operations to remove cataracts from my eyes.)
4. And we will, of course, be buried or cremated to music too.
5. It should be noted, however, that commercial radio has not been absorbed into such corporate structures. This is in part because it is, for political reasons, a much more tightly regulated sector (with, in Europe, some remaining public service obligations) and in part because in the USA until very recently copyright law was such that broadcasters didn't need to be licensed to play records nor did public venues need to pay mechanical rights fees to transmit broadcasts. Up to now there have therefore been fewer economic imperatives and more regulatory obstacles to record companies taking over radio stations or vice versa. Now that US copyright laws are beginning to be harmonised with those elsewhere in the world – following WIPO agreements and the USA's belated signature to the Rome Convention – music radio's place in the US music business may well change, particularly given the Federal Communications Committee's 1990s deregulation of the radio industry. The rise of Clear Channel, as a company dominating both the radio and live music industry in the USA and, now, investing in live and radio music markets in Europe, may be an indication of things to come. Clear Channel is already heavily implicated in record companies' record release and promotional strategies and has begun its own form of music production (through the planned digital release of live concert recordings). What effects this will have on copyright income flows remains to be seen.
6. In practice record company discretionary charges have sometimes been so high that it has been cheaper for advertising agencies to rerecord the song to sound the same as the original, thus only having to pay a fixed fee to the song's composers/publisher. ('Heard It on the Grapevine' on Levi's pioneering TV commercial was apparently made this way.)
7. 'Indie bands have found a new, if unlikely, saviour in Andy Gulliman, a producer from an ad agency [Bartle, Bogle Hegarty]. Tracks he picks for major campaigns can mean the difference between obscurity and a No 1 hit.' See Stephen Armstrong 'The brand played on', *The Guardian Media*, 19 November 2001: 4.

8. I was once shown (in confidence) the list of synch deals done by a British dance act on the release of its first CD. The group had one international top ten hit; the CD sold a few thousand copies. Every track on it, though, was licensed for use on film or TV. Among other things tracks were used for the opening credits on BBC documentaries and lifestyle shows, on TV adverts in South Korea and Spain, as incidental music in cable features and HBO films in the USA. This kind of music use has become routine – Moby famously licensed every single track on a CD to advertisers even before the music had been released to the public.

9. Consider, for example, what is involved in a TV programme like Channel 4's *Teachers*. The musical soundtrack is obviously a crucial part of its appeal, both as a television programme and as a DVD. The tracks involved in a *Teachers* season are also sold on a compilation CD using the *Teachers* connection as a key part of its sales appeal, and Channel 4 has an interest in this music as part of the way it establishes its station identity. The negotiations between the various rights-holders involved here as to who has a licence to do what – TV production company, Channel 4, rights-owners of the tracks used, producers of the DVDs and compilation CDs, and so on – cannot really be described as deals between 'the television industry' and 'the music industry'. Rather, all the players involved are part of the entertainment industry.

10. Court cases can, indeed, be a useful source of information about the costs of deals not usually open to public scrutiny. A 1999 US court case concerning the disputed ownership of the 1979 Spoonie Gee track, 'Spoonin' Rap', revealed that it had been licensed for a fee of $90,000–$100,000 each time for use in a couple of films, for $242,124.50 for use as a sample, for $85,499.82 each time for use on various European rap anthologies. Such licensed uses undoubtedly earned the songs' composers and publishers rather more than the record's original sales, which presumably explains why rights ownership was only now being contested, twenty years after its release. (I take this information with thanks from a private communication from Frank Kogan.)

11. See Monopolies and Mergers Commission (1996). The PRS's *Distribution and Date Review* was summarised in *PRS News* 52, 1998 and *Music and Copyright* 143, 9 September 1998.

12. For details of this case see Ware et al. (2000: 225–6).

13. Heather Tomlinson, 'Video ban. Indies in row with MTV over plan to slash payments', *The Guardian*, 5 February 2004: 23. See also Ajax Scott; 'MTV and indie labels play a different tune', *Music Week* 14 February 2004: 6.

14. See the Scott article mentioned in Note 13.

15. This hasn't happened to me with lyrics, but Richard Hamilton's then agents refused Howard Horne and me permission to include one of his images in our book, *Art into Pop*, on the grounds that this was an inappropriate context!

16. In practice what this means is that an academic seeking permission is likely to be charged excessively; an academic not seeking permission (on the grounds

that such use is fair) is unlikely to be pursued. In other words, the scholar's real problem may be the caution of the academic publisher. Walter Everett's *The Beatles as Musicians–Revolver through the Anthology* (1999) contains ninety-three extracts from Beatles' songs quoted without permission. The publisher, Oxford University Press, was not sued. As Everett himself has noted, for OUP to agree to this strategy he had to prepare a meticulous argument as to why his use was fair *and* have the support of a strong editor and the publisher's legal counsel. There are a few other examples of academic books using musical or lyrical quotations extensively without permission and without legal consequence, but, perhaps unsurprisingly, given their limited resources, most academic publishers aren't risk takers.

17. As reported in *Rolling Stone* in March 2003. Reference courtesy of Steve Pick's mailing to the emplive.com discussion group.

18. It should be pointed out in this context that because the BBC has blanket licences for music use from PRS and MCPS it can use music relatively unrestrictedly in its programming. Hence the growing use of pop extracts even on news and current affairs programmes: it sometimes sounds as though BBC producers are under instructions to use music as often as possible to justify the size of the fees already paid. On the other hand, this doesn't solve the rights problems once BBC programmes are sold on to other markets. There are certainly cases of programmes (*Tutti Frutti*, most famously) that have had a very restricted showing since the first broadcast because of the terms of the original music licences.

19. Eils Lotozo; 'Private intellectual property: Keep Out!', *The Philadelphia Inquirer*, 15 October 2003. Available from http://www.philly.com/mld/inquirer/news/magazine/daily/7014772.htm

20. Legally, at the moment, the answer certainly seems to be yes. Recent cases suggest that the most minimal melodic similarities can be taken as a reason for handing over a percentage of a song's earnings to a complainant, but historically courts have tended to accept the presence of generic melodies and lyrics in pop, and not taken similarity to imply infringement. See Frith (2002: 200–7).

21. The other way of fixing an image is death. For an interesting account of how the dead Elvis became more valuable in rights terms than the live Elvis had been see Wall (1996).

22. See the Lotozo article mentioned in Note 19.

References

Frith, S. (2002), 'Legality and the music industry', in M. Talbot (ed.), *The Business of Music*, Liverpool: Liverpool University Press, 195–216.

Frith, S. (2003), 'Music and everyday life', in M. Clayton, T. Herbert and R. Middleton (eds), *The Cultural Study of Music*, New York and London: Routledge, 92–101.

Laing, D. (2003), 'Jukebox', in *Continuum Encyclopaedia of Popular Music of the World, Volume 1. Media, Industry and Society*, London and New York: Continuum, 513–15.

Lange, D. (1981), 'Recognizing the public domain', *Law and Contemporary Problems* 44 (4): 147–78.

Monopolies and Mergers Commission (1996), *Performing Rights* Cm3147, London: HMSO.

Wall, D. (1996), 'Reconstructing the soul of Elvis: the social development and legal maintenance of Elvis Presley as intellectual property', *International Journal of the Sociology of Law* 24: 117–43.

Ware, J., Sprawson, R. and Enser, J. (2000), 'The music industry in 1997–8', in E. M. Barendt and A. Firth (eds), *The Yearbook of Copyright and Media Law 1999*, Oxford: Oxford University Press, 222–34.

CHAPTER 11

Infringers

Lee Marshall

Introduction

This chapter is concerned with those people who ignore or disregard copyright law in their daily practices. You may therefore be expecting to find discussions of Mafia-style crime syndicates in Eastern Europe and China pirating massive numbers of the latest chart CDs as part of a portfolio of illegal and socially undesirable operations.[1] Or maybe it will cover the sneaky bootlegger, profiting by illegally recording and distributing live concerts (Marshall 2004b). Perhaps the chapter concerns itself with rap artists who 'sample' snippets of earlier songs in producing new hip-hop hits (Sanjek 1994; Vaidhyanathan 2001: 132–48; Bentley 1989). All of these expectations are reasonable and they all, in one form or another, involve individuals overstepping the boundaries of copyright law (although research on the organised crime gangs allegedly involved in music piracy is verified only by the legitimate music industry). However, this chapter does not discuss such activities. Instead, it concentrates on something closer to home: you. Well, you and millions like you. I say this because, chances are, if you are reading this book then you probably have an interest in music. If you live in the developed world, are relatively young and have an interest in music, then you are likely to have consumed music in a manner that is not only unauthorised by rights-holders, but also in a manner that they find extremely problematic.

Such a focus is not intended to dismiss other forms of piracy as insignificant. For two reasons, however, they are less significant at this particular historical moment. Firstly, individual use of copyrighted material is extremely high on the legitimate record industry's political agenda at this time (McCullagh 2001; Borland 2001). Secondly, the personal use of copyrighted music brings up extremely important issues about the nature of copyright and the rights that non-rights-owners can reasonably expect from it. When these two reasons coincide, the result is the current position in international music copyright: an attempt by the music industry (along with other content industries, such as film studios) dramatically to increase rights-holders' powers at the expense of the rights of those who listen to music, watch DVDs, use computer software, read books, and so on.

The chapter is divided into four parts. In the first part, I shall define different types of piracy and outline some of the recording industry's current concerns regarding the personal use of copyrighted material. Following this, I shall question whether such concerns are well-founded by arguing that we must take into consideration how people use music in their everyday lives if we are fully to understand the effects of piracy. In the third section, I will question the basic assumptions of the industry argument through a discussion of the notion of 'fair use' within copyright law and by discussing how previously acceptable actions have come to be labelled as piracy. Finally, I shall detail how current industry campaigns to increase the strength of copyright protection are dramatically reducing potential fair uses of copyrighted music.

Piracy in the Music Industry: Definitions and Current Concerns

Although currently the most controversial types of music piracy are file sharing and CDr burning, it is important to bear in mind that there are different forms of piracy. As will become apparent in what follows, 'piracy' is a contested and value-laden label given to activities which involve the unauthorised reproduction of copyrighted material. The term is of little analytic use, however, as it covers a wide range of activities with different characteristics and effects (Marshall 2004a). In particular, it is important to recognise two important variables of 'piracy'. The first is the *scale and commerciality* of unauthorised copying – it can range from the individual, non-commercial copying of one tape all the way up to large scale counterfeiting operations producing thousands of copies for commercial sale in street markets, computer fairs, and so on. The second important variable of music piracy is the similarity of the copied music to official music industry products. This allows us to take into consideration the differences between, for example, counterfeiting (where pirated products are deliberately designed to look like official products) and tape trading (where recordings of live concerts are swapped between collectors and valued precisely because of their difference from legitimate releases). Such an awareness also allows us to acknowledge the differences between individual CD burning when a copy is made as a substitute for the official album (sometimes with covers being scanned/downloaded to make the CDr look 'original') which has the same character as counterfeiting (even though the latter is on a different scale), and compilations of tracks done by one person for another, which are individualised collections rather than a direct copy of a music industry release.

With these variables in mind, we can distinguish between six different types of 'piracy' in the music industry:

1. *Counterfeiting*: The commercial copying of legitimately released albums, including the cover art. In this instance, the copy is intended to look like, and substitute for, the official album.
2. *Pirating*:[2] The commercial copying of the *sounds only* of one or more official releases. In this form, the unofficial product is not intended to look like an already released one (though it may give the impression that it is sanctioned by the record label) but will take its music from legitimately released albums. For example, a CD that takes songs from Eminem's first three albums but is titled 'Slim Shady's Greatest Hits' and has a unique cover would be a pirate recording.
3. *Bootlegging*: The commercial recording, reproduction and distribution of music that has *never been released* by official record labels. The bulk of such material comes from live concerts and studio out-takes. Although produced commercially, bootlegging occurs on a smaller scale to both counterfeiting and pirating. Bootlegs are given their own distinctive covers and are not intended to be mistaken, nor act as a substitute, for officially sanctioned products.
4. *Tape trading*: The swapping of tapes (or more commonly today, CDrs) featuring the same type of recordings as bootlegs. This is a non-commercial activity where collectors trade recordings on a one-for-one basis.
5. *CDr burning/home taping*: The individual, non-commercial, copying of officially available music on a CDr or analogue tape. This could be a direct copy of a complete album (much like a counterfeit), or a collection of different tracks (much like a pirate recording).
6. *File sharing*: The 'sharing' of music (both officially released and that which would appear on bootlegs) via the Internet, particularly utilising peer to peer (P2P) software such as Kazaa and, most famously, Napster. Individual songs, rather than complete albums, are the unit of sharing (although of course individuals can download all of the tracks from one album if they choose, and can find them).

The definitions get less clear the further down the list we go. Where do web sites that host illegal files fit into this? How 'commercial' are burning and file sharing? How do we differentiate between the student who makes a copy of a CD for his mum and the student with 3,000 MP3 files on her computer to share? It may be that CDr burning has a bigger impact on record sales than bootlegging, even though the latter is a commercial form of piracy rather than an individual one (see Marshall 2004a). The recent history of music piracy has made these questions central to the future of the music industry.

Current Music Industry Concerns:
CDr burning and File Sharing

In the last decade of the twentieth century, three technologies emerged that pushed piracy to the top of the recording industry agenda and, in particular, made the distinction between commercial and individual piracy less clear. These were recordable CDs (CDr) and MP3 compression algorithms, combined with P2P protocols.

Since the release of the Compact Disc in 1982, digital quality music has conventionally been available in a read-only format. When you bought a CD from a store, you could listen to it, but that was it: you could not record onto them or alter them in any way. If you wanted to record music to listen to in the car, on a Walkman or to share with a friend, you had to use the analog audio tape technology which had been introduced in the 1960s. These were less user friendly than CDs as they had no track markings, were more fragile and of a lesser sound quality that deteriorated with each play. Although Sony released Digital Audio Tape (DAT) in the mid-1980s, and Philips launched the Digital Compact Cassette (DCC) in 1992 neither of them, for a variety of reasons, became a popular consumer format. For around fifteen years, if you wanted digital quality music, it was only available in a passive, consumption-centred format.

This changed with the invention of the recordable CD. CDrs contain a layer of dye which, when burned by a laser, mimics glass-pressed CDs from official pressing plants. Recordable CD technology was first developed in 1988 as a means of storing computer data. However, the first CD recorder sold in the US cost $149,000 and the technology only became affordable for general domestic use as part of a computer system around 1998.[3] Today, a CD burner for a PC costs around the same as three chart CDs.

During the same period, two other digital technologies were being developed that would have profound implications for the music industry. In 1987, the Fraunhofer Institut Integrierte Schaltungen in Germany began developing a compression technology that would enable digital music to take up a smaller quantity of data than regular audio data and which could then be used in the distribution of digital video. The institute patented their MP3 algorithm in Germany in 1989, it became part of the MPEG standard for digital video, and MP3 technology was patented in America in 1996.[4]

MP3 technology meant that music files offering 'near-CD' quality could be much smaller than conventional CD files and it began to be utilised on web sites containing pirated tracks. The success of MP3, however, and its *de facto* position as industry standard in digital music distribution depended upon the invention of another technology– peer to peer file sharing – and, in particular, one piece of software: Napster. Napster was invented by 19-year-old college student, Shawn Fanning, as a way of helping him share MP3 files with his friends.[5] Instead of searching for MP3s hosted by another web site, Napster put one person's computer in touch with other people's MP3 collections. By connecting individual computers through Napster's central servers, it was possible to search through thousands of different MP3 files, which could then be downloaded to your hard drive directly from someone else's. The principle of peer to peer is that there is no middle man involved, just a series of interlinked nodes (peers) in a vast network.[6]

The combination of these new technologies has resulted in an increase in the amount of copying that individuals are able to do and, in the major record labels' view, are doing. Whereas in the past you may have copied tapes from a few of your friends, now you have access to thousands (if not millions) of people's record collections. And whereas in the past, if you liked one of those tapes of your friend's CD, then you needed to buy the CD to listen to it in digital quality, now you can copy your friend's CD directly onto CDr, with no loss of sound quality; or you can download it on MP3. And as you may not want to sit in front of your computer to listen to music, you can even burn your MP3s onto CDr, or buy a DVD player that plays MP3s which you can attach to your stereo (or buy a personal MP3 player, or an MP3 player for the car . . .). The logical result of all this is that people do not need to buy CDs any more: they can easily obtain CD quality music without going near a record shop.

This is certainly the concern of the music industry. At the 2003 MIDEM recording industry convention in Cannes, IFPI president Jay Berman blamed 'online theft' for the fact that only one album had sold more than 10 million copies world-wide in the previous year.[7] The IFPI's 2002 Music Piracy report states that 'piracy is the greatest threat facing the music industry today' (IFPI 2002) and the most significant form of piracy, according to the industry, is the combination of file sharing and CDr burning.

The Effects of Piracy

There is no doubting the popularity of these new technologies: at its peak, Napster had 1.5 million people connected to its servers simultaneously, each sharing 220 files on average (330 million files) (King 2001). An estimated 239 million blank CDrs were sold in Japan in 2002, compared with 229 million official CD sales (IFPI 2002). In Germany, blank CDr sales reached 486 million in the same year.[8] And the surge in popularity of these new technologies has also coincided with a decline in the global sale of music. Global sales declined 7 per cent in 2002, the second consecutive year that sales had fallen. Some territories have registered quite dramatic declines: 23 per cent in Argentina, 16 per cent in Spain, 10 per cent in the USA, 9 per cent in Germany and Japan. Internet and CDr piracy are held to be the principal explanation for this decline, with Berman stating: 'The industry's problems reflect no fall in the popularity of recorded music, they reflect the fact that the commercial value of music is being widely devalued by mass copying and piracy.'[9]

The coincidence of these phenomena may make such causal relation-ships appear common sense. However, it is important to remember that the notion of 'piracy' is an ideological construct that performs important rhetorical strategies for the recording industry (Krestchmer 2000). I shall discuss this further in the next section: here, I want to question whether CDr burning and Internet file sharing are having the effect on legitimate musical consumption that the record industry suggests and I shall do this by offering some reasons why the simple causal relationship between increased piracy and decreased sales may not be quite so simple.

Firstly, there are a number of other possible explanations for the decline in global record sales aside from an increase in file sharing and CD burning. In terms of wider economic factors, the global recession at the start of the twenty-first century could adequately explain a small drop in sales of a leisure commodity. A second possible explanation is that we may also be witnessing the end of the CD boom: the record industry was in a slump just before the introduction of the CD and has been carried along on the strength of its back catalogue for almost twenty years. It may be people have now stopped replacing their vinyl in which case the CD format will no longer be such a fillip to sales which may be reverting to 'normal' levels. The slump in music sales is also because record labels have found themselves in a more competitive market-place: the sales growth of video games and DVDs (the most successful leisure technology ever) means that CDs face increasing competition for consumer attention. While the record industry has been able to take advantage of the DVD format – sales of pre-recorded music videos have increased during the last two years – some of the $11.6bn spent on DVDs in the US alone in 2002 would surely otherwise have been spent on CDs.[10] Another technology that is impacting significantly upon record sales is the mobile phone. As Bricklin (2003) points out, young people spend more money and time on cell phone usage than ever before (you see more people using phones in the street than using personal stereos – including personal MP3 players) which again reduces time and money available for music.

The record industry recognises some of these facts, but it views them as less significant than piracy, particularly file sharing. However, what is more significant than these economic arguments is the fact that we do not know what effects individuals' use of file sharing has on their overall musical consumption. In its anti-piracy proclamations, the record industry seems to assume a fairly static demand which is compromised by every downloaded file. But the number of files downloaded (2.8 billion a month at Napster's peak) far outweighs the decline in record sales. If piracy has the impact that the recording industry suggests than there should have been a far greater decline in sales than has been experienced.

The reason we do not fully understand the impact that unofficial consumption has upon individual music consumption is because we have not asked these individuals how they use unauthorised music. There have been some market research surveys on whether downloading makes people buy fewer or more CDs but, even leaving aside the partiality of some of these reports,[11] they are not particularly useful for understanding the effects of piracy because they treat musical consumption as an *economic* activity when it is actually a *social* one. Such reports "reduce musical activity to buying, selling and stealing records" (Frith 2003: 208) when in reality the 'bare fact' of music consumption masks a wide variety of social practices. People *use* music rather than merely consume it.

In general, I think that there is not enough research on how people use music in their lives.[12] And it is certainly the case that there is insufficient research on how people use personally-recorded material rather than purchased commodities.[13] People record albums they own for convenience (to listen to in the car, on the train and so on). They record current hits off the radio rather than buying singles, as such hits are likely to be ephemeral anyway. They produce their own compilation tapes (and now compilation CDrs) both for their own benefit and for their friends (a friend of mine gives a compilation tape out with his Christmas cards each year). This last example is crucial for the argument of this paper. Music consumption (an economistic word that deflects from the fact that what we are actually talking about is music enjoyment) is a social activity which is more often than not engaged in with other people. This sociability makes the *sharing* of music a key feature of musical social relations. Music is on in the background at parties, in teenagers' bedrooms, at the pub. People talk about music almost as much as they listen to it ('How can you like that?') and a significant part of this musical enjoyment involves the use of 'pirated' music: making compilation tapes for potential lovers (there isn't an officially released record that says exactly what you feel), sharing your own tastes with friends ('You've got to hear this!'), copying your friends' CDs to expand your own collection. *Music copying is an integral part of music consumption.* This means that it is also intricately bound up with legitimate purchasing; not only as a direct stimulus through 'sampling' music before purchasing (this was a central plank of Napster's legal defence) but also because the people who copy music are those who consume most music of all types – individuals who purchase two or three CDs a year from Woolworths or Wal-Mart probably do not do much home copying, whereas those who do a lot of home copying also buy a lot of records. Two separate reports by Mintel state that: 16 per cent of the UK population buy more than ten CDs a year but this 16 per cent buys 65 per cent of all CDs sold; and that 15 per cent of the population copies music regularly (Brown et al. 2001). There is likely to be a significant overlap between these two groups: those who do the most copying also do the most buying.

Interestingly, Brown et al.'s 2001 study suggests that there is little difference between how people use MP3 files and how they used analog tapes in the past. Similar types of reasons as those discussed above (sampling; control of playlists; sharing musical tastes) were offered by those who regularly downloaded MP3 files. The study also showed that individuals do not just download MP3s, but instead use downloading as a complement to other consumptive practices. This indicates another possible reason why downloading is not displacing official sales: perhaps downloading is actually replacing home taping! If this is the case, then the amount of unauthorised copying remains constant but shifts to new practices and technological forms.

The central argument of this section is that we cannot understand the *effects* of piracy in the music industry unless we understand the *meanings* that people attach to their unauthorised copying activities. Simply assuming that an increase in file sharing results in a decline of CD sales is not satisfactory: not only does it overlook that it may merely be a displacement of one type of copying to another; it also ignores the fact that unauthorised copying plays a central role in the social activity of music enjoyment and thus acts as a stimulus for official sales.

The ideology of piracy

To a certain extent, none of the above matters. In terms of the importance of piracy for the recording industry, what matters is not its economic effects but its rhetorical impact. We will never be able to ascertain the economic effects of piracy accurately (which is not to say that we should not try to be more accurate than we currently are), but piracy is not primarily an economic concept: it is an ideological one. Copyright protection is not a natural right, nor is it absolute: it is a socially mediated relationship between publishers (and, in this case, the recording industry), artists and the public. The particular rights granted and withheld by copyright at any particular time reflect wider power relations between these parties: 'copyright' is not a static thing, it is a constant struggle between competing interests. This struggle is often of a legislative nature – interested parties must persuade law makers (and law enforcers) of the reasonableness of their copyright claims. And it is for this reason that the notion of piracy is extremely important – if rights-holders can persuade governments (and the public) that they are losing billions of euros through piracy, and that such losses have a detrimental impact not only on the industry, but also on artists, employees and local and national economies, then they have a greater chance of gaining legislative support for strengthening copyright. 'Piracy' is thus a key rhetorical tool for the content industries (Krestchmer 1999, 2000).

If copyright is a struggle, then one side is definitely on top early in the twenty-first century and I will discuss this in the final section. However, if copyright is a constantly changing legal form, then so too is piracy and here, I intend to discuss how what is viewed as piracy is changing. To do this, we need to discuss the concept of fair use in copyright law.

Copyright is at heart a commercial regulation. When copyright first emerged during the eighteenth century, copyright statutes were designed to ensure the circulation of books by protecting publishers against other publishers (Patterson 1968; Feather 1994; Lowenstein 2002). The limited monopoly that publishers were granted was a necessary burden on the public in order to ensure the dissemination of literature. However, as more and more reproductive technologies have developed (photography, sound recording, motion pictures, photocopying, audio tapes . . .), the scope of copyright has greatly increased. But copyright owners do not (yet) have complete control of copyrighted works; there remain a number of limits on copyright's scope designed to ensure that the public is still able to make use of copyrighted works. One of these is temporal: once the term of copyright has expired, the work falls into the 'public domain' where it is free to be used by anyone. Another significant limit to copyright holders' powers is the concept of 'fair use'.

The idea of 'fair use' developed over the course of the twentieth century and is now legislated in many countries including the United States, United Kingdom, Australia and Germany.[14] The principle of fair use, as already discussed in Chapter 5, is that activities undertaken for specific purposes do not constitute infringement of copyright. Such instances include criticism and review, parody, research or private study and reporting current events. One important element of fair use (which in part emerges from the instances just mentioned) concerns individual copying of copyrighted works. In general, fair use exempts individual copying from those activities which infringe copyright. Sometimes this is expressly legislated, such as in France where 'copies or reproductions reserved strictly for the private use of the copier' do not infringe rights-holders' rights (Goldstein 1994: 172).[15] However, even in territories where private use is not explicitly excluded from infringing activities, it is generally believed that fair use exempts individual, non-commercial copying from copyright infringement.

There have been many instances of copyright lawsuits where the dispute concerns whether the activity in question is covered by fair use. In their chapter in this book, Steve Greenfield and Guy Osborn draw attention to one of the most famous American copyright cases of recent years, concerning the rerecording of Roy Orbison's 'Oh Pretty Woman' by the rap group 2 Live Crew. In 1994 the Supreme Court ruled that the rerecording was fair use as it was a parody of the original song, and the principles underpinning this judgement are worth reiterating here.[16]

In the USA, four criteria are utilised when deciding whether the use of a copyrighted work is fair:[17]

1. The purpose of the use (non-commercial use is more likely to be fair than commercial use);
2. the nature of the work (copiers can use more from scholarly works than from fiction);
3. the amount copied as a proportion of the whole work (copying smaller sections is more likely to be fair);
4. the effect that the copying has on the market for the original work (usage that may decrease the original work's sales – for example, a competing computer programme – are less likely to be considered fair).

Among copyright scholars and practitioners, there are two main ways of understanding the fair use doctrine. The first of these is that fair use is a central concept in copyright law that helps maintain the balance between creators and the public in copyright law:

> [Fair use is] part of the implicit *quid pro quo* of intellectual property; we will give you this extremely valuable legal monopoly . . . In return, we will design the contours of your right so as to encourage a variety of socially valuable uses. (Boyle 1996: 139)

Fair use thus ensures that public use of works (the original purpose of copyright and what Netanel (1996) describes as copyright's democratic function) is not prohibited by an over-emphasis on the rights of rights-holders (for examples of this approach, see Netanel (1996), Vaidhya-nathan (2001), Jaszi (1996), Boyle (1996)). Copyright protection has increased dramatically over the last twenty-five years and fair use is the essential bulwark of users' rights and prevents the total control of copyrighted works by rights holders.[18]

The second main way of interpreting fair use is that it represents market failure, that is to say the failure of market mechanisms to maximise social welfare. In this understanding copyright should, if possible, prevent *all* unauthorised copying because the rights-holder should be compensated whenever someone uses the protected work. However, it is economically unviable to account for every single use of a work (by domestic users, for example) because the costs of keeping track of how individuals use copyrighted materials would not be met by the small licence fees that would be charged. Fair use thus exists as a 'hard-edged economic instrument that will excuse an unauthorized use of a copyrighted work as being a fair one any time it is too costly for the parties to negotiate a license' (Goldstein 1994: 170; see Gordon (1982) as an example of this approach).

These two interpretations of fair use are fundamentally opposed and have a decisive impact upon the interpretation of unauthorised usage of copyrighted material.[19] If the first interpretation is adopted, then the unauthorised use of material – for example making one copy of a CD for private non-commercial use – is an essential part of the copyright balance between creators and users and is not an infringing activity. Under the second, such an activity *is* copyright infringement but cannot be adequately policed and is thus overlooked.

Such ideological conflicts are not merely of an academic interest; they play a critical role in how copyright law is being shaped today and I will return to this in the final section. However, they also play a part in shaping how we understand the notion of piracy, particularly in the recording industry. 'Piracy' is an act that infringes copyright: it is illegal and receives widespread moral condemnation. Traditionally, the term has been used to label the actions of those who reproduce large quantities of records and CDs – counterfeits, pirates and bootlegs. None of these 'pirates' would be able to utilise fair use as a legal defence. Individual, non-commercial copying, however, has traditionally not been piracy but part of a range of activities that is deemed non-infringing. In some cases this has been explicitly legislated – the US Audio Home Recording Act (AHRA) permits individuals to make one copy of an original recording, but not a copy of a copy – while in others it has been considered part of a wider fair use remit.

However, as Jessica Litman points out, in the last few years there has been a rapid expansion in what gets labelled as piracy. Instead of referring to the *illegal* copying of copyrighted works, the term is now being used to describe the *unauthorised* copying of copyrighted works:

> The content industry calls some things that are unquestionably legal "piracy" . . .
> They've succeeded in persuading a lot of people that any behaviour that has the
> same effect as piracy must *be* piracy, and therefore must reflect the same moral
> turpitude that we attach to piracy, even if it is the same behaviour that we all called
> legitimate before. (Litman 2000: 8)

There is, however, a wide difference between illegal and unauthorised usage. Indeed, in the first interpretation of fair use, unauthorised use is a good thing as it facilitates the dissemination of cultural works, spurs the creation of new works and enables socially useful activities such as parody and investigative journalism. However, it is the second interpretation of fair use – fair use as market failure – that is currently most prominent in copyright rhetoric and in the final section of this paper, I want to discuss how the current situation is drastically diminishing fair use provisions in copyright law and the effects that this may have on music users' rights.

Napster and the decline of fair use

Recent technological developments and record labels' related rebranding of certain new activities as piracy are combining to create a situation that threatens further to reduce individual rights concerning their use of copyrighted music. Rather than understanding unauthorised copying as one practice within the whole range of music fandom (as well as one that stimulates the dissemination and creation of further work, as originally intended by copyright law), the recording industry is successfully lobbying legislators and law enforcers to allow them to increase their control of copyrighted works and make individuals liable for *any* copying they do. In this section, I will briefly discuss two important facets of this process: the restriction of the fair use doctrine and the integration of digital rights management (DRM) in CDs and DVDs.

The restriction of fair usage of music can be seen in the legal case that was brought against Napster by a group of American record labels (*A & M v. Napster* 2001). Napster, to date the most famous of the P2P applications, was unleashed to the world in August 1999 and a lawsuit from a variety of record labels was issued in December 1999. A preliminary injunction against Napster was issued in March 2001, though this was subsequently overturned (but later reinstated). Napster was declared bankrupt during the injunction process as it could not reach a settlement satisfactory to the labels.

In the injunction hearings, Napster was charged with 'vicarious and contributory copyright infringement', meaning that the program itself did not infringe copyright but that it knowingly aided others in infringing. Napster's defence centred on the argument that its users were not infringing copyright because they were making personal, non-commercial copies of songs. Such an activity, of course, has traditionally fallen under the remit of fair use, and is explicitly allowed under America's AHRA. The defence had a significant legal precedent: in 1979, Disney and Universal Studios had sued Sony for contributory copyright infringement over Sony's new VCRs which allowed people to record movies from TV broadcasts. The US Supreme court found for Sony, arguing that the ability to 'time-shift' films (recording them to watch later) was fair use, and as there was no copyright infringement by VCR owners, Sony could not be found guilty of contributing to infringement.[20]

Napster's argument that individuals' personal copying of copyrighted songs is fair use was rejected by the court which held that 'repeated and exploitative copying of copyrighted works, even if the copies are not offered for sale, may constitute a commercial use.' Indeed, because she accepted the record label's arguments that individuals' downloading occurred 'to save the expense of purchasing authorized copies', the judge ruled that individual use did count as commercial (quoted in Dossick and Halberstadter 2001: 37).

At this point, it is important to recall the argument made in the second section of this paper: the unauthorised use of copyrighted music is a social rather than an economic practice. People use music in a variety of ways – unauthorised as well as authorised – and these uses have a variety of different effects on the sales of music. Yet in this instance, uses that had been accepted as fair were now regarded as copyright infringement because the courts accepted the industry's unsubstantiated claim that unauthorised sharing of MP3s was affecting official CD sales.[21]

The instances that have been given here are from America, but the trend is discernible across all territories: individual usage is gradually being removed from the list of acceptable uses of copyrighted material. Those who argued that fair use was merely the result of high transaction costs are winning the argument: as it becomes technologically possible to trace *every* usage of a digital file, then it becomes possible to charge for *every* usage of a song.

This is being reinforced by the incorporation of digital rights management mechanisms into new technology. DRM involves technological devices that prevent the copying of copyrighted material. DVDs, for example, are protected by a Content Scrambling System (CSS) algorithm. Copy protected CDs are also being developed by the recording industry.[22] These technological measures have been buttressed by legal ones: the Digital Millennium Copyright Act (DMCA) in the USA and the European Union Copyright Directive (EUCD) both contain laws that make it illegal to invent software or hardware that breaks these technological locks.

The instigation of DRM technology presents three challenges to individual users' rights. Firstly, the technology has limited the usability of DVDs and CDs. The CSS system means that users cannot watch DVDs on computers using the Linux operating system, while there have been a high number of copy protected CDs returned to retailers because they do not play on ordinary CD players. CD copy protection also interferes with error corrections on CD players. Secondly, DRM cannot distinguish between fair and unfair copying. The right to make an individual copy – expressly legislated in some countries – is not possible under DRM. And as it is illegal to break the DRM lock, then any successful attempt to make a copy of a protected work is *de facto* illegal, regardless of fair use considerations. A Norwegian teenager who broke the CSS system in order to watch DVDs on his Linux computer was charged by the Norwegian Economic Crime Unit at the request of the US DVD Copy Control Association, the Norwegian Motion Picture Association and the Motion Picture Association of America.[23] The third feature of DRM that is detrimental to public rights is that even though copyright is a time-limited protection, DRM is perpetual. And even though the work may be out of copyright so you can use it however you want, it will still be illegal to break the technological lock.

The recording industry has made much of the threat that new technology poses to the future of music. The Internet's threat to popular music is not digital anarchy, however, but digital totalitarianism. As James Boyle (2000) writes:

> The biggest threat to the cultural potential of the internet is not digital piracy but the continuing attempt by the music industry to change technical standards and legal rules so as to build its current business plan into the law and the technology of the medium itself.

Charging for every individual use, and allowing no unauthorised uses of music is a threat to free speech and future creativity and demonstrates a misunderstanding of the role that music plays in our lives.

Notes

1. 'Pirates are often members of organised criminal gangs who use the regrettably easy profits from music piracy to finance other criminal activities such as drug dealing and arms trafficking.' Speech by Iain Grant, IFPI Head of Enforcement to the European Parliament, 23 April 2003. Available from http://www.ifpi.org/site-content/press/inthemedia10.html (last visited 13/5/03).
2. There is obvious confusion between 'piracy' as a generic term for all infringing recordings and 'pirating' as a specific type of illegal recording. I have used the term because it is recognised by the official industry (the definitions of 'counterfeit', 'pirate' and 'bootleg' can, for example, be found on the RIAA's anti-piracy web site).
3. http://www.oneoffcd.com/info/historycd.cfm (last visited 14/4/03).
4. http://www.mp3–mac.com/Pages/History_of_MP3.html (last visited 14/4/03).
5. For more on the history of Napster, see Alderman 2001, Chapter 6.
6. This was not strictly true of Napster, as files passed through Napster's central server on their journey from one peer to another. This is what made it possible to shut Napster down, both technologically and legally. Later applications such as Gnutella, Freenet and Kazaa are actual P2P applications as they do not involve a central server.
7. Full text of his speech is available at http://www.ifpi.org/site-content/press/inthemedia08.html (last visited 13/5/03).
8. http://www.intellnet.org/documents/1200/040/1245.html (last visited 15/4/3).
9. In Brad King (2002). See also http://www.wired.com/news/business/0,1367,54767,00.html (last visited 13/5/03).
10. http://www.dvdinformation.com/news/press/010903.htm (last visited 13/5/03). This is an extraordinary increase in consumer spending (DVD was introduced in 1997) even allowing that some of the spending on DVD displaces spending on VHS.
11. For example, Forrester Research, 2002, 'Downloads Save the Music Business' (http://www.forrester.com/ER/Research/Report/Summary/0,1338,14854,00.html, last visited 12/5/03). Reports submitted to the court in the Napster case, offering arguments both that downloading affects CD sales and that it does not are available from http://news.findlaw.com/legalnews/lit/napster/ (last visited 13/5/03).
12. Some exceptions to this are Tia DeNora (2000), Andrew Bennett (2000) and Daniel Cavicchi (1999).
13. The only such study before the emergence of file sharing of which I am aware is part of Paul Willis' *Common Culture* study (1990). There have been a small number of studies on file sharing, of which Brown et al.'s (2001) is the most useful, but much more work needs doing in this area.
14. It is important to point out that there is not one overarching idea of 'fair use' to which all different countries adhere. Rather, there are large differences in

the philosophical underpinning and practical ramifications of fair use in different territories. For example, fair use in the US offers a set of broad principles (discussed below) which can be used to determine whether an activity is fair, whereas in the UK, 'fair dealing' lists a number of specifically defined acts which fall into this category rather than offering general principles. My thanks to Martin Kretschmer for pointing this out to me.

15. Goldstein's book contains a discussion of how the notion of private copying has developed in American copyright cases.

16. For more information on the 2 Live Crew case, see http://www.benedict.-com/audio/crew/crew.asp and http://library.lp.findlaw.com/articles/file/00102/005704/title/Subject/topic/Intellectual%20Property%20Law_Copyright/filename/intellectualpropertylaw_1_233

17. http://library.lp.findlaw.com/articles/file/00102/005704/title/Subject/topic/Intellectual%20Property%20Law_Copyright/filename/intellectualproper-tylaw_1_233

18. Some useful discussion on fair use concerning music copying (particularly in the UK) can be found at the Campaign for Digital Rights web site (http://ukcdr.org).

19. There is at least one more interpretation of fair use, one to which I adhere, that is closer to the first understanding outlined above than the second. In this third interpretation, the concept of fair use is inherently biased towards rights-owners and illustrates the reversal of copyright law's priorities from public usage to private control. Before the introduction of fair use, a wide variety of activities were not considered infringements but were instead seen as achieving the legal purpose of copyright – the public use of creative works. If an activity was not expressly prohibited, then it was not protected by copyright law. However, once the notion of fair use is introduced, it implies that all uses not explicitly covered by fair use are *a priori* infringing. The 'slack' between protected and not protected is assumed to belong to the rights-owner rather than the public. This shifts the balance of interest in copyright law from the public to rights-holders. This can be seen in the TRIPs agreement (Trade Related aspects of Intellectual Property) which holds that all signatory states (all members of the World Trade Organisation) can only allow for exceptions to copyright infringement in specific special cases. For a full discussion of this approach, see Marshall (2004b forthcoming) and Litman (1987: 883–4).

20. For more on the Sony case, see Abrams (1983) and Goldstein (1994).

21. The record labels' submission to the court quoted a report that CD sales had fallen in record shops close to university campuses (university students are heavy downloaders), but the report did not take into account the fact that CD sales for online retailers had substantially increased on campuses (Bricklin 2003).

22. http://ukcdr.org/issues/cd/

23. In what is currently being seen as a landmark case, Jon Johansen was

eventually acquitted by a Norwegian court, though had the case been heard in the USA, he would have been guilty of breaking the DMCA. For more on this case, see http://www.eff.org/IP/Video/DeCSS_prosecutions/Johansen_DeCSS_case/

References

A&M Records, Inc. v. Napster, Inc., (2001), No. 00-16401 (9th Cir. Feb. 12).

Abrams, H. (1983), 'The historic foundation of American copyright law: exploding the myth of common law copyright', *Wayne Law Review* 29 (3): 1120–91.

Alderman, J. (2001), *Sonic Boom: Napster, P2P and the Future of Music*, London: Fourth Estate.

Bennett, A. (2000), *Popular Music and Youth Culture*, London: Palgrave.

Bentley, L. (1989), 'Sampling and copyright: is the law on the right track?', *Journal of Business Law*, March: 118–25 (part 1) and September: 405–13 (part 2).

Borland, J. (2001), 'Copy-protected CDs quietly slip into stores', *Cnet.com* Available from http://news.cnet.com/news/0–1005–202–6604222.html (last visited 24 July 2001).

Boyle, J. (1996), *Shamans, Software and Spleens: Law and the Construction of the Information Society*, London: Harvard.

Boyle, J. (2000), 'Britney Spears and online music fears', *Financial Times*, 24 May.

Bricklin, D. (2003), 'The recording industry is trying to kill the goose that lays the golden egg'. Available from http://www.bricklin.com/recordsales.htm (last visited 13/5/03).

Brown, B., Geelhoed, E. and Sellen, A. (2001), 'The use of conventional and new music media: implications for future technologies', *Proceedings of Interact 2001*, Tokyo, Japan.

Cavicchi, D. (1999), *Tramps Like Us: Music and Meaning among Springsteen Fans*, Oxford: Oxford University Press.

DeNora, T. (2000), *Music in Everyday Life*, Cambridge: Cambridge University Press.

Dossick, H. J. and Halberstadter, D. (2001), 'Facing the music: the fate of Napster in Federal Court will have far-reaching implications for the distribution of all forms of entertainment over the internet', *Los Angeles Lawyer* (April), 34–40.

Feather, J. (1994), *Publishing, Piracy and Politics: A Historical Study of Copyright in Britain*, New York: Mansell.

Frith, S. (2003), 'Illegality and the music industry', in M. Talbot (ed.), *The Business of Music*, Liverpool: Liverpool University Press, 195–216.

Goldstein, P. (1994), *Copyright's Highway: The Law and Lore of Copyright from Gutenberg to the Celestial Jukebox*, New York: Hill and Wang.

Gordon, W. (1982), 'Fair use as market failure: a structural and economic analysis of the *Betamax* case and its predecessors', *Columbia Law Review* 82 (8): 1600–57.

International Federation of Phonographic Industries (IFPI) (2002), *Music Piracy Report*. Available from http://www.ifpi.org/ (last visited 13/5/03).

Jaszi, P. (1996), 'Goodbye to all that – a reluctant (and perhaps premature) adieu to the constitutionally-grounded discourse of public interest in copyright law', *Vanderbilt Journal of Transnational Law*, 29 *(May): 595–611.*

King, B. (2001), 'Farewell free downloads', *Wired.com*, Available at http://wired.com/news/print/0,1294,44412,00.html (last visited 18 June 2001).

King, B. (2002), 'Slagging over CD Sales', available at http://www.wired.com/news/mp3/0,1285,51880,00.html (last visited 13/5/03).

Kretschmer, M. (1999), *In Defence of Piracy*, unpublished paper.

Kretschmer, M. (2000), 'Intellectual property in music: a historical analysis of rhetoric and institutional practices', *Studies in Cultures, Organizations and Societies*, 6 (Harwood) special issue: 'Cultural Industry' (P. Jeffcutt (ed.)): 197–223.

Litman, J. (1987), 'Copyright, compromise, and legislative history', *Cornell Law Review* 72 (July): 857–904.

Litman, J. (2000), 'The demonization of piracy', *CFP 2000: Challenging the Assumptions. Tenth Conference on Computers, Freedom and Privacy*, Toronto Canada, 6 April 2000. Available from http://www.law.wayne.edu/litman/papers/demon.pdf (last visited 22/6/01).

Lowenstein, J. (2002), *The Author's Due: Printing and the Prehistory of Copyright*, Chicago: University of Chicago Press.

McCullagh, D. (2001), 'New copyright bill heads to DC', *Wired.com* Available from http://www.wired.com/news/print/0,1294,46655,00.html (last visited 13/5/03).

Marshall, L. (2004a), 'The effects of piracy upon the music industry: a case study of bootlegging', *Media Culture and Society* 26 (2): 163–81.

Marshall, L. (2004b forthcoming), *Bootlegging: Romanticism and Copyright in the Music Industry*, London: Sage.

Netanel, N. W. (1996), 'Copyright and a democratic civil society', *Yale Law Journal* 106: 283–387.

Patterson, L. R. (1968), *Copyright in a Historical Perspective*, Nashville: Vanderbilt University Press.

Sanjek, D. (1994), ' "Don't have no DJ no more": sampling and the "autonomous" creator', M. Woodmansee and P. Jaszi (eds), *The Construction of Authorship: Textual Appropriation in Law and Literature*, Durham: Duke University Press, 343–60.

Vaidhyanathan, S. (2001), *Copyrights and Copywrongs: The Rise of Intellectual Property and How it Threatens Creativity*, New York: New York University Press.

Willis, P. (1990), *Common Culture*, Milton Keynes: Open University Press.

Useful Websites

British Phonographic Industry: http://www.bpi.co.uk/
Campaign for Digital Rights: http://ukcdr.org/
Electronic Frontier Foundation: http://www.eff.org/
Findlaw Napster archive: *http://news.findlaw.com/legalnews/lit/napster/*
International Federation of Photographic Industries: http://www.ifpi.org/
Recording Industry Association of America: http://www.riaa.com/

Where now for copyright?

Lee Marshall and Simon Frith

Despite the wide-ranging discussion within the preceding chapters, you may be feeling that the book has not answered the question on this topic that most people want answered: what is going to happen to the music industry given the tumultuous challenges that it is now facing? Can the recording industry survive?

Such a question is, of course, as unanswerable as it is enticing. The simple response is that it will survive – if people continue to make music, then there will always be someone making money off it – but this response is deceptively simple because it may be that the structure of the music industry will be very different in a very few years' time, particularly if the copyright regime comes under serious threat.

In this brief afterword, we want to speculate what impact future copyright changes may have on popular music. Such speculation, of course, will never be entirely right: new technologies, creative practices and economic interests will emerge that shape the politics of copyright discussed by Dave Laing. Copyright is a hot topic at the moment, both within academic discourse and (through a variety of issues) within popular discussion. And, from the content of this public debate, two kinds of copyright dystopia are being projected – copyright totalitarianism and copyright anarchy. So, how might both affect popular music?

Copyright totalitarianism

The first possible future is the Orwellian one. Music is delivered to us through a variety of digital transmissions, all of which are 100 per cent traceable. Sophisticated data banks record what you played, how often, when and on what devices. Each individual usage is charged and you are billed at the end of the month. If you fail to pay your monthly subscription to the recording provider, you are unable to listen to any of the recordings you have previously bought. If you try and send a copy of a song to a friend, digital signatures within each file will record it and charge you with infringement or, more likely, bill your friend for his new copy. Software or hardware that nullifies the digital signature will be illegal and web sites that offer such services quickly shut down. Digital tracing highlights a previously unrealised popularity in Scottish folk music and rights in old folk songs are quickly established. Many folk clubs are threatened with closure because they cannot afford the performance royalties they now have to pay. Following a sudden resurgence in the popularity of Enrico Caruso, rights-holders persuade legislators to increase the term of copyright in sound recordings to 175 years because it is unfair that his great-great-great-great-grandchildren derive no benefit from the belated rerecognition of their ancestor's talents. Although even older recordings do eventually fall out of copyright, the only copies available are fenced in by digital rights management devices and the technology to liberate them is illegal. Sampling is remembered as a historical curiosity – a form of postmodern music making that was very popular in the last decades of the twentieth century but died out in the first decade of the twenty-first when some controversial samplers wound up in jail.

Copyright anarchy

The music industry, as well as other content providers, has long since given up on utilising copyright as a means of protecting their business interests. Judges began to turn against the recording industry's attempts to prosecute individuals because they argued that a law ignored by so many should be repealed. Investment in digital rights management declined because someone would always invent a key to break the new lock and make it available on Kazaa. All music is now easily copyable and distributable by anyone with a computer, mobile phone or television. This has hit the major record labels hard – they are much smaller operations than at the end of the twentieth century – but has resulted in a proliferation of micro-labels – small independent labels serving localised niche markets. As a general development, music has become less mainstream. For consumers, while they freely copy recordings and download from P2P services, there is a feeling that music isn't as important as it once was, that finding good new music among all of the tunes swirling around is just too much hard work. And, with little possibility of gaining a deal with one of the old majors, and without taste-shaping media such as national music magazines any more, musicians find it hard to make their work widely heard or valued.

The reality, of course, will be somewhere in between. What should be clear from our glimpse at copyright anarchy, however, is that *some* form of copyright protection is necessary. Without a form of protection to encourage investment, it is difficult to imagine any form of industry structure that would enable artists to communicate with listeners beyond their immediate locale. Some artists – stars and amateur musicians – see this as a good thing, particularly if the 'local' describes a community of interests (linked via the Internet) rather than simply immediate geographical neighbours, but this is to discount one of the reasons why copyright law developed in the first place: to promote the *dissemination* of knowledge beyond the author's immediate circles. Creators need publishers to get their work known (to do it oneself would leave no time for creation); and readers and listeners need publishers to provide some sort of initial guide to what is out there to be heard and read (otherwise there would be no time to do either). It is noticeable that those musicians who have most effectively used web communities and by-passed record companies are those who have already got a fan base, are already known to their potential listeners because of the work, however long ago, of a record company.

However, although copyright is clearly a necessary incentive to companies to invest in music and in organisations for its dissemination, its current formation seems to offer little incentive to musicians to create. In fact, what is evident from the preceding chapters is the number of ways in which copyright has become a disincentive to creativity, a barrier for musicians. Whether it is new musicians losing control of their work because of the inequalities of power in contract negotiations, traditional musicians gaining no reward at all for their creative endeavours, or samplers being treated as aesthetic thieves, the consistent view emerging from the second half of this book is that the current copyright landscape is a hindrance for creators.

This does not address the normative issue, however: how should copyright strike a balance between creators, users and investors? The suggestions implicit within the preceding chapters are sometimes contradictory. For example, while Marshall argues that we need to decrease copyright rights to facilitate users' interests, the logic of Seeger's paper is that there should be *more* rights – though probably of a different nature – in order to protect traditional musicians. Wallis criticises the weak position of the composer in the music food-chain, but Toynbee's paper suggests that it is the performer who needs more protection. If we were to follow all of these approaches, copyright would become even more bloated than it is now.

There does seem to be convergence between the authors here on some points, however. Firstly, there is the suggestion in many of the papers that the role of the creator should take on more prominence in copyright as a bulwark against commercial pressures. Martin Kretschmer and

Freidemann Kawohl argue that there is a conflict of interest between artists (who have an interest in wide dissemination of their work) and publishers/record labels (who have an interest in exclusive rights to a work). This is illustrated by Greenfield and Osborn's account of how the imbalance between creator and investor in copyright structures contractual arrangements in the music industry. Jason Toynbee suggests that in the future, artists may use 'copyleft' licences to maintain an aesthetic link with their work while limiting the economic claims of its usage. In these papers, the separation of aesthetic and economic interests is important for shaping a new copyright regime.

Another area of general agreement is that the term of copyright has become too long, and there are suggestions in various chapters for a much shorter copyright – perhaps even as short as ten years. Shortening copyright would have a dramatic impact upon the recording industry, which has survived for a generation on the profitability of its back catalogue. Such a move would not solve all the problems discussed in this book, however. For example, samplers would still be prevented from utilising recent hits in making new music (and with a shorter period of time in which to enforce their rights record companies would undoubtedly charge higher fees for licences and police unlicensed uses even more fiercely than they do now). There would still be limits on, say, hip-hop's capacity to make immediate social parody. In general, though, a strongly protected shorter period of copyright could provide record labels with adequate returns on their investments while rewarding creators and facilitating new forms of creativity.

This would also prevent the rhetoric of piracy from portraying large sections of the population as criminals. Since these chapters were originally written, the concerns voiced in the final chapter seem even more prescient. In September 2003, the RIAA filed lawsuits against 261 individuals it accused of sharing music files over P2P networks. Many of these cases have been settled before reaching trial, with settlement figures of approximately $3,000 being reported.[1] They were followed in January 2004 by a further 532 suits. The British Phonographic Industry has said it may well adopt the RIAA strategy if it proves an effective deterrent. Maybe copyright totalitarianism is the way we are heading?

Perhaps, but it is worth recalling the words of Martin Kretschmer and Friedemann Kawohl at the end of their chapter in this volume:

> Within a generation, copyright laws will be unrecognisable . . . copyright *practice* is already changing, as, in their various ways, bootleggers, DJs, samplers, consumers and performance artists invent new forms of cultural engagement. Copyright law must eventually follow.

There currently seems to be a radical disjuncture between the law and the social practices it supposedly governs. Copyright law has an effect on how we act but it does not determine our actions. When we consider the law (any law), we do not just obediently follow it, but bend it and, significantly, follow the law as we think it should be. If copyright law is counter-intuitive, if it contradicts widely-held beliefs about creative freedom and reinforces widely-held beliefs about the avaricious nature of the recording industry, then it is unlikely to be followed. Many musicians and most music consumers seemingly do not believe in existing copyright laws, and so rights-holders are trying to make us believe in them through legal threats and technological locks. The outcome of this struggle cannot be predicted; it depends upon the particular power relations involved. And, as Toynbee rightly concludes, wishful thinking apart, to promote copyright change requires us to acknowledge that there are powerful actors out there with vested interests in strengthening the existing regime. On the other hand, precisely because what is at stake here is profit rather than principle, the existing copyright regime will stay in place only for as long as it is economically effective. If it becomes financially unviable to prosecute vast numbers of consumers, or too expensive to keep adding further technological locks because the last one has been broken, then the law will change. And, if that happens, then the structure of the music industry will change too.

Note

1. http://www.wired.com/news/digiwood/0,1412,61989,00.html
   (last visited 2/2/04).

Index